11.00

Essay Index

THE TIME OF TENNYSON

THE TIME OF
Tennyson

ENGLISH VICTORIAN POETRY
AS IT AFFECTED AMERICA

BY

Cornelius Weygandt

KENNIKAT PRESS, INC./PORT WASHINGTON, N. Y.

Essay Index

To

A. M. W.

The Position of Poetry

THIS book is an appreciation, against an American background, of the poetry of Great Britain and Ireland written during Victorian times. Tennyson and Browning and Arnold had as warm a welcome in the States as in their own country. They were poets of our tongue, and as such, to be accepted here as fellows of Emerson and Longfellow and Poe, as a part of our racial inheritance. So we had accepted Burns and Byron and Wordsworth before them, and so we were to accept Kipling and Yeats and Masefield after them. The lesser poets of 1835 to 1885 were accepted by us, too. The Hon. Mrs. Norton was recited in little red schoolhouses all through our country. Mrs. Hemans was sung in drawing rooms and at church sociables; and Tupper's *Proverbial Philosophy* made its way to the most remote places. For forty years I have been a resolute attender of auctions, and at no auction have I neglected to look over what books the home had cherished. I have found importations of early English editions of many of the poets and surprisingly early reprints of them in America.

All the major poets I came on first in my father's library. He had bought, from the eighteen-fifties, the great Victorians as their successive volumes appeared, and in his middle years he turned to the Georgians, so that when I was old enough to be interested in poetry I found all the great from Wordsworth to Arnold on his sanctum's shelves. I inherited in 1888 my mother's father's library of eighteenth-century poets, Pope and Somerville, Gray and Collins, Macpherson and Burns. I know, through family tradition, what these several authors were to my people, and I have talked to scores on scores of folks all over the States as to how the volumes of the poets I saw in their homes found their way there and as to what they meant to those who had them always at hand.

vii

The books themselves, by their condition, their thumbed paper, their marked passages and turned-over page corners, often told of how they had been read.

It has always been my belief that poetry should be as much a matter of daily concern to people as food and sport, gossip and outings, songs and cards, church and stage. It was such a matter of common concern to cultivated Americans in the eighteenth century. Poetry lost place among us after the heyday of Scott and Byron. Its appeal revived again through the efforts of the lyceum lecturers of the mid years of the nineteenth century, although certain of the writers were then listened to, Whittier for one, as propagandists rather than as poets. The preoccupation of Tennyson with ethical matters had a tendency to win readers to verse because of its burden of preaching rather than because of its poetry. The art for art's sake attitude was largely a revolt against the habit of judging a work of art for its morality rather than for its beauty. The dominance of the novel in Victorian times was, too, inimical to poetry. It was not until novel and short story and drama had found their just values in public estimation, after the World War, that poetry was to come back to its proper place.

CONTENTS

Indebtedness is acknowledged to Charles Scribner's Sons for permission to use quotations from George Meredith, Robert Louis Stevenson, William Ernest Henley, and Alice Meynell.

THE TIME OF TENNYSON

CHAPTER I

What Is Poetry?

THE question, "What is poetry?" is not easy to answer. It is easy to point to "The Twa Corbies" and to say: "This is poetry." It is easy to point to the seventy-third sonnet of Shakespeare and to say: "This, too, is poetry." It is easy to point to "L'Allegro" of Milton and to say: "This again is poetry." Yet to say why these three poems so different in subject and intention and art are all three of them poetry is another matter. It may be the quickest way to the answer, if an answer is to be found, will be to analyze the three, with ten other poems, like these well known and admittedly poetry, to find what qualities they have that are alike, what common denominator there is among them. It will be more illuminating, perhaps, if this anthology in little be representative of the wide range of poetry, poetry of different forms, and poetry from various periods of English literature.

What is it that makes "The Twa Corbies" poetry? It is a ballad, very condensed, in which two ravens explain that they will dine off the body of a "new slain knight." His "lady fair" knows how he came to his death, but she has taken "another mate." The nineteenth and the last line of the twenty that make the poem give a picture of what will be when the birds have made their "dinner sweet":

> O'er his white banes, where they are bare,
> The wind sall blaw for evermair.

Those lines give the upshot of it all, restrainedly, bitterly, with the right hardness of words. There is grotesquerie in the poem, brutality almost, but all is in keeping with that wild Border life

3

out of which the ballad comes. There is a rejoicing in the uncertainty of life, in the fickleness of woman, in the lack of fidelity even of man's friend the dog. There is here a rejoicing kindred to that in the abomination of desolation that informed so much other Scottish writing and so much Puritan preaching down until yesterday. There is a lonely sort of music in the lines; there are felicities of phrase there; there is striking imagery; there is a greyness of tone contrasted most artfully with the golden hair and blue eyes and white shoulder-bones of the hacked man. There is the unforgettable couplet at the end, as lonely lines as there are in all English poetry.

The oncoming of age is the concern of the famous seventy-third sonnet of Shakespeare. Time, change, the little while man has to know the sun, the weakness of last years, the love of life that is all the greater when the days of life are numbered: these have been themes of poetry from Old Testament days. Shakespeare needs no new theme, but with image on image of clear beauty; with a rhythm that marches, that delays, that hesitates and trembles with every shift of emotion; with an insight into human nature swiftly revealed; with his mastery of every power of the poet, he drives home a sense of the inevitable approach and of the finality of death such as cools the hottest blood. John Davidson points out that this poem grows in part out of its rhyme scheme, that the rhymes suggest its images and breed much of its music. What of it? There is in evidence in this poem, as always where Shakespeare is himself, such a lordship of language as no other poet can approach. It is instinctive, this command of language, wholly unstudied, natural.

All the world is shut away from the man writing save this one consideration: he is wholly absorbed in what he is doing. The poet is possessed by his subject, and by the afflatus which descends upon a man in the moment of creation. He is in an ecstasy, but he is master of himself all the while. No glow of imagination, no matter how great, can cloud his clear vision of things as they are. Need I quote the great onset of the sonnet to remind you of its noble numbers?

That time of year thou mayst in me behold
When yellow leaves, or none, or few, do hang
Upon those boughs which shake against the cold,
Bare ruined choirs, where late the sweet birds sang.

"L'Allegro" is a poém "of slow endeavoring art." That is its maker's own phrase in his "On Shakespeare." Milton here acknowledges the master's "easy numbers," in contradistinction, one cannot help thinking, to his own. The opening of "L'Allegro" is far from easy. It is labored, rhetorical, choked with classical references. Soon, however, the verse begins to clear, and, though the ode observes all the formalities of its structure, and can forget its dignity only for whiles, it brings us treasure after treasure. In a moment of unbending from his considered stateliness he writes "heart-easing mirth"; in another "Laughter holding both his sides," and in a third "the light fantastick toe," all three of them to become an integral part of our language.

Milton is a suburbanite rather than a countryman, but he gives us country pictures quite a few: the cock who "stoutly struts his Dames before"; "dappled dawn," a phrase written with the eyes on the object; whistling ploughman and singing milkmaid; and "Russet lawns and fallows grey Where the nibbling flocks do stray." He rises to ecstasy at the close of the ode, in considering Shakespeare on the stage, an ecstasy that reaches its height in:

Lap me in soft Lydian airs,
Married to immortal verse
Such as the meeting soul may pierce
In notes, with many a winding bout
Of linkéd sweetness long drawn out.

There is a deliberate aloofness about "L'Allegro," as there is in all Milton, an aristocracy of mien, a pomp and circumstance. Despite its joyousness and lightness of subject, it is a poem written as if it were to be recited as part of a ritual, as *Comus* was written to be played as part of a celebration at Ludlow Castle. It is not an intimate kind of poetry, but it is of the very fiber of Milton's being. He must be at attention in the ode. That he feels necessary in writing such a form, as worthy men we all know think they must walk weightily and look severe on public occasions. "L'Allegro" is strait-jacketed by the ode form, but it is poetry deeply felt and with vision. It has from beginning to end a kind of processional music, with airs breaking out now and then to relieve its solemnity.

Have we come upon as yet, in the discussion of these three poems, any qualities recurrent in all three, which may be what make them poetry? Certain likenesses there are in all three. In each we note a man writing in whole-souled preoccupation with his subject, fashioning a something he has experienced in life, from a corner of the world that he has made his own, into a thing of beauty. In each poem a cry of the human heart, which is the end of all brooding upon life, is heard breaking out, over loneliness and death in one poem, over the prospect of age in another, over the spectacle of laughter in the third. In each poem the poet is obeying laws recognized as the laws of the form of poem he is writing, ballad, sonnet, and ode. In each poem there is a music of verse distinctive, individual, commanding. In each of the poems are phrases so universal in their applications that they have become part and parcel of everyday speech and writing. It is not because of the poetical qualities of these phrases, perhaps, that they have become necessary in daily usage, but it is a fact nevertheless that ten such phrases have passed into speech from verse to every one from prose, if we except phrases from the King James Bible. Large portions of that version have the voice and feeling of poetry, are in fact poetry, and will be found so printed in Henley's anthology *From Chaucer to Poe*. Nor can we call the whole-souled preoccupation with the subject an exclusively poetical quality. That is a quality Poetry shares with all literature of power. What makes these poems poetry is to be found, in part, in the way that intense preoccupation breaks out in a heart's cry that is burdened with an elemental passion. There is a something more than a passion in each of them, a something that is an agony or an ecstasy. The way in which each quintessentializes some phase of life, draws "a kind of quintessence from things," is another quality that makes them poetry. The phrase is Sir John Davies', who used it of the soul. It was Coleridge who saw that it might be applied, "even more appropriately, to the poetic imagination."

It seems to me that we can say now, at least tentatively, that poetry is the statement of a strongly personal and poignant emotion in words that sing, that it is of near kin to ecstasy, and that it quintessentializes some part of life that the poet has discovered for himself.

A consideration of another ten poems will perhaps make these deductions more certain. These ten shall be Herrick's "Gather ye rosebuds," a song; Gray's "Elegy in a Country Churchyard"; Landor's "I strove with none," an epigram; Emerson's "Rhodora," a flower piece of realistic rendering; Poe's "The Haunted Palace," an allegory; Browning's "The Last Ride Together," a love lyric; Whitman's "The Ox-Tamer," a bestiary of modern sort; Kipling's "The 'Mary Gloster'," a character poem; Frost's "An Old Man's Winter Night," an eclogue in little; and Ledwidge's "An Evening in England," a "music and moonlight" description of nature.

There are in Herrick lyrics so light in tone and of subject so trifling that some readers cannot distinguish them from *vers de société*. It is their serious art and their joy in living that lifts them above such verse. The poems on the theme "Eat, drink and be merry" have been legion all the long centuries there has been poetry in the world. In English literature the note is struck in Chaucer; it is loud in the Elizabethan lyric; it is at its best, of more recent years, in Herrick and Fitzgerald and W. H. Davies. The familiar "Gather ye rosebuds" brims with it. No familiarity can take away its freshness from this poem, no repetition of it can find a flaw in its form. It is a perfect poem chiseled out of life.

> Gather ye rosebuds while ye may,
> Old Time is still a flying;
> And this same flower that smiles today,
> Tomorrow it is dying.

These lines may be quarreled with because they have an under-
current of sadness in them, but so has everything in life. Man is
epicurean chiefly because epicureanism emphasizes the happy side
of things. No cultivation of the code can blot out the other side
of things. Man has always been keenly aware that work has been
his portion, with little time for play, but that work is after all the
symbol of life, that there are worse things than work, that "the
night cometh when no man can work." Herrick has chosen to be
the poet of what hours of play there are, but he has never forgotten, as no preacher can forget, that "the night cometh." It
should always be remembered that "Gather ye rosebuds" is, after
all, but a variant of the teaching of "Ecclesiastes." The verses have
nearly all the characteristics man most cherishes in poetry: lyrical
cry, beauty of form, music, and a reading of life.

One reason that Gray's "Elegy" makes so great an appeal is
that it is a poem of evening. Man knows more about evening than
about any other time of day because it is the time after labor is
over. It may be a time for rest or it may be a time for larking,
or love, or revelry. It is in any event a time in which he has
leisure to look about him and to admire the spectacle of the world,
even should it be only as a background for a girl. There is little
time for looking about, and for taking in the splendor of midday,
at the twelve o'clock lunch hour. Man is too busy eating or too
tired at nooning to think of much else than of refreshing himself
for the long labor of the afternoon. In the evening he can relax
after supper and chores, and build up enough energy to be aware
of the beauty of earth and sky. He has the chance, if he will, to
be alone in the evening. If he should be with his family, he is less
likely to have his attention diverted from the spectacle of nature
than on his way to work of mornings, or at nooning. On his way
to work he is often hurried or only half-awake or concerned with
his newspaper. At the lunch hour there is a herding together, talk,
gossip, and newspapers again, if the man lives in the city. The
evening has the advantage of being long, too, and a man has time,
if with others, to be talked out and so to fall back for something

to think of on afterglow or fall of night. In the evening somehow, man is less hard, less a driver, less dominated by the mob than at other times of day. Coventry Patmore does not believe men look round them at all, "except once a lifetime," when they are in love. "That," he says, "that, and the child's unheeded dream is all the light of all their day." That is, I think, an extreme view. Man from the earliest times has felt, in other moods, the charm of evening, and of the oncoming of night, when "the stars around the moon look beautiful." In his shirt-sleeves, on the front steps or in a rocking chair on the porch, and puffing a pipe, all America admires the world, in a fashion, of summer evenings. And since few of us in America are more than two generations from the farm, we know or have heard tell of the look of the country just short of dusk. Not only our own lives but the lives of our ancestors have prepared us for Gray's "Elegy."

I have talked and talked, and with malice aforethought, over Gray's "Elegy," to try to account for its extraordinary popularity. It brings to people of all sorts and conditions of life a pleasantness and peace and a consolation for things gone wrong such as does no other poem. It does more than that. It arouses a reverence for itself and a belief that it is the last word in poetry. I have labored to show it is associated with such leisure and such beholding of the beauty of the countryside as falls to the lot of most men, but such associations only begin to account for its appeal. That appeal defies analysis. There is an element of appeal, certainly, in its concern with the common man. The "village Hampden" and the "mute inglorious Milton" flatter Tom, Dick, and Harry reading, and rereading, the poem. Until yesterday all America met the elegy in school and a large part of America had to get it by heart. Its very familiarity is one of the reasons it pleases. Its clarity is another. Here is a poem every mother's son of us can understand. It is liked, too, because it invests familiar things with beauty. It is liked, again, for its music, so similar to that of an organ voluntary in church. Although surprise, change, new experiences, delight us in poetry as in life, there are times when the heart yearns for the familiar. The "Elegy in a Country Churchyard" satisfies this long-ing. All the deep feeling for the countryside in it wins a response from the deep feeling for the countryside there is in most men, even if they prefer the city both for work and play. Not until Masefield wrote "August, 1914" was there another English poem that summed up the appeal of rural England as did the elegy of Gray. Its feeling, its methods of presentation, its burden of thought, may all be obvious, as its many detractors maintain, but you cannot get away from its wide-spread and long continued fame. If any English poem is sure of its place this elegy is.

The elegy is, of course, colored by the temperament of Gray, a grave man and a serious. Evening after evening of his life, the many sights of evening and the much brooding over it, are quintes-sentialized in the poem. There is a subdued and deep-seated melan-choly in it, the very sadness of evening light. This sadness and melancholy are caught in its music and are plangent in the lyricism of its august and forthright lines.

There is, in certain poems, much that is to be overheard as well as to be heard. There is much to be read between the lines. There are suggestions, intimations, cryptic sayings, symbolism, things to be understood not only by mind and heart but by whatever it is that is beyond these, spirit, if you so choose to call it. There are other kinds of poetry that say their say out clearly, that give you precise intellectual concepts of things and acts and thoughts, that make no appeal to anything beyond what the senses reveal to us. There are certain people who like no other sort of poetry, people to whom riddling is intolerable, recondite allusions mere pedantry, mysticism stuff and nonsense. To such people Pope is the first of poets, Landor second only to Pope, and Austin Dobson worthy of such forebears. Cold poetry close to rhetoric is their first choice, and they will delight in it in direct ratio to the grandiloquence of its sentimentality. Such men are sometimes afraid to acknowledge that they admire Owen Meredith's *Lucile*, but they do admire it. They declare "The Charge of the Light Brigade" the best of Tennyson, "In Flanders Fields" of Macrae the outstanding poem in English that came of the World War, and "The glory that was Greece And the grandeur that was Rome" the greatest lines in American literature. Those two lines are great lines, but they are all but rhetoric. The rondeau of Macrae and the battle piece of Tennyson are stirring poems, but they are not of the first order of poetry.

The epigram is a favored form of poetry with such readers. They delight in Landor's "Rose Aylmer," and they hold his equally famous quatrain perfection itself:

> I strove with none, for none was worth my strife;
> Nature I loved, and next to Nature, Art;
> I warmed both hands before the fire of life;
> It sinks, and I am ready to depart.

No matter what one's preferences in poetry, one must own that these lines realize wholly the intention of the poet writing them. They are finished in form; they sum up a man's life with explicit clarity; they are gravely high and mighty; they gradually freeze more and more into rhetoric, until, in the third line, the feeling is fastbound. Poet after poet has spoken of the fire of life, and Landor but rings a change on the old figure. Phrases of such sort, no matter how craftily shaped to the theme of a poem, seem still on the outside of it, veneered on the thought or emotion rather than inevitably the outcome of the thought or emotion. Rhetoric results when words in a poem, or any form of literature, say more than the underlying thought or feeling warrants, or when the writer resorts to words only for his effects. The writer sometimes has by nature the habit of resorting to words. That is the case of Swinburne. Sometimes he realizes that feeling is wanting, and tries to offset the lack of it by large phrases. That is the way of Sir William Watson. The maker of rhetorical poetry seldom uses his own rhetoric. Swinburne is an exception. Rhetoric, indeed, is most often a diction and an imagery supposed to be inseparable from poetry in one age and inherited in another age by poets who have not the imagination to create their own imagery, or the taste

and power of selection to choose their diction from the speech of
their own time and from the best writing of all time. The words
listed in such lists of "stunning words for poetry" as the Rossettis
played with dim and tarnish quickly. "Pencraft," in the sense that
Sir William Watson uses it, as the power of using nobly traditional
words and falls of sound and imagery, would stereotype poetry
and keep the poet writing to-day in the diction and on the subjects
that Milton chose. The poets who are beginnings are almost never
rhetoricians in their best work. It is only when they feel con-
strained, through some outside influence, to adopt the tune of the
time, that they lapse into rhetoric. Landor is by no means the only
offender.

Emerson's "Rhodora" owes its chief fame to one line, "Then
Beauty is its own excuse for being." There is more to the poem,
of course, but such a reading of life as that line would be enough
to keep a poem alive down the ages. The poem describes the rhodora, a flower of the heath family that is closely akin to the rhodo-
dendron, and gives the very atmosphere of the swampy place in
which, in May woods, you find it in bloom. The poem has failed
to make the rhodora known to all Americans, but that so shy and
out-of-the-way a flower is known at all widely is largely due to
it. Emerson had the gift of caring for many of the little things
of out-of-doors, and you, reading the poem, feel the joy he had
in this little thing, the rhodora, at sight of its rose-purple flowers
spreading their "leafless blooms in a damp nook." There are other
good lines than the famous twelfth, one of them so memorably
musical that it refutes in itself the contention that Emerson had
no ear. That line, the thirteenth, is an address to the rhodora:
"Why thou wert there, O rival of the rose?" It presents a variation in *r* sounds comparable to that in *v*'s of Poe in "The viol,
the violet and the vine" which so delighted Ernest Dowson. It is
the discovery about beauty, though, that sends us to "The Rhodora" again and again. What would else be only a descriptive poem
interesting to those who know the flower is lifted to a place in the
consideration of the world by that line.

It is music and the sense of otherwhere that underlie the charm of Poe. In "The Haunted Palace" the allegory is alienating, as allegory always is. From the nursery up we dislike the tale with a moral, and we are always a little suspicious of any hidden meaning. If the poem says one thing and means something else too, or another thing altogether, we are never sure about it. Such a poem bothers us, tends to confuse us, is taking us in maybe, in some way, ridiculing us even. And yet there has been allegorical poetry, symbolic poetry, riddling poetry, from the beginning. "The Haunted Palace" has the color of medieval times. Not even Campion's "Tourneys and great challenges of knights" gives us more of the fanfare and trappings of chivalry. The palace towers before us:

> In the greenest of our valleys
> By good angels tenanted.
>
> . . . . .
>
> Banners yellow, glorious, golden,
> On its roof did float and flow,
> (This—all this—was in the olden
> Time long ago.)

It disconcerts us a little to feel, as stanza follows stanza, that there is a meaning behind the description of the palace. We soon guess, of course, that it is the mind of man the palace symbolizes, a mind in which "wit and wisdom" give place to a "hideous throng" of disordered thoughts. We turn back to the opening stanza, where, for a while, we are in the company of concrete, clearly put things, and to the second stanza with its medieval bravery. We delight in the romance of it, the sense of otherwhere, and the music, a music all compounded of "soft Lydian airs." There is a strong individuality in the verse, a note all Poe's own, and a poignant lyric cry.

It is from Browning, of course, that I shall take the love poem to analyze. But which one shall I take? My choice might be "Porphyria's Lover," but there is madness in it. Or "Meeting at

Night." Or "In Three Days," the experiences of which have fallen
to all. Or I might take "Love among the Ruins," in which the
"girl with eager eyes and yellow hair" waits for him in the little
turret above the sheep pastures. I should choose this last surely
did not the short line alternating with the long line jolt me as I
read. That is the way it is almost always with Browning. In a
poem that you like very much there is a something that prevents
you from being wholly content with it, from admiring all of it.
I had best trust to the memories of forty years ago and pick out
"The Last Ride Together." It has not the abandon of "Meeting
at Night," or the agony of waiting of "In Three Days," or the
sharp contrasts of serenity and passion of "Love among the Ruins."
It is a little too vocal, it is almost declamatory, but it is direct,
simple, and clear. It recites the plea of a lover, to the lady who
has dismissed him, for a last ride together, her acquiescence to
his plea, their ride, and the hope that she will relent. It is a poem
that many men have had by heart in their youth. It has consolation
in it for failure, it ponders life, and it records discoveries about
life. It is a common experience to contrast:

> The petty Done, the Undone vast,
> This Present . . . with the hopeful Past.

It is a weakness of us all to comfort ourselves with the thought
that most of the other fellows are no more successful than we
have been:

> What hand and brain went ever paired?
> What heart alike conceived and dared?
> What act proved all its thought had been?
> What will but felt the fleshly screen?

"The Last Ride Together" puts poetry, sculpture, and music over
against love and life, and it finds life is better than any art and
that love is the best thing in life. It challenges the poet, who holds
"things beautiful the best," with "Sing, riding's a joy, For me I
ride." It rallies the sculptor:

"And that's your Venus, whence we turn
    To yonder girl that fords the burn!"

It raises the question, "The Last Ride Together," with the
so many and so varied tones of voice in it, of whether to-day a
poem is for the ear as well as for the eye, whether a poem is a
poem until it is spoken any more than a play is a play until it is
played. I am not sure of the answer. If I myself care greatly for
a poem I must read it aloud to some one, if it is a short poem.
If it is a long poem I feel that it must remain largely a thing for
the eye. Even with all the "barding," as Frost calls it, the reading
by poets of their works in public, there are no conditions in our
modern life under which a very long poem can be satisfactorily
read aloud. The blank verse play can, sometimes, be heard in the
theatre, but the "Michael" of Wordsworth, *The Wanderings of
Oisin* of Yeats, and *The Daffodil Fields* of Masefield are too long
for any kind of reading that has yet been devised.

There is a wide difference of opinion of how poems short
enough to be recited or read should be read or recited. Should
there be in the presentation something of the art of the old-fashioned elocutionist? I have heard Browning's "Glove" read with
such art to tumultuous applause. Should a poem be interpreted as
a modern actor plays a part, not only with gestures and changes of
voice and of expression, but after a study of all the shades of feeling expressed in the poem? I have heard O'Reilly's "Bohemia"
so interpreted to tumultuous applause. Or should poetry be read
as the poet who wrote it hears it? Yeats reads his verse in one
way; Noyes his in another way; Masefield his in still another.
Frost's way of reading suits Frost's verse, and James Stephens's
way his verse. I have heard the elocutionary minded sympathize
with all five of these poets because they "do not understand how
to put the stuff over." The fact is, of course, that they do. They
have one and all the power to win an audience.

"The Ox-Tamer" of Whitman is further from the conventional form of the poetry of his time than are other good poems

of his. I had thought to consider the description of the song of
the wood-thrush, section thirteen of "When Lilacs Last in the
Dooryard Bloomed," or "With husky haughty lips, O sea," but I
finally settled down to "The Ox-Tamer," after long weighing of
"Italian Music in Dakota" and "The Dead Tenor." "The Ox-
Tamer" has in it the tones of the human voice. It is exactly the
sort of thing one of my neighbors in New Hampshire would
say to another when the slow-moving teams of the two meet upon
the road. It tells of a man, hardly described at all, who has the
gift of quieting steers and of breaking them to the yoke.

See you! on the farms hereabout a hundred oxen young and old, and
    he is the man who has tamed them

. . . . .

How they watch their tamer—they wish him near them—how they
    turn to look after him!
What yearning expression! how uneasy they are when he moves away
    from them.

The poem up to that point is narrative and descriptive. Now it
turns lyric:

Now I marvel what it can be he appears to them (books, politics,
    poems depart—all else departs,)
I confess I envy only his fascination—my silent, illiterate friend,
Whom a hundred oxen love there in his life on farms,
In the northern country far, in the placid, pastoral region.

The poem is poignant in its presentation of the dumb beasts'
trust in their tamer. It is deeply personal in its owning of the
poet's envy of the man's way with the oxen, and in the manner
the mingled pathos and wonder of the relationship of man and
beast described has taken hold of him who has seen it. The poem
is a bit of life discovered for himself by Whitman, with only one
companion piece in our literature, Borrow's description of the
Irish horse-breaker.

    "The 'Mary Gloster' " is a poem as plain as a pikestaff. There is nothing in it that you have to reread to understand, though you will reread it all if you care for poetry that gives you characters. You get to know Sir Anthony quickly, an emphatic seaman who has won his way, by fair means and foul, to more than a million, and to the position of a merchant prince. He is dying when you meet him and talking to his son, whom he despises because the youth is "Harrer and Trinity College," and interested in art, and not in ships and money-making. He is laying an injunction upon his son to bury him at sea from the "Mary Gloster," the ship named for his wife and in which he laid the foundation of his fortune. His body is to be shot overboard where his wife, in her youth, was buried at sea in Macassar Strait.

"The 'Mary Gloster' " is a dramatic monologue. All of it has the quality of talk. It is strident and overemphatic, but so was Sir Anthony. It is vulgar, but so was Sir Anthony. It is obvious, but so was Sir Anthony. Kipling has caught the man vividly, a man at once unscrupulous, high-hearted, and sentimental. There are lyric moments in Sir Anthony's narrative of his life. He recalls the wife of his youth. As he thinks of her death he cries out, as such a man would: "My heart, how young we were!" As he recalls her burial at sea, he cries out: "Tiny she looked on the grating—that oily, treacley sea!" He keeps in character always, most in character, perhaps, in the cry recurrent throughout the long poem, a cry of disappointment in his son: "No help, my son was no help." There is passion in this old cry of disappointment, than which there is none heard oftener at life's end. There are readings of life in the poem, some of them shocking to the thin-skinned. There is a throb in the lines, insistent as that of the sea.

There is no poem in which a phase of American life is quintessentialized more completely than in "An Old Man's Winter Night." It is a scene from the life of farm-country going back, a scene that recurs in a thousand instances every year in New England alone. The poem is a dramatic lyric. All out-of-doors is one character, the old man the second, the scared cellar under him the third. The poem has that sense of ominousness, that sharp loneliness, that very color of place that, until it was written, were known only to those who were neighbors of the old men hanging on to the farms longheld of their people. It is written out of a full knowledge of its material and of the background to that material. Its rhythm is wholly at one with its subject, it has the somber tone of its place and time, the needed resignation to the inevitable. It has in it a reading of life, in the placing of the old man's relation to the world, so memorable that it cannot out of mind after a first meeting with it. That reading of life is: "A light he was to no one but himself." There is a loneliness in the line as great as the loneliness of the couplet that brings "The Twa Corbies" to an end. The close of Frost's poem, too, is impressive:

> One aged man—one man—can't keep a house,
> A farm, a countryside, or if he can,
> It's thus he does it of a winter night.

The deep sympathy and understanding of the poem never near sentimentality; it has the right hardness of texture; its form is perfect; it achieves a beauty of a kind that was not in poetry in English before its creation.

Francis Ledwidge contents those who love the music-and-moonlight kind of poetry. He follows on the old main highway of the English poets, with Keats beckoning him on. His is a soft and insinuating verse, sweet, dew-drenched, savorsome on the lips. It is a verse thrillingly aware of all the beauty of the world; its maker's senses are keen, not only sight and hearing and touch, but taste and smell as well. There is a slow and delicious music to his lines that soothes you as does a light stir of air at noon, a music that leaves you in a kind of poppied and half-conscious ease. "From its blue vase the rose of evening drops" steals on you like an opiate. "The dim silence falling on the grey" is a caress. There is splendor, lessened by a suggestion of rhetoric, in "Night tells her rosary of stars full soon." You foresee the moon is about to rise, and it does, and lovelily. "The moon Leans on one horn as if beseeching ease." It is a beautiful poem of the traditional sort, "An Evening in England," but there is no genius of place in it, no tang of bog or sharp bite of salt air, nothing to individualize it save its music. There is deep feeling in the poem, ecstasy even, and music, and music, and music. It is pure poetry of a long-credited order.

It may be that I should have considered other forms of poetry than those I have considered. The thirteen poems analyzed include no more than half of the forms and kinds of poetry. The narrative kinds of poetry have been little discussed, epic and *fabliau* and realistic narrative and episode not at all. Dramatic poetry has been discussed hardly at all, yet the blank verse play has given us, obviously, as great poetry as we have, and play in rhyme, and dialogue, and debate all have their place. The philosophical poem, the credo, gnomic poetry generally, the riddle, the hymn, and the many other forms of religious poetry have not been taken up and weighed. Occasional poetry, too, has been left out. Yet the thirteen poems we have analyzed, in their thirteen different forms, represent many phases of life over a period of three hundred years and more. One and all these thirteen poems reveal that human nature has not changed at all during the long years of modern English literature.

The common denominators to all thirteen poems are naturally those we found in the three first analyzed. They are the heart's cry breaking out in the verse, what Matthew Arnold called "lyrical cry," music, a something very like ecstasy, fresh imagery, memorable sayings, and the rendering of the quintessence of the subjects considered. There is, of course, that absorption by the subject noted above and the strong stamp of personality.

Poetry is, then, so far as one reader of it can see, the statement of a strongly personal and poignant emotion in words that sing, of near kin to ecstasy, and possessed of the power to give the quintessence of the subject considered, a subject from some corner of the world that the writer has long pondered and made his own.

And if it be objected that this definition fits lyric poetry only, then I say that the lyrical element in poetry is what makes poetry of whatever kind poetry, that poetry can no more be great without the lyrical element in it than prose literature can be great without poetry in it. Which is only saying again that the lyric element is the animating breath of all literature. This is not saying that the lyrical form is the greatest kind of poetry. It is saying, I repeat, that no poetry can be great without the lyric element. The old teaching was that dramatic poetry was the greatest kind of poetry because it was a fusion of lyric and epic poetry, an apotheosis of the two· made one.

It is so necessary to be clear in this discussion of the nature of poetry that I must restate the essential facts about it. Poetry is, then, I say a third time, the statement of a strongly personal and poignant emotion in words that sing. The emotion from which a poem comes must be completely possessive of the poet, and its writing must have the very color of his personality. What he feels must be revealed through his temperament, and in rhythm. To be great the poem must be original, it must strike a new note. What the poet puts into a poem comes to him in a sort of ecstasy, an ecstasy breaking into words almost of its own impulse. The poem must have such instancy to the heart in matter, and such magic in its phrasing, that it asserts itself as part of its reader's experience as well as of its writer's. It may be outside of the reader's experience at a first reading, but it must have such a way with it that he is led back to rereading on rereading until it becomes a part of him.

Poetry, to be great, must achieve a new beauty, a beauty of words and of music, of images and of color that has not been before. Poetry must have suddenness and an element of surprise. It may intoxicate or astound; it may bewilder or bewitch; it may widen horizons or concentrate attention on a near thing not before realized as a wonder; it may transfigure familiar things, or it may strip them of illusions: but, whatever it does else, it must make us feel. Poetry is all the better poetry if it goes further and makes us see and know as well as feel.

A poet who counts makes some corner of the world his own, and he gives us its quintessence in poems so clear against the skies that we can no more forget them than we can the evening star, or firebells, or a loved face. Such a poet will make discoveries about life, have insight into hidden things, reveal truths unknown before.

The material of poetry is not restricted to any particular kind or kinds of subject. Its material is not only all that is "romantic," not only what can be presented to an accompaniment of "music and moonlight," but all life that has been lived and felt passionately, and that can be told of in awakening and rhythmic language. Incalculable harm has been done to poetry by an insistence that it is concerned only with what is elevated and noble, that it is difficult to understand, that it can be appreciated only by rare natures, that it is not for the man in the street. There are many who with the best will in the world do all the arts a disservice by insisting that they must be approached reverentially. If the fine arts are ever to be universally loved, they will have to be made familiar things, as much a part of daily life as work and play and talk, as fellowship and sport and adventure.

There was a time when our English talk had in it much of poetry. It was from the talk of its time came the cadences and tones of the King James Bible, its words that are pictures, its color of life. And there was a time, much less distant, when there was talk that kindled into poetry in many a corner store and tavern in America. The "Rude poets of the tavern hearth" of "Monadnock" is not an idle phrase. There were fantasy and imagination, there were vividness of idiom and a winning fall of words, there was lyric feeling, in that recurrent discussion of a long winter's evening in Ansel's store, on "Whether you take milk from the cow or the cow gives down her milk." And there was the old chant of our tongue, the authentic voice of poetry, in that comment of Frank the auctioneer as he cried a pair of snowshoes at Alonzo Bickford's sale.

"Oh ho! What do you think of them?" he began, holding up the shoes one in each hand, and both in fine fettle. "Filled in, both of them, and with rawhide. You don't need 'em now, but it's coming winter. Hear it now in that wind is whistling by. Get these snowshoes now, and be ready against when it's here."

There was gusto in his words, because of the good workmanship of the shoes, and because he loved crying an auction. There was rhythm in his words, because he was of the old stock of New England and because he was little read. He inherited the traditional speech of his countryside, a speech unvitiated among the oldest generation by much reading of newspapers and cheap magazines. Talk was to him more than the half of life, a something in which he had as much pride as in his political influence, his young wife's cleverness, and his three yoke of Herefords.

It was Synge who emphasized the fact that poetry should deal with "the strong things of life" to show through such dealing that "what is exalted or tender is not made by feeble blood." He went on to say: "It may almost be said that before verse can be human again it must learn to be brutal." His belief is that poetry must broaden out again in its scope to what it was when men like Chaucer and Shakespeare, Villon and Burns, men far from cloistered, delighted in it and delighted through it.

Masefield was Synge's friend, and the sharer of intimate talks with him on art and life. And it was undoubtedly in the spirit of what Synge advocated that Masefield wrote *The Everlasting Mercy* and *The Widow in the Bye Street*. Kipling, uninfluenced by Synge, had already come to somewhat similar conclusions, and had written a poetry that certainly was not of "feeble blood," and that was at its best, exalted. John Davidson had taken common things and mean, and had made them into what was fine and uncommon, in poems as different as his version of "Tararaboomdeay" and *The Testament of an Empire Builder*. Hardy helped the cause of the widening of the scope of poetry with "The Fire at Tranter Sweatley's," "The Dance at the Phoenix," and "A Tramp-woman's Tragedy." W. H. Davies brought again the voice of the sturdy beggar into English poetry. All these infusions of rough and low life and of the rough and low things of life into poetry were in the very spirit of the long teaching by precept and example of Walt Whitman.

The tendency away from purely lyrical poetry to a kind of dramatic narrative more or less realistic, in the early years of the twentieth century, helped to widen the appeal of poetry. For a generation, at any rate, in late Victorian times, the lyric had reigned supreme. Such narratives as were then approximately popular were romanticized writing brought into being by *The Idylls of the King* and by the Pre-Raphaelite ballads. It was the spectacle of Shakespeare as well as the old teaching derived from the Greeks that gave dramatic poetry the place it held so long. Because our greatest poet was a dramatist and because we hold long to traditional teaching and because drama had the acclaim of the town, the reign of dramatic poetry lasted well into the eighteenth century. From the time of Burns on, however, the lyric grew steadily in popular and critical favor, and it established its preëminence after Scott turned to prose as the medium of the romantic tale. Scott and Byron were the last popular writers of unetherealized narrative in verse until the day of Kipling and Masefield. T. E. Brown, somehow, never got the hearing you would have expected from the quality of his Manx tales.

To-day Frost is so sure that the dramatic is the thing that he can say, in the introduction to *A Way Out* (1929): "Everything is as good as it is dramatic. It need not declare itself in form, but it is drama, or nothing." It has already been pointed out that there is a lyric element in all dramatic poetry. It is this same lyric quality that makes a narrative dramatic by bringing the speaker before you in his own person. The lyric quality is as necessary to all poetry, I repeat, as poetry is necessary to essay or novel or play in prose if these forms shall be great. What made lyrical poetry in late Victorian times a thing of less wide appeal was the feebleness of its blood, or the aloofness of its material from the common interest of men. Poetry has been made a something other than a matter of coterie appreciation by our latter-day poets' concern with the whole of life.

CHAPTER II

Poetry the First of Our Arts

POETRY is the first of the arts of the peoples who speak English. Its only rival is the architecture of cathedrals and cottages in the old country and of village homes and farmhouses in America. Salisbury Cathedral, rose-red in the evening light, and rising from its water meads, lark-high to heaven, is as beautiful a building as there is anywhere in the four countries of Great Britain and Ireland. The butcher shop in Selborne Village under the north downs in Hampshire, straw-thatched and white-walled, is as perfect in its humble kind as Salisbury Cathedral with all those pinnacles springing so lightly aloft. A Pennsylvania farmhouse, under a cedared hill and against a snowy landscape, is simplicity itself in its straight lines and its restful gray of mica-schist. A manse in a village street in New England, white of clapboards and green-shuttered, and cool in the half light of the spreading elms about it, is another triumph of simplicity. It is low, earth-clinging, long, and every detail of its stoop and front door and heavily mullioned windows at one in restraint and balanced beauty.

There are good things in plenty in the other arts that have flourished in the civilization of the English-speaking peoples. Only in architecture, though, and in poetry, do these arts stand out with unquestioned superiority when compared with similar arts in other civilizations. German music has a higher place in the world than English music. French painting has a higher place in the world than English painting. Greek sculpture has a higher place than English sculpture. The acting, dancing, and oratory of other peoples rank higher than the acting, dancing, and oratory of the English-speaking peoples.

No one can contend that the homes of the people of the English civilizations the world over compare in beauty, even at their best, with the English poetry created cotemporaneously with the building of those homes. And though the public buildings of America, and England, and Australia, and South Africa, that have been built of recent years are, many of them, beautiful and noble structures, they do not compare for nobility and beauty with English poetry cotemporaneous to them. Castles and manor houses, scores of them in England, are places of pilgrimage. For themselves and apart from their associations, but like English timbered cottages and Pennsylvania farmhouses and New England village homes, they are few of them so fine as the poetry that has come out of the times in which they were built.

There have been no cathedrals built in English-speaking countries in modern times that can compare with Salisbury Cathedral, but even Salisbury Cathedral itself is not such a triumph of art as the *Canterbury Tales* of Chaucer or the plays of Shakespeare. All of life, practically, is in the *Canterbury Tales*. *Troilus and Cressida* is an analytic realistic novel with characters that are "figures against the sky." "The Knight's Tale" has epic quality. Short story, sententious essay, lyric poem, all have place in these tales that present us with so vivid a cross-section of fourteenth century England.

In Shakespeare we have all of life projected so dramatically that all the world has taken all of him to heart. There is analysis of life in the sonnets so deep as to be terrifying. There are the world's greatest portraits of men and women in the plays. There is a mastery over speech, and a splendor of poetry in his writing that no other man has attained to. There has been no long period of time since Shakespeare's day in which there have not been great figures in English poetry. There have been buildings of great beauty erected since Elizabethan times, public buildings, castles, country-seats, colleges, churches, blocks of city dwellings, office buildings, hotels, cottages, but you cannot claim that they are rivals in beauty and significance to the great post-Elizabethan poets, that they are the honor to England that are Milton and Herrick, Gray and Wordsworth, Shelley and Keats, Tennyson and Browning, Kipling and Hardy, Masefield and A. E. Housman.

The range of poetry is wider than the range of architecture or, for that matter, of any of the other arts. It concerns itself with everything in life, little or big, new or old, worldly or unworldly. It is impossible, therefore, to reduce the themes of poetry to a table of topics. Bacon is said, in his essays, to have considered all the great things in life, and his list of titles to the essays to be a list of such great things. Poetry, however, is just as much concerned with things that men in great place hold inconsequential as with those they hold consequential. One wonders what Horace Walpole, for instance, thought in his heart of Burns writing about a mouse upturned by the plough. The long preaching on the sparrow's fall must have had some effect, but the conventional values that the centers put upon things in life are apt to prevail. The poets have, like the clerics, been many of them against the world and its ways. So it is that nowadays in poetry we do not find the laudation of war and power, leadership and high place, that were general in times when poets were hangers-on at courts or clerics dependent on some lord's bounty or impecunious men about town who could not publish except under patronage. In the old days the poets who lived by the theaters or by hackwork generally were more independent than these others, but they had nothing like the freedom of a Whitman or a Masefield.

A Kipling can still write:

> Four things greater than all things are:
> Women and horses, power and war.

Yet the declaration is generally accepted as more than half youthful smartness. It is, of course, possible that what the poet means to say is that women are topic number one, in smoking-room gossip, sport topic number two, politics and business topic number three, and war topic number four. Or it is possible to reverse the numbering, interpreting Kipling's order as climacteric. It is true that love is still the inspiration of more poetry than any other topic.

It is equally true that there is not enough poetry of sport. It is difficult to get poetry out of politics or of trade. A consideration of either generally results in satire.

The poet long ago realized the truth of Bacon's statement: "It is a strange desire, to seek power and to lose liberty." The modern poet, therefore, has little interest in a man's lust of power over his fellows. Freedom is so precious to him he would never think of exchanging it for power. The poet is sometimes recognized to-day by an appointment to some public office, generally in the diplomatic service, but those who have sought political power are very few indeed.

That there will eventually come more poetry out of man's modern way of making things seems likely, as out of the revival of small trades in that general development of artisanship into artistry of which there are so many symptoms about us.

There were laudations of war written by poets during the World War, but they were largely outnumbered by laments over war and bitter satires on the men who were responsible for war.

The old theme of patriotism, too, has weakened as an inspiration for poetry. It is not so much that any feeling of internationalism or what not has taken its place, as that it is, like religion, difficult material for poetry. It is almost true to say that the mob spirit must be present for us much to enjoy the "Onward, Christian Soldier" of Baring-Gould or Riley's "American Flag." I have heard ten massed bands playing the hymn and all a city's crowded center singing it, but the effect made was not the effect of poetry. I have heard Riley recite his verses at a college banquet in after-dinner mood—before 1917—and the success of the recitation was as great in its way as the success of the thundered hymn, but its effect was not the effect of poetry.

The prevalent themes of poetry to-day seem to be: the joy of living; love; the sense of the brevity of all good things; the beauty of the world; the inner realities of things, truth about life as revealed by vision and insight; and the otherworld, the supernatural, dream.

Poetry, of course, is to be found in prose as well as in verse.

There are passages in the Bible, a great many of them in the Old Testament, in the "Psalms," in "Job," in "Isaiah," in the "Song of Solomon," and in "Ecclesiastes" that are very noble poetry. There are passages in the prose of Sir Thomas Browne, of Carlyle, of Emerson, of W. H. Hudson, and of Dunsany that can be compared, for their poetry, with these great passages in the Bible. It is not with poetry in prose that I am concerned in this book, however, but with poetry in verse. It is poetry in verse that captures and retains the greatest moments of life in the fewest words. It is Browning who says:

> How good is man's life, the mere living! how fit to employ
> All the heart and the soul and the senses forever in joy!

and Stephen Phillips who echoes him with a line:

> How good it is to live even at the worst.

The mere sense of being alive, of breathing fresh air, of basking in the sunlight, of drinking in the scent of spring woods or summer clover, the sense of renewed energy after eating, the play of lithe muscles—all these things, high or low as you may call them, have called forth poetry. It is Sturge Moore who begins a child's poem: "How nice it is to eat." There is much poetry about idling. As W. H. Davies says:

> What is this life if, full of care,
> We have no time to stand and stare?

Walt Whitman's "Song of the Open Road" is full of this joy in the sense of being. It is often associated, of course, with other impulses, with the joy of wandering and the joy in new horizons.

> Afoot and light-hearted I take to the open road,
> Healthy, free, the world before me,
> The long brown path before me leading wherever I choose.

The love of man and woman has been for so long a main theme of poetry that to many people it is the chief theme of poetry. It is unquestionably true, of course, that, the world over, great love stories have stood out among the greatest stories of all peoples. And the time seems little likely ever to come when men will forget Helen of Troy, or Hero and Leander, or Tristram and Iseult, or Sigurd and Brynhild, or Romeo and Juliet, or Richard Feverel and Lucy, or Angel Clare and Tess, or Heyst and Lena. These, of course, are great love stories all, and whether they are those of unidentified old authors, or those of Shakespeare and Meredith, of Hardy and Conrad, they are all stories presented with lyric ecstasy.

The lament over the little while man has to live, over the quick fall of bloom, over the brevity of all good things, is a note constant to poetry of all times. One thinks of the fourteenth chapter of "Job":

Man that is born of woman is of few days, and full of trouble.
He cometh forth like a flower, and is cut down: he fleeth also as a
    shadow, and continueth not.

One thinks of:

> And since to look at things in bloom
> Fifty springs are little room,
> About the woodlands I will go
> To see the cherry hung with snow.

And one thinks of "Nothing gold can stay."

Beauty, too, is one of the fundamentals of all poetry. The beauty of the world, I mean, the joy the poet has in external nature in her rarest moods. As my mind turns to this subject, there arises before any line of verse a prose passage of Synge in his *Aran Islands*. He is in a coracle, a skin boat, in a rough sea going from Aran toward the mainland. The beauty of the whole scene is so great that he cries out, "The black curragh working slowly through this world of grey, and the soft hissing of the rain, gave me one of the moods in which we realize with immense distress the short moment we have left us to experience all the wonder and beauty of the world."

The necessity of beauty has been recognized throughout the English-speaking world ever since industrialism on a large scale and the herding of men together about great factories began to threaten the existence of the beauty of countryside and the beauty of old buildings. Keats gave us the slogan that has been sounded ever since in "A thing of beauty is a joy for ever." Emerson's "Beauty is its own excuse for being" helped to keep consideration of the matter before America. Ruskin's pleas for beauty bore fruit in both America and England. There is hardly a poet of all the many of our tongue who has not written well of the beauty of the world. Often the lines imprisoning such beauty from nature are all that one remembers of all a man's writing. So it is of a many-volumed poet—all I recall is the two lines: "A touch of red on the hardwood trees" and "The white-throat's lonely whistle in the rain."

The discoveries about life that poetry makes are one of the easiest qualities of poetry to discuss. Here you are dealing with very definite things, with things that are clear intellectual concepts, things that do not depend on one's imagination or feeling for their appreciation. One recognizes at once the truth of statement after statement about life in *Hamlet*.

> To thine own self be true
> And it must follow as the night the day
> Thou canst not then be false to any man

will serve for sample. Wordsworth is another of the poets with vision. We all know: "Thoughts that do often lie too deep for tears." And as we look back on childhood we agree that: "Heaven lies about us in our infancy." This "Ode on Intimations of Immortality from Recollections of Early Childhood" has in it as many memorable lines as any English poem. There is hardly a one of us who, remembering some hour of hours of yesterday, or day before yesterday, or from years long gone, will not say: "It was with me as it was with this man writing:"

There was a time when meadow, grove, and stream,
The earth, and every common sight
    To me did seem
Apparelled in celestial light,
The glory and the freshness of a dream.

George Meredith gives us a phrase that well describes this
sort of revelation. He calls such a revelation a reading of life.
That is the title of one of his volumes of verse and he himself
is full of such readings. A long one is:

Blood and brain and spirit, three—
(Say the deepest gnomes of earth),
Join for true felicity.

It may take some experience of life to realize the truth of what
Masefield says in:

All beauty in a little room may be
Though the roof lean and muddy be the floor,

but years of living and seeing drive home its truth. "Keep up
your heart, the day's as yet but noon" is a ringing burst of Masefield. Robert Frost has line after line of such caliber. We all know
the man who is "A decent product of life's ironing out." We may
not all agree with that other declaration of his that "The best
way out is always through," but we all recognize it as a splendid
challenge. Another such challenge is the line of John Davidson,
"And one against the world will always win." Another equal
challenge from Davidson is "Business, the world's work, is the
sale of lies."

There is, too, the poetry of otherworldly things, of supernatural things, of things of romance, of "perilous seas in faery
lands forlorn," on which we look out from magic casements. There
is glamorous poetry of this sort in Spenser, in Blake, in Coleridge,
in Rossetti, in Yeats, in De La Mare and Ralph Hodgson. Spenser
conjures up worlds unlike any we know in "The Cave of Mam-
mon" and in "The Bowers of Bliss":

The joyous birdes, shrouded in cheerful shade,
Their notes unto the voice attempered sweet;
Th' Angelicall soft trembling voices made
To th' instruments divine respondence meet;
The silver sounding instruments did meet
With the base murmure of the waters' fall.
The waters' fall with difference discreet,
Now soft, now loud, unto the wind did call;
The gentle warbling wind low answered to all.

Blake can ask of the

Tiger! Tiger! burning bright
In the forests of the night

whether he was of God:

Did he who made the Lamb make thee?

Lines like these have a strangeness and wonder of which no
familiarity can rob them. Read a hundred times they are still
things of mystery, like the worlds beyond the stars, or the impulses that lead staid folks to wild actions.

There is strangeness and wonder and otherworldliness in poem
after poem of Coleridge. We all of us recognize these qualities as
one of the sources of the charm of "The Ancient Mariner," and
they are so emphasized as to be almost repellent in "Christabel."
In "Kubla Khan" there is such a concentration of pure romance
as we may come upon in scarcely any other place.

In Xanadu did Kubla Khan
A stately pleasure-dome decree:
Where Alph, the sacred river, ran
Through caverns measureless to man
Down to a sunless sea.

Nor is there often in any poetry, mystery-haunted or not, such
music as that in another passage of this same poem:

> The shadow of the dome of pleasure
> Floated midway on the waves;
> Where was heard the mingled measure
> From the fountains and the caves.

Strangeness and wonders were always at the beck and call of Rossetti. We find them in:

> The blessed damozel leaned out
> From the gold bar of Heaven.

There the strangeness and wonder are in the picture the words paint and in the quality of the sound of the lines. In "Love's Nocturn" it is difficult to analyze just why,

> Darkness and the breath of space
> Like loud waters everywhere

strikes at your heart as it does. There is a cold that creeps into your bones in: "In the shaken trees the chill stars shake." There is the magic of a world beyond this world we know in "The Withering of the Boughs" of Yeats:

> I know, and the curlew and peewit on Echtge of streams:
> No boughs have withered because of the wintry wind;
> The boughs have withered because I have told them my dreams.

In "Winter Dusk" of De La Mare it is a ghost brings the other-world into the quiet of the nursery where a mother is reading fairy stories:

> Dark frost was in the air without,
>   The dusk was still with cold and gloom,
> When less than even a shadow came
>   And stood within the room.

I have not dwelt on the beauties of rhythm in poetry because I take it that we are all agreed great poetry must have such rhythm. It is as much the rhythm of the poet as his attitude

toward life that makes up that new note we must find in a poet
to acclaim him as one of the great. Five times it seems to me in
poetry in America we have heard such a new note; first in Emerson, again in Poe, and still again in Whitman. Then there came
Emily Dickinson, with such discoveries as "Success is counted
sweetest by those who ne'er succeed," and with such lyric ecstasies
as that in her description of the humming bird

> A route of evanescence
> With a revolving wheel;
> A resonance of emerald,
> A rush of cochineal.

And in our own time has come Robert Frost. There is a new
music in "Stopping by Woods on a Snowy Evening." The poet
wonders if his little horse does not think it queer to stop here by
the frozen lake "without a farm house near," on so dark a night,
and the snow falling all about:

> He gives his harness bells a shake
> To ask if there is some mistake.
> The only other sound's the sweep
> Of easy wind and downy flake.

> The woods are lovely, dark and deep.
> But I have promises to keep,
> And miles to go before I sleep,
> And miles to go before I sleep.

One can distinguish a new rhythm as one can distinguish a
new attitude toward life in a poet. We never had before the day
of Spenser, for instance, the rhythm of Spenser, or before the
day of Milton the rhythm of Milton, or before the day of Keats
the rhythm of Keats, or before the day of Poe the rhythm of
Poe, or before the day of Swinburne the rhythm of Swinburne.
Each of these men brought about a new music of words in English. We never heard before Poe:

Helen, thy beauty is to me
Like those Nicæan barks of yore,
That gently, o'er a perfumed sea,
The weary, wayworn wanderer bore
To his own native shore.

Nor did we have before Swinburne such a rhythm as that we find in:

In a coign of the cliff between lowland and highland,
At the sea-down's edge between windward and lee,
Walled round with rocks as an inland island,
The ghost of a garden fronts the sea.

The clarity of Milton's blank verse, its sureness of accent, its spaciousness, mark it apart from all blank verse before its time, but it is its processional rhythm that most influenced the poets who imitated it. The grand style of his sonnets and the sonorous roll of certain of his odes owe, too, a large part of their impressiveness to their rhythm. Before Milton there had been nothing in English poetry like:

Oft on a plat of rising ground
I hear the far-off curfew sound
Over some wide-watered shore,
Swinging slow with sullen roar.

Melancholy has there its most musical presentment. There are mingled in these lines the melancholy of bells at evening over great estuaries with mist gathering off shore, the melancholy of oncoming night, the melancholy inseparable from the intimations of death in the scene and the hour.

Poetry has come into new honor and dignity in these past thirty years. When Yeats wrote *The King's Threshold* (1904), the poet had not always a place at the table of the king. That play was a protest against the lawmaker, the warrior, and the priest being more highly regarded than the poet. Since that time Yeats, by his readings of his verse, and by his talk about the place of poetry in life, and by his winning of the Nobel Prize in 1923, has helped toward this new honor and dignity of poetry. Yeats was the first English poet to come here "barding," after Arnold's visits in the eighteen-eighties. Since the time of Yeats have come Noyes, and Masefield, and Wilfrid Gibson and others; and our own poets Frost, and Vachel Lindsay, and Carl Sandburg have carried on the good work.

There was a time when the phrase "There is more truth than poetry about that" was not questioned. To-day it is questioned. Poetry is no longer generally regarded as a thing of music and moonlight merely, a gilding for the grey of things, mere picturesqueness of phrasing, and the beating-up of a beautiful syllabub of words. Masefield has made it very apparent that there is a poetry of common things. He can write sea chanties in low language and he can write sonnets that are studies of many phases of beauty. He can put a rowdy moment in such words as

> Your nose is a red jelly, your mouth's a toothless wreck,
> And I am atop of you, banging your head upon the dirty deck,

and he can write:

> I have seen dawn and sunset on moors and windy hills
> Coming in solemn beauty like slow old tunes of Spain:
> I have seen the lady April bringing the daffodils,
> Bringing the springing grass and the soft warm April rain.

Masefield is even one of the best sellers of our time, with Wilfrid Gibson a close second.

I can well remember how strange it seemed when during the Venezuela crisis of 1896 a sonnet of William Watson was cabled to America. Later it became inevitable to cable important poems such as "For All We Have and Are" of Kipling at the outset of the World War, and his verses, "Great-Heart," on the death of Roosevelt. Newspaper men now go down to the docks in New York to meet incoming poets and to interview them, and the proprietors of lecture bureaus demand fees in four figures for some of them. Mountains are named for poets. Where I live in the summer I look out upon Mt. Larcom, named after Lucy Larcom, and Mt. Whittier, named for the poet of *Snowbound*. The Whittier Highway runs from West Ossipee to Meredith just north of these two mountains.

It has been only in the last two generations that men have come to realize that without the words of the poets few men can talk well or write well. The poets have given us nearly all the phrases we use. Go to a performance of *Hamlet* and you will hear a hundred such phrases. "Rich, not gaudy"; "the primrose path of dalliance"; "indifferent honest"; "caviare to the general"; "tear passion to tatters"; "outherod Herod"; "the lady doth protest too much"; "the insolence of office"; "frailty, thy name is woman"; "more in sorrow than in anger" will make a ten that will serve. It is from Shakespeare and the Bible and Milton, from Wordsworth, Tennyson, and Kipling that we get the words we use daily.

Poetry can say infinitely more in a few words than any other form of writing. There is a whole love story in the line of Yeats: "She put on womanhood, and he lost peace." Swinburne puts a truth about the dead that knells like a funeral bell in the line, "They have the night who had like us the day."

So it has been in all the long heyday of poetry in English,—the most of what is important to the race and the world; the best said, has been in verse. There have been periods when the power of English poetry has lessened, but there has been no period since the times of Elizabeth in which there has not been written English poetry of beautiful imagery and arresting music and full of discoveries about life. Poetry, as I said at the outset, is, above everything else, the great artistic heritage of the race.

All the other forms of literature, the novel, the play, the essay, the short story, depend upon poetry. If there is not poetry in a novel, it is not great; if there is not poetry in a play, it is not great; if there is not poetry in an essay, it is not great; if there is not poetry in a short story, it is not great. No form of literature can be great without poetry in it.

We have come into that happy state when poetry is no longer a thing to be avoided. It is becoming more and more a thing of daily use. It will shortly be as necessary to us as food and clothing. Even the most self-conscious among us need have no longer the fear that by their interest in poetry they betray themselves as highbrow or apart from their fellow-men. Poetry is taking its place among the things we cannot get along without. The day is fast approaching when all the world of cultivated people will admit the necessity of poetry.

CHAPTER III

The Debt to Wordsworth

IT IS a curious chance that made Coleridge and Wordsworth, the fellows of the *Lyrical Ballads,* the two main influences over the poetry of the century following the publication of their joint collection of verse in 1798. The direct influence of each was equally wide-spread, the indirect influence of Wordsworth more wide-spread. Wordsworth was owned not only as master, but as the liberating force that set poets free of masters, and allowed them to develop their own individualities, to be themselves. The influence of Coleridge was the influence of the romantic quality of his poetry, of his tone, and of his ballad forms and methods. The influence of Wordsworth was from his infinite humanity; his concern with many humble sorts of men; as well as from his concern with nature, his knowledge of beasts and birds and "the vegetable world." There was, too, the influence of his mystical ecstasy over out-of-doors. There was, too, the influence of his homely and commonplace words, words used sometimes flatly, but, at his best, with such a simple surety that no poetry has ever known a more perfect felicity of phrase or a greater lyric sweetness.

Poetry is at its utmost in "To the Cuckoo" and "The Solitary Reaper." There are those unappreciative of the intensity of response in the human heart to the little incidents in the great ritual of nature. There are those who see nothing but a happy reaction to an insistent bird-cry in

> Thrice welcome, darling of the Spring!
> Even yet thou art to me
> No bird, but an invisible thing,
> A voice, a mystery.

What such indifferent folk miss is half of life. Man from the earliest times has waited and waited and waited through long winter and slow-coming spring for the bird-voice that would tell him of the approach of the time of the drying up of frost-bound and wet land, of the season of quickening life and growth in all nature, of those good days when he could go to sleep out of doors in some sunny nook out of the wind and take no hurt from cold and damp. Man has waited for the cuckoo as he has waited for the nightingale. Let us not forget that even so early as the "Riddles" associated with Cynewulf men of Viking sort were so moved by the voice of "the evening-singer old" that they sat listening "with bent heads" to the wonder of that tumultuous hindered song.

Nor do all and sundry, especially in this age of the dominance in criticism of mere city-dwellers, realize to the full what is implied and symbolized and conveyed subconsciously as well as consciously to those to whom associations are of first importance, by the "yellow primrose" passage in "Peter Bell." I am not of those who ridicule "Peter Bell," but even did I grant that the man in the street had reason to laugh at it, I should maintain it justified itself for the three lines:

> A primrose by a river's brim
> A yellow primrose was to him,
> And it was nothing more.

It was the old gentleman with the patriarchal beard who made clear to me the meaning of those lines, though he was unaware of what he was elucidating. He sat just across the aisle from us in the church of my childhood. He had lived long in the island of St. Thomas in the West Indies. One morning as we left church he heard some one complaining of the dandelions in the churchyard sward. "You should be glad of them there," he said to the objector. "When I was in St. Thomas, I tried always to have dandelions in a border of my flower-garden. They meant home to me, God's country of Pennsylvania, more than did any one thing." I was a boy just in college then, beginning to find joy in the poetry of Wordsworth for the record in him of the out-of-doors I so loved. It was the associations that you had with a flower that were at the bottom of half your love for it.

All America loves ·lilacs because they are the dooryard shrub of all America, and yesterday all America had a dooryard. It takes two generations, at any rate, for knowledge of a known and loved thing to die out of a family. Those of us now sixty are no more than a generation from the village or the farm, those of us thirty no more than two generations from such good places. Nothing in all Whitman gives him so firm a place in the affections of his countrymen as his praise of lilacs, his preoccupation with lilacs, to him, as to most of us, the symbol of the dooryard. Arbutus or mayflower, call it which you will; plum and pear and apple-bloom; damask rose or sweetbriar or moss rose; that hardy perennial we call Bouncing Bet in Pennsylvania and chimney pink in New Hampshire; summer heliotrope and white phlox—not one of these so widely known plants or shrubs of the dooryard is so universally loved as the lilac bush with its flowers purple or white making sweet all the neighborhood of the house in April or May or June, whenever it is that spring is at full tide in this place or that or another.

It may not be necessarily a thing of beauty, or of so lovable a beauty as a yellow primrose, that stirs us so deeply. I was traveling west one time in a train from Denver to Oakland. Two Australian boys had been for two days just nice college boys in the casual but close acquaintanceship common on such trains. In the Sacramento Valley a chance gust of wind brought in the aroma of sun-warmed red gum. It went to the heads of the boys like wine. That scent was Australia to them, and they were immediately bubbling to all of us at our end of the car of home and old days. There was now an intimacy to their talk it had not even approached before.

That fragrance of red gum was to them what the sight of the yellow primrose was to Wordsworth. It was the symbol of home and of childhood's day and of friendliness; it brought back memories of all kinds of little familiar things they had not thought to disclose to strangers. Australian red gums are so common in California that many of us must know and like them. Their scent is delicious, aromatic, stimulating, and their high pillars of greenery, with leaves drily rustling in that cloudless, sunny weather, and upturning their whiter undersides in the puffs of air, a feature of the landscape, and not without beauty of a kind. Red gums are not, however, a thing one can take into one's affections as one can a flower. Yet, to these boys, the red gums were, because of their associations, a thing to bring tears to the voice, even if they were successfully fought off from the eyes. Associations are, I repeat, to many of us, a large share of life. They bring up memory after memory; they are, in a sense, all compact of memories. And memories, as one grows older, become more and more of life. They are, at the least, a third of life. There is the joy in the living of the present. There are the hopes for the future. There are the memories of the past.

"The Solitary Reaper" is instinct with memories. Wordsworth passed the girl who inspired the poem as she was at her work. He had reached the loch country on a tour of the Highlands. She was on the slopes above an inland water, "reaping and singing by herself." It was the Gaelic, no doubt, she sang. It was a melancholy strain. He wonders what is the burden of her song.

> Will no one tell me what she sings?
> Perhaps the plaintive numbers flow
> For old, unhappy, far-off things,
> And battles long ago.

The appeal of these lines is to something very elemental in us, very primitive. They stir us as if by an appeal to ancestral memories, to things experienced by our forebears generations back and preserved in what of us has come down from those so long before us.

What concerned the town was far less to Wordsworth than what concerned the country. His sonnet on Westminster Bridge proves that he could appreciate the beauty that man has made for man. Better, though, he loved the beauty that existed in country places long lived in by man, but owing that beauty largely to the contrast between man's clearing and planting, his ditching and draining, and the woods and lakes and mountains as nature made them. Canon Rawnsley's careful collecting of Wordsworthiana in the Lake Country has shown conclusively that the poet was not an easy man to "crack" with, that he could not be all things to all men, or hail-fellow-well-met with the dalesman whose fields he crossed and whose lanes he followed in his daily walks. That it was just his manner that was offish and not his heart many of his poems prove. I cite three such, "The Leech-Gatherer," "Simon Lee," and "The Waggoner." Perhaps the truth was that people he could foregather with comfortably had to be poor or in trouble or outcast. There is no offishness in his writing, though, as there is in that of Milton, say, or Landor, or Yeats. It is not difficult to feel chummy with Wordsworth as one reads him.

That there is something in Wordsworth, however, that is anti-pathetical to some people, no one who has taught literature for years can fail to have found out. And as it is among students so it is with the general reader. J. K. S. tells us that there are two voices in Wordsworth, one of the authentic poet and one of an old bellwether bleating among the rocks. The satirist, as usual, has gone too far. At his worst Wordsworth is no more than plati-tudinous, gravely discovering that two and two make four. That is a way half of the world has, but the very people who suffer it in their neighbors profess to be driven nearly frantic by it in the poet.

Such folks find offense even in most carefully sifted selections from Wordsworth, such as that of Matthew Arnold. This book tells the tale, though, of his greatness, as, indeed, do all the an-thologies whether of his work alone, or of all English poetry. Palgrave includes forty-one poems of Wordsworth in *The Golden Treasury* (1861), more than of any other poet, not even excepting Shakespeare. Shakespeare is here represented by thirty-three poems, and Shelley by twenty-two. Altogether there are two hundred and eighty-eight poems in *The Golden Treasury*, so the selections from Wordsworth total at one-seventh of all the lyrics included.

Quiller-Couch, in his *Oxford Book of English Verse* (1900), gives forty-three poems of Shakespeare and twenty-seven of Wordsworth, but at that devotes only one page less to Wordsworth than to Shakespeare. George Moore will have none of Wordsworth in *An Anthology of Pure Poetry* (1925) on the ground that Wordsworth never wrote an "objective poem," one about the world of things only, but always colored his verses with "ideas, thoughts, reflections." Moore's belief is that "ideas, thoughts, reflections," pass quickly. His three are not, of course, things of a kind. Ideas, which are the attitudes of a time to "morality, patriotism, duty, and religion," are passing things, but there are thoughts and reflections, the summing-up of man's experience of life that have been part and parcel of man's heritage down the ages. Even with such a belief as he professes Moore can find only two lines of comment among forty lines of objective description in "The Green Linnet."

Moore's exclusion of Wordsworth does not trouble me at all. I sympathize, for that matter, with his stressing of things rather than ideas as the material of literature. Moore goes too far, I think, in his theory of objectivity by excluding thoughts on things and reflections on things. Insight and vision are ruled out, too, all that part of the poet that is prophet and seer. Moore would have the poet singer of external things only, objective poet only. Yet with the poet barred from singing of his experience of life, and of his brooding over life, and of his concern with mysteries, English poetry would not be the incomparably rich treasure house that it is. Moore has forgotten for the nonce that poets have always been riddlers. There is cryptic writing and prophecy aplenty in the old bards of his own Ireland. You have but to put Moore's theory of objectivity only for poetry in relation to the great spectacle of English poetry to see what a starveling it is.

A lifelong reading and rereading of Wordsworth makes it impossible for me to reduce the number of his poems that must be included among the best lyrics in English below fifteen. There must be in my anthology "I heard a thousand blended notes," "Up! up! my Friend and quit your books," "Tintern Abbey," "My heart leaps up when I behold," "It is a beauteous evening," "The Green Linnet," "The Solitary Reaper," "To the Cuckoo," "She was a phantom of delight," "I wandered lonely as a cloud," "A flock of sheep that leisurely pass by," "Loud is the vale!" "Ode on Intimations of Immortality," "Two Voices are there," and "O nightingale! thou surely art."

The years 1797-1807 were his golden years. After 1831 he wrote, indeed, verse as good as the verse of his second order of accomplishment, as the average of his verse from 1807 to 1831. But after 1831 he wrote no verse of the first order. "Yarrow Revisited" (1831) is as good as "Yarrow Visited" (1814). In 1831 Wordsworth was a guest of Scott, already a stricken man. He had foregathered with Scott on his previous visit to Scotland, and the contrast of the then and now in Sir Walter moved Wordsworth to the depths. This deep feeling brought something of the old power to his "Yarrow Revisited." The best of all the later poems, however, is "Extempore Effusion upon the Death of James Hogg" (1835). It laments the passing of Scott, too, and Coleridge, and Lamb, Crabbe, and Mrs. Hemans, and in its recollections of old days with these poets almost recaptures the spirit of the years in which he had first known them.

There are phrases akin to those of his heyday in still later verses, in verses written from 1836 to 1847, and a couplet or two that soar, but no poem spoken in that authentic mountain voice no English poet has surpassed. That dove heard cooing "near Arno's stream," and the cuckoo that he listened to with delight at Laverna could not lift his verse to the old rapture. Vallombrosa, that Milton sang, Wordsworth could not sing nobly in old age, and even his own lake country, loved intensely to the end, could not inspire him as once it did. The last poem of all, the ode to

Prince Albert that his duty as laureate compelled him to write, is no more than perfunctory.

The thoughts whose expression required periphrasis before Wordsworth gave them to us in phrases of final brevity are all but all in the writing before 1832, most of them, indeed, in that before 1807. At thirty-two he wrote "My heart leaps up," whose nine lines have in them three phrases in universal use now. They are "my heart leaps up," "The child is father of the man" and "natural piety." What I am concerned with now is not the poetry of these lines, but simply the phrases in them entered into the language and become of daily use wherever English is spoken. You may believe that they would not have attained such universality had they not been high poetry, but I am not sure that such belief is justified. Lines of Pope and a saying of Horace Greeley with no poetry at all are quoted round the world. The gift of "enriching the English language," as W. H. Davies calls it, is not necessarily the gift of poetry. Wordsworth made phrases the world could use. He was well enough read and middle-manned, from 1830 to 1840 at any rate, for needed phrases of his to have a wide hearing. The world took what it wanted of him of that sort. It took also, and it has always kept in mind, whole sets of verses of his as well as many of his best poems. "The Happy Warrior" is not of his best, but as recently as 1928 it was called upon to do yeoman service for one of the candidates for the presidency of the United States. The glib youth of to-day says, as he offers a drink of this, that, or the other to the girl to whom he is dancing attendance, "Drink, pretty creature, drink." So said his father and his grandfather and his great-grandfather before him.

The best things of Wordsworth, then, are on everybody's lips. The ode "Intimations of Immortality from Recollections of Early Childhood" has alone given us a half-dozen quotations of so frequent use that we hardly realize that some of them are quotations at all. They are "The glory and the freshness of a dream"; "The things that I have seen I now can see no more"; "There has passed away a glory from the earth"; "Our birth is but a sleep and a forgetting"; "Heaven lies about us in our infancy"; and "Thoughts that do often lie too deep for tears." There are also in the poem observations on the beauty of the world and readings of the meanings of things to ponder over, to take to heart, to bring back to mind again and again for our profit and delight. There are at least another half-dozen phrases from the ode in frequent use: "Shades of the prison house"; "the light of common day"; "obstinate questionings"; "a season of calm weather"; "primal sympathy"; and "the philosophic mind."

There is another Wordsworth of the so-called "philosophic poems," of "The Prelude" and "The Excursion," and still another Wordsworth of the blank verse narratives of the sort of "Michael" (1800) and of "The Two Brothers" (1800). The Wordsworth of neither can appeal, perhaps, as does the Wordsworth of the lyrics and the odes, but in both the philosophical poems and the blank verse narratives he succeeded wholly in what he put his hand to. The philosophic poems, too, outside of their consideration of values in life, are a kind of ordered and idealized autobiography, indispensable to those who would understand the whole nature of the poet. In "Michael" Wordsworth has written the simplest, barest, most unadorned narrative of high intent that we have had from its time to ours, when there arrived those equally simple and bare and unadorned narratives of New England life in *North of Boston* (1914).

There is mountain air about "Michael." The poem has the lift of the heights, a sunniness tempered by the coolness of upland pastures, and scents of clover and of grasses close-nibbled but flowering on short stems.

What the influence of Wordsworth's praise of mountains and of lonely places has been on life the world over it is impossible to estimate. He rediscovered the Swiss Alps and the Lake Country for his own people and for us in America. His writing made both directly and indirectly for the fame of our American mountains, the White Mountains and Green Mountains and Adirondacks first, and then the Alleghanies on southward through Pennsylvania to North Carolina, and ultimately the Sierra Nevadas and the Rockies. Emerson and Thoreau, John Burroughs and John Muir, Emily Dickinson and Robert Frost developed interests in nature first roused by Wordsworth. In England Tennyson and Arnold went to school to him, as did Richard Jefferies and W. H. Hudson, and Sir William Watson and Edmund Blunden. Wordsworth, though he saw the fustian in Macpherson, owed not a little to *Ossian* (1761+). He owed much of his appreciation of wild nature to the Highlander, and something of his appreciation of his own Lakeland to Gray, who wrote well of it in his *Journal in the Lakes,* which was written in 1769 but not published until 1775, four years after his death. It is interesting to note that Hardy felt himself to be of this succession. In one of the notes he made in his extreme old age, in 1918, he writes: "It bridges over the years to think that Gray might have seen Wordsworth in his cradle, and Wordsworth might have seen me in mine." In his "Apology," prefixed to *Late Lyrics* (1922), Hardy quotes Wordsworth twice and elsewhere in his writing by reference and by practice shows he had taken his precepts to heart.

Wordsworth owed something of the loving particularity of his interest in birds and flowers to Gilbert White. There was, of course, only a slight inheritance from White, or, for that matter, from anybody in the past in his writing. He added to the tradition in which he worked far more than that modicum of what is new that suffices for originality in most writers. Wordsworth was a beginning, like all writers of first power, a beginning as much as Chaucer or Shakespeare, as Hardy or Hudson.

Wordsworth was of that main line of English poets, of natures passionate yet controlled, and of standards of art based upon tradition, that began with Chaucer and that has never wanted worthy adherents from his day to Frost's. Shakespeare, because he bulks largest as a dramatic poet, seems not so surely of the line as Spenser, yet Shakespeare was of the line. Milton was of it, and handed on its precepts to Dryden, who was of it by his odes and occasional poems and translations, but who wrote no great poem in the traditional manner. Pope's thin voice and restricted interests did not allow him to maintain the standards of this old main line of English poetry, but he held to it so far as it was possible for him so to hold. There are echoes of the old manner in "Eloisa to Abelard" and "Verses to the Memory of an Unfortunate Lady." Gray had moments when he was able to speak out as he would speak, but they were all too few. He, however, handed on the tradition in his odes and in the undying "Elegy." He was the most immediate predecessor of Wordsworth in the main line of English poetry. Burns was first of all the satirist of a parish, and then the artist in whom culminated Scottish folksong. He was hardly in the English line at all. Yet he had many affinities with poets of this line, in his reliance on tradition, in his love of country-side, in the Biblical background common to him and Milton and Gray and Wordsworth.

There has been no break in the line from Wordsworth's day to ours, on either side of the Atlantic. As I have pointed out, Emerson, lacking in art as he was, was of it as surely as Tennyson, as lacking in material as Emerson was in art. Arnold and Clough were of the line, and Bryant and Whittier. So were Robert Bridges and Laurence Binyon, Madison Cawein and Bliss Carman, John Masefield and Lascelles Abercrombie, William Vaughan Moody and Robert Frost. There have been those of the line with leanings toward rhetoric and those with leanings toward homeliness of speech, but they have been at one in their concern with normal life and dignified art, in their carrying-on of the great traditions of the past.

It is the crowding of men into cities through the human instinct of herding together and through economic pressure that more than any other cause has brought about the deluge of nineteenth-century nature books. Men are driven away from the crowded centers for the tonic of untainted air and for prospects other than those of the canyons between skyscrapers. The country is still necessary to health and happiness. And if men cannot get to the open places as often as they would, they seek to content themselves with reading about such places.

Nature study in the schools has had its influence in bringing about the week-end exodus from town that is so prominent a feature of urban life at the kindly seasons of the year. The automobile, and the good roads it necessitated, have been factors in making possible the country cult now in vogue. The discovery of the value of sunlight in medical treatment has had a share, too, in the emphasis on forest and countryside and shore in the writing of our generation. The "scout" movements and the development of the idea that everybody should take part in sport, and not content himself with looking on at sporting spectacles, are elements in the popularization of out-of-door life and of the writing about out-of-doors. Skiing and other winter sports are adding to the country cult.

The direct influence of literature in bringing about concern with country things begins, as I have intimated, with Wordsworth. The reading of his verse has sent very many to the country. So has the reading of Thoreau's *Walden* (1854), a book that owes not a little to Wordsworth. These two men have been responsible for thousands of outings in America and hundreds of attempted returns to the land. Few who read Wordsworth, of course, have the high rapture over landscape and country things generally that he knew. Many, though, have tried to find in countryside and wild places what Wordsworth found.

His poems had, too, an influence on landscape gardening, and on painting. Some hold, for instance, that the pictures of Turner's second period owe certain effects of light to the light caught in the *Lyrical Ballads*. Turner was so much greater a hero to Ruskin than was Wordsworth that Ruskin could hardly realize just how great Wordsworth was. Ruskin quoted Wordsworth often, and at length, and owed much of his own enthusiasm over Lakeland and the Alps to the master, but he would not cry him up as he should lest he detract somewhat from the appreciation of Scott, whom Ruskin admired only short of idolatry. Wordsworth was not romantic enough for Ruskin, yet Ruskin found more to quote from him than from Sir Walter. Ruskin gave Scott the palm even in poetry because he felt Scott's was a larger nature than Wordsworth's. He was afraid that "Wordsworth was often affected in his simplicity." Yet Ruskin could at the same time "perceive the intense penetrative depth of Wordsworth." He knew "Tintern Abbey," quoting the lines beginning "Nature never did betray the heart that loved her." It must be that he had taken to heart the great passage just preceding this he quoted. Perhaps it was that Ruskin had so completely absorbed this passage that its thoughts seemed trite to him. This passage from "Tintern Abbey" does not give complete presentation to what nature was to Wordsworth. It would take the quoting of many poems to do that, but the passage does concentrate in shorter space what nature was to him than does any other passage. He describes what his attitude toward nature was in boyhood, and then what it was in youth, when

> The sounding cataract
> Haunted me like a passion: the tall rock,
> The mountain, and the deep and gloomy wood,
> Their colours and their forms, were then to me
> An appetite; a feeling and a love,
> That had no need of a remoter charm,
> By thought supplied, nor any interest
> Unborrowed from the eye.—That time is past,
> And all its aching joys are now no more,
> And all its dizzy raptures. Not for this
> Faint I, nor mourn nor murmur; other gifts
> Have followed; for such loss, I would believe,
> Abundant recompense.

Wordsworth goes on to show how this passion for nature turned to a spiritual ecstasy in the presence of natural beauty, an ecstasy in which nature was enjoyed not only for itself but for what it symbolized in human life. This later stage he thus describes:

                                For I have learned
To look on nature, not as in the hour
Of thoughtless youth; but hearing oftentimes
The still, sad music of humanity,
Nor harsh nor grating, though of ample power
To chasten and subdue. And I have felt
A presence that disturbs me with the joy
Of elevated thoughts; a sense sublime
Of something far more deeply interfused,
Whose dwelling is the light of setting suns,
And the round ocean and the living air,
And the blue sky, and in the mind of man:
A motion and a spirit, that impels
All thinking things, all objects of all thought,
And rolls through all things. Therefore am I still
A lover of the meadows and the woods,
And mountains; and of all that we behold
From this green earth; of all the mighty world
Of eye, and ear,—both what they half create,
And what perceive; well pleased to recognize
In Nature and the language of the sense,
The anchor of my purest thoughts, the nurse,
The guide, the guardian of my heart, and soul
Of all my moral being.

It is this phase of his attitude toward nature that carried his influence furthest. The accuracy of his descriptions of raven and cuckoo, celandine and daffodil, were influential, too. They show that accuracy need not take away from writing witchery and glamour.

His concern with humble types has justified a similar concern on the part of many who have come after him. The drovers and pitmen of Wilfrid Gibson are studied after Wordsworth's "characters," and Masefield owes only less to him than to Chaucer in his poacher and navvy and sailor. Abercrombie's "Staircase" shows the influence of Wordsworth, and Binyon's "Driftwood Gatherers," and Benson's "Shepherds," and Hardy's "Tramp-woman's Tragedy," and Edward Thomas's "Lob." A. E. Housman owes to Wordsworth much of his simplicity and directness, and even Yeats, not an enthusiastic admirer of Wordsworth, owes to him, in part, his interest in the brown mice that bob about the oatmeal chest. So, too, one can find in De La Mare and W. H. Davies touches one believes would not be there were it not for Wordsworth.

The sonnets of Wordsworth on public affairs are echoed in every other sonnet on such topics you come upon, though such sonnets, Sir William Watson's for instance, often take on a rhetoric foreign to Wordsworth's nature.

It is the ecstasy over nature of Wordsworth, however, his finding there satisfaction for the spirit, that has won him his most perfervid following. It was this ecstasy that won Emerson more than any other attribute of Wordsworth. There was in Emerson's regard for him, though, a liking for the man as well as an infinite respect for the prophet. Wordsworth had surprised Emerson by his simplicity when Emerson called upon him at Rydal Mount in 1833, and by his willingness not to shine. Wordsworth was more "just folks" and much less of the don than Emerson expected him to be. Emerson, his own writing shows most clearly, had been reading Wordsworth from early youth, but it was not until after Wordsworth's death that he paid full tribute to him. It is in *English Traits* (1856) you find the passage: "Where is great design in modern English poetry? The English have lost sight of the fact that poetry exists to speak the spiritual law. . . . The exceptional fact of the period is the genius of Wordsworth. He had no master but nature and solitude. 'He wrote a poem,' says Landor, 'without the aid of war.' His verse is the voice of sanity in a worldly and ambitious age. One regrets that his temperament was not more liquid and musical. He has written longer than he was inspired. But for the rest, he has no competitor."

On that call upon Wordsworth in 1833 Emerson had found his recitation of his verses almost laughable. Yet he refrained from laughter and came to see the simple dignity of the man. It had been well had he taken to heart Wordsworth's words about what was best among his verses, those that "touched the affections . . . for whatever is didactic,—what theories of society, and so on,— might perish quickly; but whatever combined a truth with an affection was . . . good to-day and good forever."

Emerson saw Wordsworth even more clearly on a second visit to Rydal, this time with Miss Martineau, in 1848: "Let us say of him, that, alone in his time he treated the human mind well, and with an absolute trust. His adherence to his poetic creed rested on real inspirations. 'The Ode on Immortality' is the high-water-mark which the intellect has reached in this age. New means were employed, and new realms added to the empire of the muse, by his courage."

Emerson owed more of his transcendentalism, perhaps, to Coleridge than to Wordsworth, but Emerson's essay "Nature" had been very different than it was had he not read his Words-worth, as had, too, a good deal of his verse. There are parallels between "Monadnock" and "The Apology" and well-known pas-sages in "I heard a thousand blended notes" and "Up! up! my friend, and quit your books." To read "Nature" is to come upon passage after passage that seems Wordsworth writing in prose. There is, of course, the tang of a wilder countryside than that of Lakeland in Emerson, but the precepts close packed together in the essays are many of them like a concentrated and pithy epito-mizing of those of Wordsworth. This that was written in Concord was no doubt approved at Rydal. "He who knows the most, he who knows what sweets and virtues are in the ground, the waters, the plants, the heavens, and how to come at the enchantments, is the rich and royal man." And is not this that follows a part of Wordsworth's decalogue, though its accent is American? "It seems as if the day was not wholly profane in which we have given heed to some natural object."

Emerson realized the full significance of Wordsworth. He saw and appreciated not only the man's transcendentalism, but his true-blue British humanity. "Domesticity," writes Emerson in

English Traits, "is the taproot which enables the nation to branch wide and high." And Wordsworth, of course, is the poet of domesticity more surely than any Englishman of his time, and with only Patmore at all comparable to him among the poets that have come after him.

There has always been a literature of humble life in English. There is the story of Cædmon the neatherd and of the genesis of his hymn in its very beginnings. There is Chaucer, and there is Langland. There is a *Shoemaker's Holiday* and there is *Pilgrim's Progress.* There is Burns and there is Crabbe. It is Wordsworth, though, inheriting from his predecessors as he did, who handed on the narrative of humble life to the Victorians and Neo-Georgians.

Of Victorians there were as many influenced by Wordsworth as of the Neo-Georgians referred to above. Some of these Victorians acknowledged their obligations by direct imitation or by open comparison of his influence. Of these are T. E. Brown, whose tales in verse chronicle humble lives in Man very like those that Wordsworth chronicled in Cumberland and Westmoreland. Robert Buchanan presented Scottish countryside and character after Wordsworth. David Gray, Buchanan's friend, owned that his "Luggie" was an attempt in the Wordsworthian manner. The De Veres, both father and son, wrote themselves down Wordsworthians. John Clare recalls effects of Wordsworth in "The Flitting" and in "The Cottager," and William Barnes in a score of poems.

I find parallel passages and likenesses of various sorts between Wordsworth and about every third poet of any parts at all that wrote after him. Clough and Ernest Myers, Sydney Dobell and Arthur Munby, Frederick Tennyson and Charles Tennyson Turner are among the small fry that followed him day before yesterday. And of those of yesterday that show allegiances of one sort or another are Stephen Phillips and Bottomley, Norman Gale and A. H. Williams, Drinkwater and John Freeman, Charlotte Mew and James Stephens.

All these poets that I have mentioned owe something directly to Wordsworth. Their writing in one place or another reveals Wordsworthian simplicity or Wordsworthian mysticism. There are besides all the many influenced indirectly by Wordsworth, those whom, in the words of Sir William Watson, Wordsworth "sang free." It is, in speaking of his own development as a poet in "To Edward Dowden" that Watson tells us of what Shelley and Keats did for him, and what Wordsworth.

> The first voice, then the second, in their turns
> Had sung me captive. This voice sang me free.

There is no way of knowing how many others may have been so sung free. The company of the confessed Wordsworthians is a goodly company, however, as large a company both in numbers and in power as any company that follows the banner of any other English poet, unless it be, as I have said, that of Coleridge.

CHAPTER IV

The Romantic Heritage

THE poetry of Wordsworth and his like is a poetry based on reality. It may leave What Is pretty much as those close to it see it, or it may sift out of the real what is most unusual in it, or what is most picturesque in it, or it may sublimate the real, or even transfigure it, but whatever it does with the real, with life as we all know it, reality remains the material of the poetry, is immanent in the finished product of the art, the completed poem.

The poetry of Coleridge, and of his following, on the other hand, is an escape from life; like the poetry Macpherson derived from *Ossian;* like the poetry of Chatterton; like the poetry of Blake. So, in the main, were the old romances an escape from life, whether you found them in the chapbooks, or in Malory, or in Chrétien de Troyes. Like their ultimate Celtic originals they embodied a "revolt against the depotism of fact" that led their writers into the bypaths and out-of-the-way places, into the loneliness of sea-headlands facing the sunset and of mountains haunted by the cries of those who had gone forth to war only to fall. The ultra-romantic poets could not content themselves with the world they knew even in its rapt moments. They must escape from it into older times of strangeness and wonder, or into an ideal world the poet's imagination created for him, and that seemed, so, more at one with his dream of what is beautiful enough to be endurable, if not beautiful enough to bring contentment.

Sometimes the escape was into some far place out of the moil of modern civilization, a pantisocracy on the Susquehanna, an atoll of the South Seas, a Himalayan community of lamas, where the conventions that cabin and confine, that dwarf and minimize life, do not exist, or where may be found that leisured calm in which the spirit may expand and burgeon and come to perfect flower. Or this escape is possible, in the eyes of some, by the creation of new institutions here in the present and prosaic hurly-burly, or by a return to old institutions by some waving of a magician's wand.

Then, this age of iron who is master of us all would be transformed into some auraed age of gold. There is always a suggestion of the supernatural in whatever mode of escape is suggested, an escape accomplished by some magic, or by some unlocking of nature's secrets that is so wonderful even many of the sophisticated cannot but be awed by its processes.

The verses of Coleridge that are most magical are of his early years, "The Ancient Mariner," "Christabel," and "Kubla Khan." He lived only to the threshold of our period, dying at the age of sixty-one in 1834. His influence is felt, though, through all the hundred years since then. Just four years after his death, Lady Charlotte Guest began to publish her translations from *The Mabinogion* (1838-1849), a book that originated an impulse almost as potent as that of Coleridge himself. Tennyson owed much to Coleridge for the manner of "The Lady of Shalott" (1832) and of "Sir Lancelot and Queen Guinevere" (1842). Glamour and tone and fall of words are all in the master's manner. Tennyson's debt to Lady Guest was most largely for the material of his idylls, though atmosphere and a sense of other-worldiness came to him at times from the Welsh wonder tales.

All the Pre-Raphaelite poets have owned their allegiance to Coleridge. Rossetti gave him one of the five sonnets he wrote to the poets he held closest, Chatterton and Blake and Keats and Shelley being the others of the company. It seemed to Rossetti that Coleridge had only six years from the threescore of his life in which he was himself. Those six years were, though, he declared, "a beacon to our centuries."

Through Coleridge the names of the old romantics run like motives through Wagner's music, Wagner, who is, after Scott, the greatest romantic of them all. Swinburne, by the bye, has three roundels to Wagner, strangely slight form in which to imprison impressions of the tranced and titanic harmonies of the great German. One roundel is general, one suggested by Lohengrin, and the other by *Tristan und Isolde.*

It is the old ballads and *Ossian* and Chatterton that haunt Coleridge oftenest. You find echoes of the ballads not only in "The Rhyme of the Ancient Mariner" and "Christabel," but in "The Dark Ladie," "The Three Graves," and "Alice Du Clos." There is a poem devoted to Chatterton, the famous "Monody," and much phrasing in his manner. There are the verses "Imitated from Ossian" and their companion piece, "The Complaint of Ninathoma." All these experiments in romance of Coleridge the Pre-Raphaelites took to heart.

They took to heart, too, the spectacle of Scott, who acknowledged with his customary frankness how much he owed to the free measures of "Christabel." It was not so much any one poem of Scott that influenced them as it was the whole-hearted concern with romance in all he wrote. You could not think of Scott without thinking of the *Border Minstrelsy* (1802) and all the strangeness and wonders therein collected. In the train of such thoughts would rise others, in which you saw him riding hither and thither through the Lowlands in search of old tales, visiting homes of all sorts to write down the songs and ballads there gathered for him. There would rise before your mind's eye pictures of his meetings with herds and people of the roads and others acquainted with outland rhymes. Such gave to him the tags and scraps and full records come to them by word of mouth, often in the very places that had bred the lines.

All the shrewdness and geniality and kindliness of Scott serve only to emphasize the qualities of bard and sage and romancer that were deep-seated in him, the suggestion of knowledge of hidden and unkenned things there was always about him. There was romance in all associated with him, in the great staghounds, so white and wistful-eyed, that he loved to walk out with, in the storied Tweed by his door, in the Eildons back of his gardens, in the spell he wove over folks far and near by the wizardry of his tale-telling.

"The glory and the dream" is seldom about the verses of Scott, but "the glory" and "the dream" are always immanent in the subjects he chooses and in the places he paints in as background to the poems. You cannot mention Teviotdale or the Trossachs but romance thrills through the words, creating in you a glow that their maker's artistry and powers of suggestion cannot. "The Sun upon the Weird Law Hill" is, I think, his happiest achievement, nearer high poetry than "Proud Maisie" or "When Israel of the Lord beloved." There is glamour in his deploring that no longer

> the landscape to mine eye
> Bears those bright hues that once it bore,
> Though evening with her richest dye
> Flames o'er the hills of Ettrick's shore.
>
> .   .   .   .   .
>
> The quiet lake, the balmy air,
> The hill, the stream, the tower, the tree—
> Are they still such as once they were
> Or is the dreary change in me?

If we read Scott in rapt mood, thinking of the man in his country-side and under the shadow of his own troubled story, there sound in our ears, as the accompaniment to the obvious march of his verses, old Scottish airs, old refrains from ballads, old cries of fighting men perishing in border forays, old laments of ladies who have died young and fair in lonely castle keeps where their lords had to leave them when called to arms by king or kin. Scott can no more be dismissed from mind in accounting for the development of romance throughout all our century of poetry than the Wagner who came after him. They are both romantics of romantics, and influences throughout all the world of European peoples.

Keats had his place, too, in the development of romance. His work, though, was all over and done and part of the inheritance of the race before our period begins. "The Eve of St. Agnes" and "La Belle Dame Sans Merci" had their share in developing the early Pre-Raphaelitism of Tennyson. Both poems are close, too, to certain manners of Rossetti and Morris and only less close to a phase of Swinburne. So glamorous, indeed, is Keats, that there is much to be said for the contention that all romance is summed up in those two lines of his:

> Charmed magic casements, opening on the foam
> Of perilous seas, in faery lands forlorn.

Although Shelley is celebrated in one of Rossetti's sonnets to his masters, he is much less an influence on the Pre-Raphaelites than Chatterton, Coleridge, or Keats. Blake is unquestionably more of a forerunner of theirs than Shelley, but not so much through individual poems of his as through the fact that he was, like their founder Rossetti, poet and painter both. There are passages in "Fair Elenor," in "The Grey Monk," in "The Golden Net," in "William Bond," and in the fiery "Tiger" that suggest Pre-Raphaelite material or falls of phrase, but there is no poem of his so like poems of theirs as the poems I have named of Coleridge and Keats. Blake's name was often on the lips of the leaders of the movement, and in their writing for *The Germ,* and in the studio gossip this or that man has recorded from meetings with them.

Pre-Raphaelitism, as applied to poetry, stands first of all for medievalism, that is, if it can be said to stand for anything more definite than the differing and changing ideals of a group of poets who looked up to Rossetti as master. Holman Hunt tells us that he and Millais and Rossetti understood Pre-Raphaelitism to mean acceptance of the attitude toward nature of the painters before Raphael, rather than of the formalism of Raphael and those who followed him. Ruskin said that the aim of the Brotherhood was to paint nature as it is, with the help of modern science, and in

the spirit of earnestness of the men of the thirteenth and fourteenth centuries.

But Rossetti's medievalism went farther than this. Steeped in
Dante and English ballad poetry, and delighting in the echoes
of old romance in Blake and Coleridge and Keats, he wrote and
painted in a spirit of reverence for art, and with a rapture that
seemed not only to him but to his friends to have been seldom
attained by post-Renaissance artists. This absolute identification of
himself with the character, and even with the mood of the people
of his imagination, who to him were as actual living beings, gives
his poetry the warmth and thrill of life; while his knowledge of
medieval conditions was such that he could present these people
against a background that has the rich color of their time.

To no other English poet than Rossetti did two contemporary
poets so great as William Morris and Swinburne dedicate their
first volumes. In his youth an enthusiastic admirer of Browning,
and of the forgotten William Bell Scott, Rossetti found himself
in 1856, at twenty-eight, at the head of a group, which did not,
however, so much imitate his work as receive stimulus from it.
Besides Morris and Swinburne there were Woolner and J. L.
Tupper, Coventry Patmore and W. M. Rossetti, all of whom had
been interested in *The Germ*. William Allingham, the Irish poet,
was Rossetti's intimate friend, and after Mrs. Rossetti's death, in
1862, George Meredith was one of the three poets who joined
Rossetti in taking the great house on Cheyne Walk.

But Meredith soon left the house to the Pre-Raphaelites, to
whose verse his verse is alien in spirit. These older poets' places in
Rossetti's friendship were taken in part, after 1870, by Arthur
O'Shaughnessy, Philip Bourke Marston, and Sir Edmund Gosse.
Walter Pater now became an intimate, and grew to owe much
to the associations; as Rossetti himself had to that of the earlier
critic of the movement, Ruskin, without whose timely aid, in the
fifties, Rossetti's career might have been far different. About the
time that Rossetti gave up living with the Morrises at Kelmscott,
which was in 1874, he began an intimacy with Theodore Watts-

Dunton, who afterwards drew him so memorably as D'Arcy, in *Aylwin*. Another friend of these years was Dr. Gordon Hake, a poet that too few know. Then came, in 1879, the friendship with Hall Caine and with William Sharp. Even to his darkest days Rossetti had the power to win young men and to encourage them in their literary aspirations.

There were a good many ties between the Pre-Raphaelite poets and Yeats, the first romantic of the turn of the century, and the leader of the Celtic Renaissance. Allingham, long allied with the Pre-Raphaelites, was an inspiration for the young poets of the Renaissance, equally with the so different Mangan and Ferguson. O'Shaughnessy, too, was of Irish descent, although his most Celtic writing was after Marie de France rather than after the old bards of the Gael. William Morris was so familiar to Yeats on the streets of Hammersmith that it was the most natural thing in the world for the young Irishman to adopt the William Morris tie and the William Morris manner of writing legendary narrative. John Butler Yeats, the poet's father, knew well, as a painter, the Pre-Raphaelite tradition, though he himself was an out-and-out disciple of Watts. The most cogent reason for the youthful allegiance of Yeats and Katherine Tynan Hinkson and Nora Hopper to the Pre-Raphaelites was, however, the latter's preoccupation with a kind of romance that seemed to the young Irish writers to point the way to the kind of romance that would best exploit their own native legends. Soon, however, drama, not wholly of Pre-Raphaelite origin, lured Yeats away from the ballad and narrative of the William Morris sort.

It was Maeterlinck's borrowings from the Pre-Raphaelites, perhaps, that put Yeats *en rapport* with his early work and that made Yeats in *The Countess Kathleen* (1892) and elsewhere adopt certain of the Belgian's principles of static drama. Later still Yeats came under the influence of the Noh plays of Japan, and now, in *The Tower* (1928) and in his later poems generally, he has developed in directions very other than those the Pre-Raphaelites suggested.

The influence of Poe upon the Pre-Raphaelites has not been thoroughly worked out. It is, indeed, an influence not easily followed. So like, however, are certain of Poe's effects to their effects, that it is easy to understand how both Poe and the Pre-Raphaelites became a joint influence over Maeterlinck. It is interesting to note, in passing, that Emerson is another great influence alike on certain poets of the Irish Renaissance, notably "A.E.", and upon Maeterlinck, Emerson, than whom and the Pre-Raphaelites there could be no poets more widely asunder.

What Watts-Dunton calls the Renascence of Wonder has gained a new vitality from the Irish Renaissance. Harking back to Macpherson's *Ossian* as it so surely does, and presenting the old legends in the simpler forms in which they are found in Standish James O'Grady's versions of the Cuchulain and Finn stories (1878-1880), and in Dr. Joyce's *Old Celtic Romances* (1879), its poets invested their writing with the glamour they found in wild glows of sunset over their bare landscape, so loved and so lonely. The school of Yeats and his fellows was called the "Twilight School of Poetry," not without warrant, though all his poems are not of day's end and evening light. That poem of his most familiar of all, for instance, "The Lake Isle of Inisfree," is concerned, for a moment, with noon, whose "purple glow" it celebrates. The fires of dawn burn in many of the verses of "A.E.", and James Stephens loves well and writes well of the warm sunniness of high noon on hillsides, goat-frequented and thymy. Dunsany, too, in his prose that kindles so often to poetry, has the colors of all the hours in his richly tinted world. Synge has celebrated, in prose that has the chant of poetry, the stormy light that flashes from the Twelve Pins to Aran. There is no end to the wonders of the Celtic imagination.

On other English poets of our day than Yeats and his fellows, the Pre-Raphaelites were an influence. Wilfrid Gibson, now so staunch a realist, is a Pre-Raphaelite in his early volumes. Gordon Bottomley has gone to school to them, and De La Mare owes something of his otherworldliness to them as he owes something of it to Poe. The verse of Arthur Symons is of other than Pre-Raphaelite origin, but much of his sound criticism of art could not have been but for them and the Pater for whom they were so largely accountable.

George Moore, too, in his critical writing is an apologist of the Pre-Raphaelite line, whether he writes of the Irish Renaissance or of earlier movements. His touchstone in poetry, though, is Shelley. There is more sturdiness in art for art's sake than the Victorian moralists expected it to develop. It was not laughed wholly out of court by Gilbert in his attack on Wilde in *Patience* (1881). It has even had the hardihood to survive the World War.

CHAPTER V

Landor and the Georgian Aftermath

WALTER SAVAGE LANDOR (1775-1864) was certainly not a Wordsworthian. One with so much of the eighteenth century in him could not be. One whose easiest and most felicitous verse was close to *vers de société* could not be. One to whom scholarship and the world of the classics and all written records whether of history or of literature were more than country life of simple sort and the fellowship of nature could not be. One who could be content with the sights and sounds, the colors and atmospheres, of Italy or of any other place than England could not be.

Yet Landor felt at times an affiliation to Wordsworth. In "To Wordsworth" (1833) he writes:

> Our course by Milton's light was sped,
> And Shakespeare shining overhead;
> Chatting on deck was Dryden too,
> The Bacon of the rhyming crew;
> None ever cross'd our mystic sea
> More richly stored with thought than he;
> Though never tender nor sublime,
> He wrestles with and conquers Time.
> To learn my lore on Chaucer's knee,
> I left much prouder company;
> Thee gentle Spenser fondly led,
> But me he mostly sent to bed.
>
> I wish them every joy above
> That highly blessed spirits prove,
> Save one; and that too shall be theirs,
> But after many rolling years,
> When 'mid their light thy light appears.

These verses may serve not only to reveal Landor's attitude towards Wordsworth, but to furnish a very fair cross-section of the stuff and manner of his art. The history of the past was more precious to Landor than the daily experience of life about him. History of men of letters had fascinated him from youth, and criticism of poetry was a something he could forbear at no time of his life. There is too much writing about writing in all his work, prose and verse. It is significant, too, that Spenser, the poets' poet, bored Landor. Such a want of appreciation reveals a want of romance in Landor's nature, and a want of delight in linked sweetness long drawn out that the great poets have always known. Landor, pen in hand, never abandoned himself to ecstasies of any sort, or to passion, or to any tumultuous joy. Choleric to a fault in life, he was, like Child Marjorie, "more than usual calm" in writing.

Like Wordsworth, too, Landor by his long life bridged over many changing eras of English poetry. Landor published his *Gebir* (1798) in the year of the *Lyrical Ballads*. He had been born before Cowper had published a poem, and he had grown up in a time in which Burns was the vogue. He saw the heyday of Scott and Byron, and of Keats and Shelley. He wrote his best work in years in which Tennyson and Browning were coming into their own, and he published his last volume, *Heroic Idylls* (1863), three years after Swinburne had broken on the horizon with *The Queen Mother and Rosamund* (1860). He belongs to the century we are considering in this book by much more important writing than does Wordsworth, who had, as we have seen, done all his best work before 1835. Landor was the intimate friend of poets of several generations, of Southey, among the Georgians, and of Browning among the Victorians. Swinburne visited Landor in Italy in 1863 to pay tribute to one he revered as the dean of English poets.

Landor had been slow to come to maturity. There has been much praise of *Gebir* (1798), part of it because of its historic importance, but no pleas can make it other than a dull tale. *Count Julian* (1812) is better as a play than *Gebir* as an epic in little, but it is confused and forced heroics for all that. His *Imaginary Conversations* (1824-1829), in prose, on which his reputation rests, were the product of his middle years, and all but all of his best verse the mellow fruit of his old age. It was of himself at seventy-five that he wrote the famous quatrain of "I strove with none." That epigram is simpler than most of Landor, less figurative, less Latinical. The epigram and its kindred are most congenial to him. His most widely known lyric is epigrammatic:

> Ah, what avails the scepter'd race,
>   Ah, what the form divine!
> What every virtue, every grace!
>   Rose Aylmer, all were thine.
>
> Rose Aylmer, whom these wakeful eyes
>   May weep, but never see,
> A night of memories and of sighs
>   I consecrate to thee.

There is a cold perfection of form about this lyric; and a repression of feeling; and a rhetorical cast of expression characteristic of Landor. The repetition of the "Rose Aylmer" is artfully managed. There is less directness than is usual with Landor. We gather, of course, that Rose Aylmer is dead, but the desolating words one deeply moved could not refrain from are not uttered.

There may not be a better lyric than "Rose Aylmer" in Landor, but there are other verses that rank higher in their kinds than "Rose Aylmer" among English lyrics. These kinds are, as I have said, epigrams, or akin to epigrams, though in intention often occasional or critical. An out-and-out epigram is:

> Death stands above me, whispering low
>   I know not what into my ear:
> Of his strange language all I know
>   Is, there is not a word of fear.

That is more consoling, perhaps, than this other slightly longer epigram:

> How soon, alas, the hours are over,
> Counted us out to play the lover!
> And how much narrower is the stage,
> Allotted us to play the sage!
> But when we play the fool, how wide
> The theatre expands; beside,
> How long the audience sits before us!
> How many prompters! what a chorus!

These epigrams seldom have such revelation of the depths of things in them. They are usually quips and saws rather than readings of life. In the ode "To Southey" (1833), though, there is one that detaches itself from its context with these words of wisdom:

> We hurry to the river we must cross,
>   And swifter downward every footstep wends;
> Happy, who reach it ere they count the loss
>   Of half their faculties and half their friends.

In "Regeneration" (1824) we find:

> The heart is hardest in the softest climes
> The passions flourish, the affections die!

We can call neither passage, though, a reading of life in the sense that we can so many passages of Chaucer and Shakespeare, Donne and Wordsworth, Meredith and Masefield.

In his "Shakespeare and Milton" (1853) Landor tells us that Shakespeare cries out "all nations spoke thro' me," to be answered by Milton with these proud words:

> True; and through this trumpet burst
> God's word; the fall of Angels, and the doom
> First of immortal, then of mortal, Man.
> Glory! be glory! not to me, to God.

There are many of the verses of Landor that begin with fine onsets. If "Regeneration," for one, were all of a quality with its first two lines, it would be a great poem indeed:

> We are what suns and winds and waters make us;
> The mountains are our sponsors.

That has large accent; that is in the grand style. "When Helen first saw wrinkles in her face" is a second and "Past ruin'd Ilion Helen lives" a third. There is more of the real stuff of poetry, however, in the "Fiesolan Idyl," "The Hamadryad," and "Icarios and Erigone."

Though Landor cared greatly for flowers and trees, he was unable to get much of their beauty into his verse. What there is of such beauty is in the "Hellenics." He cared greatly for dogs, too, but only once, in the verses, "Gallio! I shall not see thee dead" (1860) did he succeed in expressing half his feeling for a loved beast.

It would seem that Landor, for all his lifelong quarrels with friends and neighbors, really did not feel things keenly. They were just surface irritations that drove him to scurrilous epigrams in Latin or to the throwing of an offending cook out of the window.

There have been those who held, Frederick Locker-Lampson chief among them, that Landor was most perfect in kind in his *vers de société*, that he was master of this lesser form as of no other. I do not so hold, but I think his excellences here fall short of no other kind of his verse save the epigram and its sort. Landor's quixotic friendships with girls and women were many all his long life, and from these come many poems that are as trifling and debonair and arch as any of their kind that we have had since Herrick. Herrick is unapproachable and alone in light verse which, for all its lightness, is lyrical poetry. Of those whose light verse is hardly poetry, but close to it, Landor has no rival to the day of Austin Dobson. There is perfection of plan and finish both in these two stanzas:

In Clementina's artless mien
Lucilla asks me what I see,
And are the roses of sixteen
Enough for me?

Lucilla asks, if that be all,
Have I not cull'd as sweet before:
Ah yes, Lucilla! and their fall
I still deplore.

"Often I have heard it said" and "To Pyrrha" are two other trifles only less successful.

Landor was very sure of the indestructibility of what he had written. He hated the crowd, and he did not miss its failure to applaud him. "I claim no place in the world of letters," he wrote to Lord Brougham, "I am alone and will be alone, as long as I live, and after." Yet he was sure that he had his place, and he was sure that his work would live. At eighty-eight he could publish:

Well I remember how you smiled
To see me write your name upon
The soft sea-sand. *'O! what a child!*
You think you're writing upon a stone.'
I have since written what no tide
Shall ever wash away, what men
Unborn shall read o'er ocean wide
And find Ianthe's name again.

It is his scorn of the crowd, his joy in his loneliness, his coldly passionate aristocracy of feeling, as much as his austere art canons that have so won Yeats in his later years. Yeats likes, too, the spectacle of Landor walking "alone on the far eastern uplands, meditating and remembering." Nor does the dry severity and hard figurativeness of the old poet repel him. He, too, is working toward such effects in his old age. Yeats, of course, never had an inheritance of eighteenth-century diction to slough off, as had Landor, yet his verse sometimes stumbled under the weight of arbitrary symbolism that it carried. There are several similarities, too, in the position of the two men. They both appeal to the few rather than to the many. They both wrote long of young loves that were unhappy. They both are most careful and painstaking artists in verse. But most of all, I think, the late admiration of Yeats for Landor is due to the spectacle Landor is in English letters.

The spectacle of Landor has little to match it in the long annals of English literature. There is Milton blind; there is Dr. Johnson ill, but dominating through sheer force of personality; there is Landor in old age poor and in exile. There is no fourth spectacle such as these. Indeed it is as a spectacle that Landor looms largest in our literature. His accomplishments in prose and verse, fine as both are, are not the accomplishments of a major writer. The spectacle he presented in old age is unforgettable. His independence, his vigor, his choleric temper, his aristocratic prejudices, his republican creed, to say nothing of his leonine appearance and his proud bearing, give him a prominence that is greater than the intrinsic merit of his writing warrants. Everybody knows that he was the original of Boythorn in *Bleak House,* and that he said of his slow appreciation: "I shall dine late; but the dining room will be well-lighted, the guests few and select." There are other sentences of his prose that are remembered as are certain sentences from the King James Bible, and from Bacon and from Browne, and from Carlyle and from Dunsany.

There is to be put to his credit the visualization of great moments in history in the *Imaginary Conversations.* These are most of them static rather than dramatic, avoidant of too tumultuous emotion, aiming in their art "to attain the balance and self-government of the Greeks." There is to be put to his credit a body of narrative verse, the best of it on Greek subjects in which we see, as Sir William Watson phrases it, "bland Attic skies True-mirrored by an English well." There are to his credit as good epigrams as we have in English, and a sheaf of accomplished short lyrics, done mostly in his later years. There are a few passages, a very few, like those in "Regeneration" and a "Fiesolan Idyl," in which he looses the shackles from his verse and lets it run pure poetry. There are twenty such passages, perhaps, in the *Hellenics* (1846), and another at the close of "Dull is my verse," whose two last lines describe so truly that strange phenomenon in the life of a poet, his poetry growing better with the years:

> The bird upon its lonely bough
> Sings sweetest at the close of day.

For years Landor had written with a swan's quill, but only in his later years were the verses worthy of such an inditing.

THOMAS CAMPBELL

All but all of the verse of Thomas Campbell (1777-1844) was written by 1832, the year in which Scott died. The effective rhetorical lyrics and the wambling romantic tales that had won him fame in the first decade of the century were things of a far past when he turned to a species of light verse closely akin to *vers de société* in his old age. He is better in this lesser kind of writing, adventured in a kind of Indian summer that came to him in his early sixties, than in the more pretentious work of his youth and young manhood.

It is useless to try to make out that Campbell is a poet according to our modern standards of judgment. You have to fall back on "the historical estimate" to place him at all among seriously intentioned poets. The old standbys "Ye Mariners of England" and "Hohenlinden" are no more than rhymed rhetoric. They are hallowed, it is true, for many people by associations with them, by recitation in all manner of schoolhouses from little red ones to big yellow ones, or by a feeling that they are a part of the ritual of war and sounding arms. "Lord Ullin's Daughter," as often recited and as dearly loved as the familiar two, is as rhetorical as either.

The Pleasures of Hope (1799) gave us the famous quotation " 'Tis distance lends enchantment to the view," but there is hardly

more left to-day of that long poem than this one line. It is difficult
now to understand what, outside of the patriotic and declamatory
poems, won him his vogue in those first years of last century.
America, of course, was flattered by his making a valley of Pennsylvania the scene of *Gertrude of Wyoming* (1809), and Ireland,
had it been a reading country, might have been equally flattered
by *O'Connor's Child* (1810), which was undoubtedly much read
and much sentimentalized over in England.

"Exile of Erin" is a fair song of the order of Tom Moore,
and there are other fair songs, "My poor dog Tray" for one,
in other manners, but in no one style distinctively Campbell's
own. The lighter, indeed, his verses, the better do they stand the
grinding of the years. "To a Young Lady," for instance, is not
half bad even to-day, and there is still a slightly cynical bite to:

> Can you keep the bee from ranging,
> Or the ringdove's neck from changing?
> No! nor fettered Love from dying
> In the knot there's no untying.

"The Parrot" too, that incident of the bird from South America
that died in its old age on being addressed in Spanish, has a way
of holding on in memory when verses much more highly intentioned fade out utterly.

Family misfortunes had their share in driving Campbell away
from serious poetry after 1810. The grind of journalism, too,
affected his creative work. He felt, though, that what he had done
to win him acclaim from *The Pleasures of Hope* to *O'Connor's
Child* should have continued his fame after he had virtually
ceased to do largely planned work. Yet he was, as a matter of
fact, fortunate in winning his reputation. For the first two decades
of the nineteenth century he was famous, famous beyond his
deserts. As Byron said in *Don Juan:*

> Sir Walter reigned before me; Moore and Campbell
> Before and after.

Campbell was bitter in his old age when the change in public taste brought about by the acceptance of Wordsworth left readers cold to rhetorical poetry. Yet certain of his poems survived. "Ye Mariners of England" and "Hohenlinden" and "Lord Ullin's Daughter" are poor stuff, but they still have place in the anthologies and they keep their maker's name known to readers of English poetry.

TOM MOORE

If Tom Moore's verses were only what they appear to be on the printed page they would be indifferent poetry. Perhaps that is all they are. In themselves, without what they have meant to four or five generations of Irishmen and Englishmen and Americans, they are just indifferent poetry, about of the stuff of most popular songs. With the response they have had from readers for more than a century coloring our mood as we read, with memories of the affection in which they have been held by those who have sung them or heard them sung in mind, we take them for what their maker would have them to be, for something much more than what they are intrinsically. Tom Moore (1779-1852) knew just about what their value was. *Irish Melodies* (1807-1835), on which his reputation rests, he was loath to have printed apart from the airs to which he wrote them, realizing that they needed the music to bring them home closely. His own singing, or chanting, or whatever you choose to call his method of presentation of them, was very successful. It was one of the shows of his time. He knew that voice, tones with color in them, were necessary to offset the poverty of words and feeling of the verses. He liked them none the less that they required so much from him, their presenter as well as their maker. He felt, perhaps, about them as an actor feels about flat lines that he can bring to life by his speaking of them, by his facial expression, by his gesture, by all the tricks of his trade. Yet as he was their maker as well as presenter his emotions must have been mixed as he "put them over."

There is no one of us at all to whom the human associations

of art are much that does not think the better of "The last rose
of summer" because of those we have heard sing it, a Patti, a
Melba, a Tetrazzini, a Galli-Curci. There is no one of us with
memories but knows that his regard for "Come, ye disconsolate,
where'er ye languish" is largely because it was sung in church
when he was young. Though Moore was a Catholic, that hymn
had a firm place in the affections of the Presbyterians among
whom I was brought up.

It is our memories that endear to us what of Moore we like.
There is no lyric of first power in all his many songs. Considered
by the absolute standard in criticism they are third-raters all, "Go
where glory waits thee," "The harp that once through Tara's
halls," "Love's Young Dream," "Dear Harp of My Country,"
"There is not in the wide world a valley so sweet," "She is far
from the land where her young hero sleeps," "Alone by the
Schuylkill a wanderer roved," "Faintly as tolls the evening
chime," "At the mid hour of night," "Those evening bells," and
"Oft, in the stilly night." The name of these familiar verses is
legion, and there is not a real poem among them. Yet, sung to
the old airs so long associated with them, they appeal to us as do
the songs of our own Foster, poor, poor verses, but wedded to
immortal airs.

Odes of Anacreon (1800) are all outmoded now, and *Lalla
Rookh* (1817) is no better to our generation than an opera
libretto. As a child I came upon the tale with so luring an Eastern
title in a squat leather-bound volume in my grandfather's bookcase. All expectancy I began looking through it in the hope of
finding yarns as thrilling as those of *The Arabian Nights,* of
course in vain. It is tawdry and pretentious to me now, as so much
else that apes the eastern convention from its day to that of *The
Light of Asia* (1879) and on to *The Garden of Kama* (1902).
Think of "Laurence Hope" and Sir Edwin Arnold and Tom
Moore, and then think of Edward Fitzgerald, and the distinction between poet and writer of popular verse becomes clear at
once.

MRS. HEMANS

Mrs. Felicia Hemans (1793-1835) was a household word in America during the second and third quarters of last century. Even into the beginnings of the fourth quarter we continued to recite "Casabianca," which we knew better by its first line, "The boy stood on the burning deck." "The Landing of the Pilgrim Fathers" was another tried and true "elocution" piece, but it was sung, too, as often as it was declaimed. Mrs. Hemans, indeed, was sung as much as Tom Moore back in the thirties and forties of last century. Even in the heart of Pennsylvania Dutchland, into which so many English things had so hard a time forcing their way, she was known and loved. At an auction in Bethlehem on May 11, 1931, I found eight pieces of hers among some twenty pieces of an inch-deep pile of loose sheets of music I bought. All that had their year of publication upon them were dated from 1827 to 1834, and as all looked to belong to that period they were, I take it, published here before her death, which occurred in 1835. Her sister, Miss Browne, had written the music to "The Messenger Bird," and to "The Pilgrim Fathers," but the rest of the settings were by New York or Boston or Baltimore composers affiliated, I suppose, with the publishing houses of music which put out the songs. Dubois and Stodard of New York published "The Messenger Bird," and Hewett of New York "The Evening Song of the Tyrolese Peasants," which was set by "D.C.L." George Kingsley wrote the music to the famous hymn, "The Better Land," published, in Boston, by Bradlee. That same publisher gave "Bring Flowers" to an expectant America. O. C. Meineke did the music for "Leave Me Not Yet" and "The Bird at Sea," which were published by John Cole of Baltimore. C. F. Cole set "O'er the Far Blue Mountain" for the same publisher.

There is no poetry in any of these verses, but just sentimentality, and more sentimentality, and still more sentimentality. They and their music and the lithographs that illustrate them are wholly of their time, and not for the ages. The steel engravings you find in *The Poetical Works, Complete,* published by Grigg and Elliot of Philadelphia, 1847, lend a little distinction to that volume, the reproduction and extension of a collection of Mrs. Hemans gotten out as early as 1835. The poetess lends her demure face, with its frame of clustering curls, as frontispiece; a vignetted landscape of the Welsh countryside in which she lived near St. Asaph embellishes the title-page; and there are other engravings, throughout the book, this one of a ship at sea and that one of a ringleted slip of a girl with outbillowing skirts and carrying a much beribboned sunbonnet. Mrs. Hemans, her verses and their place in the hearts of men, the age in which she lived and the sentimentalities she encouraged, are all of a yesterday that today has been willing to forget.

HARTLEY AND SARA COLERIDGE

What seemed the frustrated life of Hartley Coleridge (1796-1849) bore fruit in a lyric and a half-dozen sonnets that the world would be the poorer for not having. There is scarcely an effect, it is true, in "She was not fair to outward view" that is not to be found in Wordsworth, but it is a perfectly realized twelve lines, a lyric that the years fail to dim. That other lyric of his the anthologists so often include, "She was a queen," has not the shorter poem's perfection, and it is even more Wordsworthian. The last line of its first stanza, "A visitation bright and transitory," seems like one rejected from that "Ode on Intimations of Immortality" in which "li'le Hartley" is so unforgettably referred to as "a six years' Darling of a pigmy size."

There is scarcely an effect in the sonnets, too, that you do not find in Wordsworth's sonnets, but no one would accuse Hartley Coleridge of borrowing these effects. What happened was that absorption into the countryside and ways and theories of poetry of the elder poet by the younger led, in the end, to his becoming an incarnation, in little, of Wordsworth. His friendliness and his failings remained his own, but all of him out of which poetry came was only an extension of Wordsworth. The sonnet that begins, "Whither is gone the wisdom and the power," and whose finest line is "The sweetness of old lays is hovering, still," is simon-pure Wordsworth. So is, too, "When we were idlers with the loitering rills" and "The mellow year is hasting to its close" and "A lovely morn, so still, so very still." Hartley Coleridge has a sure place among the sonneteers, but discipleship to Wordsworth won him that place.

The anthologists are almost as kindly to Sara Coleridge (1802-1852) as to her brother Hartley, but she is by no means so much of a poet. She has facility, ease of expression, an outlook of her own, but she has made no discoveries and she is mistress of no new music. Her best lines are about a cow seeking her heifer that has been offered up in sacrifice.

> The stall where late her darling lay
> She visits oft with eager look:
> In restless movements wastes the day,
> And fills with cries each neighb'ring nook.

That records a phase of farm life that is constantly recurring. It has the pathos in it of the sorrows of dumb beasts, sorrows that must be borne without comfort from others of their kind. It just misses, however, doing what it sets out to do. It fails of inevitability. It flats.

She attempts, too, another universal theme, that of the mother who, delighting in the innocence and happiness of her child, is thinking of the future in which she shall be separated from him and in which he must lose his innocence. She is not so successful with the troubled human mother as with the mourning bovine one. Moralizing kills the poetry that might have been. Content yourself with those poems of hers you will find in the anthologies. You will think less of her if you read *Phantasmion* (1837).

The poetry that was in the first two generations of the Coleridge family is running thin in the verse of the present-day Coleridges. "Anodos," as Mary Coleridge (1861-1907) called herself, had a little vogue in the *Shilling Garland* days of the nineties.

Published there, her *Fancy's Guerdon* (1897) is competent verse if unmemorable. In the *Collected Songs and Lyrics* (1930) of the Hon. Stephen Coleridge only the sapphics show workmanship worthy of his name. The distinct impression I carry away from the volume is of that so amusingly English rhyme "Bear" and "Cassiopeia."

BERNARD BARTON

You are in pleasant company when you are reading Bernard Barton (1784-1849). Yet, having read him once through a sense of duty, you never read all of him again. You look through him on a second reading, not to find certain poems you remember and would recall in detail, but just because you remember the pleasant men you met in the verses on that first reading, the author and the friends and the poets he liked. You met Izaak Walton in them, and Quaker worthies, William Penn among them, and Evelyn and Cowper, and Crabbe, Gilbert White and Lamb and Wordsworth. You have glimpses of wallflowers and winter evenings by the fire, the home of Barton's forefathers at Ive-Gill in Cumberland, and country walks hither and yon. His verse is easy, not too closely wrought, pensive, gentle and quickly forgotten.

Unimpressive though it is on the average, and yielding no poem for an anthology of the best, the verse of Bernard Barton had a little popularity in its day. There were ten volumes of it from *Metrical Effusions* (1812) to *Household Verses* (1845) dedicated, by permission, to Queen Victoria. The books were named with damning exactitude, *Metrical Effusions* being all that "metrical effusions" connotes, and *Poems by an Amateur* (1818) being just that. Fitzgerald of *Omar Khayyam*, his son-in-law, wrote a critical estimate of the poet for his "literary remains" in 1849. That last volume was reprinted in Philadelphia in 1850, as *Poems by Bernard Barton* had been in 1844, and *Poems* (1820) in 1821. Before Whittier Barton was the most considerable Quaker poet, and, as was only natural, he was held in high honor in Philadelphia, even to this day the center of Quakerdom.

LEIGH HUNT

Leigh Hunt (1784-1859) was still a poet to reckon with fifty years ago when I was a boy in school. We recited "Abou Ben Adhem" there, and when we went to college, forty-odd years ago, we were lectured to on his essays and on "The Story of Rimini." We met "Jenny Kiss'd Me" in the anthologies and patronized it as a something a little better than *vers de société*. Now Hunt is hardly read at all, prose or verse. If he is mentioned it is as an influence on Keats or for his indiscreet book on Byron. Once in a while some one compares his version of the Paolo and Francesca story to Boker's or Stephen Phillips', but hardly to praise it. Arthur Symons has, it is true, picked out five words of his prose for especial approval, saying that "like sleeping Kings of Lethe" contains "more poetry than any five hundred lines of Hunt's formal verse." The words are, of course, as depreciative as they are appreciative. Who will read his essays or autobiography for passages that are poetry will have a long search. The deadly facility of the man turned nearly everything he wrote to journalism.

THOMAS HOOD

There was no poet, save Burns and Longfellow, of whom more sets of verses were familiar in the days of my youth, in the circles I knew, than Thomas Hood (1799-1845). We read, or had read to us, or recited, or had sung to us, "Fair Ines," "Ruth," "The Dream of Eugene Aram," "The Song of the Shirt," and "The Bridge of Sighs." "I remember" was dinned into our ears at every school recitation hour, until it became a companion piece to "The Old Oaken Bucket." It was the well I so loved that made the latter dear to me, and the identification I could make of the poet's home with my home that made "I remember" so instant to me.

Father, of course, half shrugged his shoulders over Hood, when we came home from school with praise of him heard there, but he did not try to minimize him to us. It was left for time to do that, and time has had its way with Hood. We write him down now as important in sociology, but of complete accomplishment only in society verse, and even there no fellow of Dobson or Locker-Lampson.

JOHN CLARE

The phenomenon of John Clare (1793-1864) is one of the most interesting in all the annals of English poetry. That a true peasant, on the soil, should come to the writing of verse before he was twenty was remarkable enough, even with the case of Burns instant to all. That he should remain the peasant throughout his publishing, continuing to work, smocked, in the fields, and in few ways, other than the writing of verse, be different from his fellow farm-laborers, was still more remarkable. That his verse should be something more than apprentice work was what was most remarkable of all. His breakdown, physical and mental, lent an added pathos to his story, and that story has now grown into a legend that must lead to disappointment in those coming to his verse through its far-heralding.

Books upon country ways and country things have been one of my delights for years. Campion, Cotton, Herrick, Pomfret; Bacon, Cowley, Browne and Gilbert White: have for me their value as writers, and then an added interest for their presentation of out-of-doors. I should, and I could, be interested in John Clare as I am interested in these men. I can, however, find little high poetry in him, much as I appreciate his chronicling of the daily life of the farm and of changing aspects of the seasons. The fact is he is not much more of a poet than Robert Bloomfield (1766-1823), though he knows much more of the detail of the countryside and of the ways of country folk than the author of *The Farmer's Boy* (1800).

My *Poems Descriptive of Rural Life and Scenery*, though 1820, is a third edition and really of 1821, as the date line under the engraving of Clare, its frontispiece, shows conclusively. This copy has seen hard usage, but there is nothing to show that it has been long in America. Clare, so far as I can find out, was not reprinted here as was *The Farmer's Boy.* One of my copies of the latter was printed in Wilmington, Delaware, in 1803, three years after its first appearance in London. Recent editors of Clare have not, I think, followed the course most likely to build up a true appreciation of him on either side of the Atlantic. They have printed many poems in *John Clare: Poems Chiefly from Manuscript* (1920) unprinted before, and reprinted a good many from the four volumes printed in his lifetime, and responsible, with his story, for what fame came to him then. The volume is far from a complete Clare, however. *The Village Minstrel* (1821) was his second volume; *The Shepherd's Calendar* (1827), his third; and *The Rural Muse* (1835), his fourth. We are glad of so generous a representation of the poems he wrote after he was put into the asylum at Northampton in 1843, but these latest poems are not so good as we have been often told they are.

The best of Clare is in the long descriptive poems of his first and second volumes such as "Evening" and "Summer Evening" and "Summer Morning" and "Rural Morning," and certain short lyrics like "The Universal Epitaph" and "What Is Life?" There is bite, mordancy, and swift attack in the "Epitaph":

> And oh! condemn me not, I pray,
> You who my sad confession view;
> But ask your soul, if it can say,
> That I'm a viler man than you.

There is like pointedness and completeness of expression in:

> And what is Life?—An hour-glass on the run,
> A mist retreating from the morning sun,
> A busy, bustling, still repeated dream;
> Its length?—A minute's pause, a moment's thought;
> And happiness? A bubble on a stream,
> That in the act of seizing shrinks to nought.

Pleasanter far are the descriptive poems in their faithfulness, and tenderness, and unsentimentalized love of all the creatures,

little and big, of the countryside, and in their appreciation of the
beauty of trees and sward and flowers. There is the sharpness of a
thing seen in:

> From the haycock's moistened heaps,
> Startled frogs take vaunting leaps;
> And along the shaven mead,
> Jumping travellers, they proceed.

That is the first time I have come upon that little incident of an
evening stroll described, in prose or verse either. And here is a
milkmaid portrayed just as she was in the Northamptonshire of a
century ago:

> And now the blossom of the village view,
> With airy hat of straw, and apron blue,
> And short-sleeved gown, that half to guess reveals
> By fine-turned arms what beauty it conceals;
> Whose cheeks health flushes with as sweet a red
> As that which stripes the woodbine o'er her head;
> Deeply she blushes on her morn's employ,
> To prove the fondness of some passing boy,
> Who, with a smile that thrills her soul to view,
> Holds the gate open till she passes through,
> While turning nods back thanks for kindness done,
> And looks, if looks could speak, proclaim her won.

That is as good poetry of its kind as Clare can write. It is
pleasing, faithful, sprightly almost, but there is not strong feeling in it. It is cruelty to man or beast that stirs him to as near to
passion as it is possible for him to come. Here is another evening
piece, one with more feeling in it:

> And from the long furrowed seams,
> Ploughmen loose their weary teams:
> Ball, with urging lashes wealed,
> Still so slow to drive afield,
> Eager blundering from the plough,
> Wants no whip to drive him now;

> At the stable-door he stands,
> Looking round for friendly hands
> To loose the door its fastening pin,
> And let him with his corn begin.

This, and the "suppering-up" of all the beasts that follows, is true pastoral poetry, as good in its secondary kind as any such we have in English.

GEORGE DARLEY

George Darley (1795-1846) wrote to Barry Cornwall asking him to cram *Thomas à Becket* "into the blazes" if the play did not force him to read it thoroughly. That surely is the test of any piece of literature of power, that it forces you to read it thoroughly. Submitting Darley, plays and lyrics alike, to that test, how many of us, devotees to poetry though we be, can honestly say, hand on heart and fingers uncrossed, that *Sylvia* (1827), or *Nepenthe* (1835), or *Thomas à Becket* (1840) forces us to read it thoroughly?

There was a time I was glad to pick up *Sylvia* and to read in it. So far and so far only has any play of Darley gotten hold of me. Now I am content to look *Sylvia* over, reading certain marked passages that I delighted in in youth. Nor can I say that any of the lyrics, even the much bepraised "I've been roaming" or "The Fallen Star" or "The Enchanted Spring," are of the poems I must read now and again to be happy, as I must certain verses of Herrick, or of Wordsworth, or of Housman. All that I can say when I come on one or another of these in an anthology, or a reference in reading sends me to it in my *Complete Poetical Works of George Darley* (1908), is that it has good stuff in it.

A man who can recapture, as can a Darley or a Beddoes, something of Elizabethan feeling or fall of words, has hardly made by those feats alone any part of life his own, and he has most certainly, by that recapture, struck no new note in poetry. If we look further in Darley than his Elizabethan quality, what do we find? He did attempt a theme in the manner of old Irish legend in "The Fight of the Forlorn," when there were few to essay such themes, but it is not in any way a notable poem.

Darley missed in his life the applause of those that cared greatly for poetry, save for a few, a Carlyle and a Mitford say, and he failed also with the crowd. His work had none of the easily understood melodrama and little of the sentimentality that made a Talfourd of his own time, or an Owen Meredith of a time a little later, popular on stage or under the lamp. He was one of the many men who miss greatness but who refuse to write that in poetry for which people will pay. Darley had to do hackwork to live, but he did that hackwork in mathematical books, and he put what was best in him into his plays. There has been a resolute attempt, in recent years, to make him out a neglected genius, but time has been just with him, as with all but all writers. When he adjured the Elizabethan convention and wrote in his own person he was no more a power. "Last Night," simple and direct as it is, and upon that most easily understood and most sympathetic of all themes, the parting of lovers, lacks poignancy and cry:

> We paced alone our fav'rite walk
> But paced in silence broken-hearted:
> Of old we used to smile and talk.
> Last night—we parted.

Poor Darley, interesting phenomenon in retrospect as he is, had as slight a hold on literature as he had on life. He was that common and pathetic figure, the man who misses happiness and success because his aims are larger than his abilities.

THOMAS LOVELL BEDDOES

The strangeness of the character and life of Thomas Lovell Beddoes (1803-1849) still lends something to his verse. We read that verse in the knowledge of his story, and we cannot prevent the story from coloring the verse. Had his life been of everyday sort he would, most likely, be to-day of little more significance than a Sir Henry Taylor or a Sydney Dobell,

As a boy Beddoes published a couple of volumes, *The Improvisatore, with Other Poems* (1821), and *The Bride's Tragedy* (1822). Nearly thirty years afterwards, and a year after his death, *Death's Jest-Book, or The Fool's Tragedy* (1850) was published by his friend Thomas F. Kelsall. Ever since then Beddoes has been a figure in the background of English poetry, but never a wholly obscured figure. Sir Edmund Gosse edited a nearly complete edition in 1890 from the poet's papers, which had been for years in the possession of Robert Browning.

The years from the time of Beddoes' graduation from Oxford in 1825 until his death were spent largely abroad. He took his physician's degree at Göttingen, and from there he moved on to Würzburg, and, later, to Zurich, where he practised his profession. He succeeded in getting into trouble with the authorities, because of his liberal politics, in Würzburg; and the troubles that followed the rising of the peasants in 1839 drove him out of Zurich shortly afterwards. Later he lived in Berlin, Giessen, Basel, Strasbourg, Mannheim, Mainz and Frankfurt. All that he was busy with, outside of his writing, in these various places, has not yet yielded to research, but there is no doubt that he consorted with curious characters in some of them. One of the strangest of his activities, dug up by Gosse, was in trying to make an actor out of a baker that he had befriended in Frankfurt. All through these wanderings, and his incidental returns to England, he was tinkering with, and rewriting, his *Death's Jest-Book*, always to him his magnum opus. We have several versions of the play, with readings so different that Gosse says it would be possible to make a variorum edition.

The best of Beddoes, every one agrees, is in *Death's Jest-Book*, in its songs. There is good poetry, too, in the blank verse that carries the action. It is the songs, though, both from this play and from the other plays, and like lyrics written in imitation of the Elizabethans, that keep Beddoes before us. The songs are in the anthologies, where their spontaneity and ease and bubbling music are in happy contrast to the studied beauty of so much Victorian poetry. They are not great lyrics, these songs, but they fall short by little of the best English songs of post-Elizabethan days. "The swallow leaves her nest" and "If thou wilt ease thine heart" are the successes among the songs of *Death's Jest-Book,* though some of the anthologies include "To sea, to sea! The calm is o'er." In another of these songs, "Folly hath now turned out of door," occur the most arresting lines in Beddoes:

> The world's no stage, no tavern more,
> Its sign, the Fool's ta'en down.

There are lines and images quite a few in Beddoes that you cannot pass over without noting. One is "The spirit of gone Eden haunting earth," and another "A pair of patchwork angels." Three others are "She was the rosy morning of a woman," "And Priam's towery town with its one beech," and "This old plebeian creature that I am."

No one has bettered the criticism of the tragic poems of Beddoes that his fellow-dramatist, George Darley, passed upon *The Bride's Tragedy* over a hundred years ago. Writing in the *London Magazine,* in December, 1823, Darley said: "The *os magna,* alone, will not do; even that which is not epic or lyric, but strictly dramatic. He exhibits no skill in dialogue. He displays no power whatever in delineation of character. If it were possible, speaking of works of this kind, to make a distinction between the *vis tragica* and the *vis dramatica,* I should say that he possessed much of the former, but little of the latter."

What Darley says of *The Bride's Tragedy* is as true of *Death's Jest-Book* (1850). This is blood-and-thunder stuff, inspired by the plays of Webster and Tourneur. It is a poorly arranged and episodic play, concerned with ingratitude, disloyalty, murder, the return of the dead, and a fool's revenge for a father and brother slain. There is power of a kind in it, it has eloquence, and sometimes that eloquence lifts toward poetry. This is almost a "lyrical interbreathing":

Speak as at first you did; there was in the words
A mystery and music, which did thaw
The hard old rocky world into a flood,
Whereon a swan-drawn boat seemed at my feet
Rocking on its blue billows; and I heard
Harmonies, and breathed odors from an isle,
Whose flowers cast tremulous shadows in the day
Of an immortal sun, and crowd the banks,
Whereon immortal human kind doth couch.

The Bride's Tragedy is another play of horrors, but without the bitter grotesquerie and the eloquences of *Death's Jest-Book*. *The Second Brother* and *Torrismond* are fragments. "Pygmalion" is a narrative poem telling the old story of the statue come to life. It is a variation from the more usual form of the tale, but it has no other interest than the puzzle interest of how it is going to end. The quatorzains are more like exercises than perfected poems. All in all, time has been a little more than just to Beddoes. In the letter, his last, that was on him when he was found, a suicide, he wrote: "I ought to have been, among a variety of other things, a good poet." The scientific spirit that was in him made him see himself as he was, as it made him speculate, quite in the manner of Darwin, about the origin of species. Beddoes was not of those, to use his own words, who "sheath their minds in scorn and self-conceit." He had missed being a good poet; he knew it, and he acknowledged his failure by his death.

WILLIAM MACKWORTH PRAED

William Mackworth Praed (1802-1839) wrote one poem, perhaps, and, surely, a score of neatly turned sets of verses that rank high as *vers de société*. The poem, if poem it is, is "Sketch of a Young Lady Five Months Old." Among the sets of verses are "The Vicar," "The Belle of the Ball-Room," "My Own Araminta, Say 'No!'," "Our Ball," and "My Little Cousins." There is tenderness in most of these verses, and humor in all of them. There is good craftsmanship, too. They are without the weariness

that creeps so often into their kind of writing. There is no deep
bitterness, or true cynicism, or inverted sentimentality in the greatest part of what he has written. He can say that his Abbot of "The
Red Fisherman"

> was thinking of scenery
> About as much, in sooth,
> As a lover thinks of constancy,
> Or an advocate of truth.

We take it, however, only as a sally, and laugh, and let it go for
what it is worth. The lines have the very accent of society verse,
its air, its poise, its artificiality, its perfection of phrase.

Another note that Praed struck seems to be that we all know
as characteristic of Gilbert. Are these lines not of the very quality
of the Savoy librettos?

> The sun shone out on hill and grove;
>   It was a glorious day;
> The lords and ladies were making love,
>   And the clowns were making hay;
> But the Town of Brentford marked with wonder
> A lightning in the sky, and thunder,
> And thinking ('twas a thinking town)
> Some prodigy was coming down,
> A mighty mob to Merlin went
> To learn the cause of this portent;
> And he, a wizard sage, but comical,
> Looked through his glasses astronomical—

That is enough, I think, to show on whose art of verse Gilbert
builded. Many of his effects are there, triple rhymes, playful
contrasts, patter, for three. The parody of old English songs that
you find in "Tit willow" has its forerunner in Praed's "Nonny
nonny" verses, which, also, you will find in this same poem
"Lillian." Praed, like most writers of light verse, has not worn
well with me in the long years I have been reading. Suckling,
Lovelace, Prior, Praed, Calverly, Dobson, J. K. Stephen, Sir

Owen Seaman, much as I have liked them, are not the joy to me for their society verse that they were when I was young. Only Locker-Lampson has stood the test of the years. That, I take it, is because he is more of a poet than any of them, unless perhaps Dobson. Cleverness is the portion of most of these men, and cleverness is of the hour. Few clever men have been great, as that student of most insight and critical acumen I ever had pointed out in a comparison of Meredith with Congreve and Sheridan, Wilde and Shaw. All five were clever, he said, but only Meredith was great. Praed, too, is clever, but once he forgot cleverness in his verses to the little lady of five, and came as close to poetry as any writer of society verse only can come. That he did really achieve poetry in "Sketch of a Young Lady" I am not quite sure, but that he barely failed of it, if fail he did, not a few will contend. So, too, it was with Prior, who came nearest to a poem in "My noble, lovely, little Peggy." It may be true, after all, that by "the hand of a child" such rhymes are "led to the throne of the King."

RICHARD HENGIST HORNE

Richard Hengist Horne (1803-1884) is one of the few minor poets who just missed being major. Time was I thought he was of the great, when I, but little beyond boyhood, read *The Death of Marlowe* (1837). I came on it at the end of the third volume of Bullen's *Marlowe*, and its blank verse fell on my ears while the "mighty lines" of the master were still echoing there. Nothing else of Horne has so sustained a power, not *Cosmo de' Medici* (1837) or *Orion* (1843), or any of the few lyrics. It was a bold attempt to put words into Marlowe's mouth. Clemence Dane was even bolder in *Will Shakespeare* (1921), and just as successful, indeed, as Horne. It was given to both of these minor poets to succeed beyond their deserts.

It is in *Orion*, however, and in *Cosmo de' Medici* that the phrases and lines occur that have become part of our inheritance. In the former are " 'Tis always morning somewhere in the world," "The wisdom of mankind creeps slowly on," and "The roar of

Time's great wings." In the latter occurs that passage on antiquity that had no rival in English until Gissing wrote the famous tribute of *A Life's Morning* (1888).

> The grandeur of Antiquity uplifts
> Each soul whose natural energies expand
> In space sufficient for its by-gone worlds.
> Greece in its infancy, and unborn Rome,
> Trac'd thro' their glorious rise and branchings vast,
> As tho' we'd watch'd seeds set in paradise
> Take root, and then inherit all the sun;
> Breed thoughts and visions, such as Time himself
> Might pause remorseful o'er his scythe, to scan.

The circumstances of Horne's life enhance the interest that his verse has in itself. His snowballing of Keats, his fighting and escape from a shark in Mexico, his wanderings in the States and in Australia, his friendship with the Brownings, the fantasticality and bitter poverty of his later years—all the stories told of him give him a place that his poetry alone could hardly have won for him. His verse has in it much to surprise and to delight, passages of dewy freshness, phrase on phrase of the beauty of the world seen under morning light, sonorous declamations, even moments of great passion nobly caught. The trouble is that these excellences are most often not inherently part of the poem or play, but asides or embroideries, like the show passages of Stephen Phillips. Always, though, Horne has largeness of utterance and a kind of Elizabethan fire.

THE HON. MRS. NORTON

Caroline Norton (1808-1877) has a place in literature higher than any writing of hers warrants. She has that place because she was Richard Brinsley Sheridan's granddaughter, and because of the belief, held rightly or wrongly, that she was the original of George Meredith's heroine in *Diana of the Crossways* (1885). She was widely read, though, and highly regarded, in England and America, as both poet and story-teller in the mid-nineteenth century. She published a volume of verse that attracted attention in England in 1829, *The Sorrows of Rosalie,* and she had success with a volume of verse published as late as 1862, *The Lady of Garaye.*

As an out-and-out Meredithian I had long been looking for verse of hers in the old bookshops, but it was not until 1923, and in far Berkeley, that I came on a volume of hers. As I sauntered out Sather Gate from the University grounds one day of July, I noticed, across the street, on a table outside a stationery shop, a brightly gilded book. I made a bee line for the gaud, noticing as I picked it up, a shepherd piping to his sheep on the binding. I turned the back around and read there "The Dream and Other Poems—Mrs. Norton." Opening the book I noted a steel engraving of the famous beauty, after Landseer. There was not only "The Dream" in the volume, but "The Child of the Islands," too. Bound together, they had found their way all the long road from the Boston where they were printed to this ultimate West just short of the Golden Gate. "The Child of the Islands," which was, of course, about little Edward, Prince of Wales, was dated in 1849, and "The Dream" 1851, so both books might have been in California since gold-rush days. The pages were stained, and corners of them turned down here and there. The book had been read.

There is humanitarian feeling in the two books such as that which informed her labors in behalf of women's rights in the England of her day, plenty of it, but no single poem of quality, not even "Bingen on the Rhine." There are few rapt moments, and fewer discoveries about life. My Aunt Rachel must, I think, have read "The Dream," for there was recurrent in her racy talk the thought that the Hon. Mrs. Norton puts in these four lines:

> Warriors and statesmen have their meed of praise,
>   And what they do or suffer men record;
> But the long sacrifice of woman's days
>   Passes without a thought—without a word.

I have underlined perhaps a dozen lines in "The Dream," for one reason or another, and not more than another dozen in all the double volume. It is the eighteenth-century quality of "Sees the low sunset gild the cultured soil" that made me notice it. It is my indifference to most dahlias that made me approve:

> Nor clustering dahlia, with its scentless flowers
> Cheating the heart through autumn's faded hours.

It is my love of little things of nature well caught in words that made me treasure "The fragile silver of the spider's web," "The pale beauty of our English heaven," and "Or young laburnum's pendant yellow chain." It is the lyric ring that poets' names have for me that made me mark the four lines:

> Then Spenser made the summer day seem brief,
> Or Milton sounded with a loftier song,
> Then Cowper charm'd, with lays of gentle grief,
> Or glorious Dryden roll'd the hour along.

There are references here and there throughout her verses to her own troubled life. These references take on poignancy if you know the details of her story, but there is no one poem, or passage of a poem, or line even, that becomes a part of you forever from the moment of its noting. She had not the art to put her suffering into song, and she made no attempt to catch there her visitations of ecstasy.

LORD HOUGHTON

It is out of our own mouths most of us are condemned. Richard Moncton Milnes, Lord Houghton (1809-1885), gives himself away in those verses of his called "The Violet-Girl":

> When Fancy will continually rehearse
> Some painful scene once present to the eye,
> 'Tis well to mould it into gentle verse
> That it may lighter on the spirit lie.

Half of the cultivated world that speaks English was brought up, I suppose, on "Lady Moon, Lady Moon, where are you roving?" Just why, unless for the tune's sake, it is hard to say. It is stale, flat, and unprofitable, like all of his verse. Yet there was a time we liked him in America, and a library copy of *Poems of Many Years*, Boston, 1846, that I know, was well thumbed back along. You will find a poem of his in an anthology once in a while, but it is not there on its merits. The sterling man that he was had nothing in him of the poet.

MINOR GEORGIANS

A good few of the lesser Georgians, most of them men not affiliated closely with either Wordsworth or Coleridge, lived on into the years we are considering, but there were few of them did any considerable work in our period. Scott and Crabbe died in 1832. Samuel Rogers (1763-1855) put out the complete edition of *Italy* in 1830, but by date of publication he is mostly Georgian, and by the spirit of his verse pre-Georgian, what we are wont to call distinctively eighteenth-centuryish. Robert Southey (1744-1843) is even less to us to-day than Rogers. Southey has suffered the most complete eclipse of any English poet once generally recognized as major. He was still collecting his verse in 1837, but his laborious practice of his unending and futile writing was about over by then.

Charles Lamb (1755-1834) and James Hogg (1770-1835), those two so differing friends of Wordsworth, were at the end of their careers, and W. L. Bowles (1762-1850) and Joanna Baillie (1762-1851), though they published in our period, hardly added to their reputation in their later years, the one in the sonnet, and the other in drama. Of their contemporaries Barry Cornwall (1787-1874) was active in the second quarter of the century, but he belongs unequivocally to the Georgian period. Thomas Love Peacock (1785-1866) is a Georgian in his novels, and he retained all his powers in prose and verse alike well into our period. His best verse might have been written at almost any time since the

Elizabethan era. It is song, at once carefree and satiric, with little relation to the point of view or standards or values of any age.

"L.E.L." (Letitia Elizabeth Landon Maclean, 1802-1838) was the rival in popularity of Tom Moore in his heyday. "L.E.L." is the writer of verse of all of her sex who most surely deserves to be called a "poetess." Jean Ingelow (1820-1897), of a succeeding generation, knew a popularity and a quickly succeeding neglect rather similar to that of her Georgian predecessor. Her best-known poem, "The High Tide on the Coast of Lincolnshire," luxuriates in the pathetic with an abandon comparable to that of "L.E.L." in "St. Valerie."

Ebenezer Elliott (1781-1849) is known because of the material of his verse, and not by the poetry of those verses. He is "The Corn Law Rhymer," a just summation of what he amounts to.

The Christian Year (1827) made John Keble (1792-1866) known before our period of all English-speaking men, but he wrote much verse through many years of that period. *Lyra Innocentium* was published in 1846. There was no hymn of his that took such a place in the affections of men as did "Lead, kindly light" of John Henry Newman (1801-1890), which was published in *Lyra Apostolica* (1834). The Tractrian movement made itself manifest as early as 1833, but so little poetry of any significance came directly out of it that a consideration of it need not detain us long.

There is a good deal of religious poetry of power in English, but little of first power. Religious poetry is at more than its average best in the well-knit platitudes of Christina Rossetti, and it reaches its highest achievement in Herbert and Vaughan and Crashaw, in Patmore and Francis Thompson. With exceptions few and far between, English hymns are poor poetry. Isaac Watts and Charles Wesley did touch the heart of the race, but it is only associations that endear their verses to us to-day. So it is with almost all English hymns. Recapturings of childhood hours they bring us; visions of faces long vanished now; memories of companionship in worship in white meeting-houses, steepled and beshedded, on hilltops in country places and in old times; but we have only infrequently "the pleasures of poetry" from any of them. Old tunes to which they were sung put a value on some of them they have not in their words, lines from them lard our talk as do lines from "Ecclesiastes" and the "Song of Solomon," "Isaiah" and the "Psalms." The lines from the Bible, though, have kindled us to an ecstasy of poetry. The lines from hymns most often do no more than make us smile with mused memories.

Familiar to me all my life have been "Nearer, my God, to thee" by Sarah Flower Adams (1805-1848); "Art thou weary, art thou languid?" by John Mason Neale (1818-1866); "There is a green hill far away" by Cecil Frances Alexander (1823-1895); and "Onward, Christian Soldiers" by Sabine Baring-Gould (1834-1924). Familiar, too, I take it, they are to a large part of the English-speaking world, and fairly representative of nineteenth century hymnology. Is there any one, however, of those who know poetry and who have associations with these hymns who can say any one of the hymns named has even approximations to poetry in it?

There are a score other Georgians other than those I have named, or will name in this chapter, who are worthy of a word of comment. An end must be made somewhere, however, and so I close the "mere mentions" with a word about four Scots. Allan Cunningham (1784-1842) and William Motherwell (1797-1835) have been brought closer to me than William Tennant (1784-1848) and William Thom (1799-1848). I have lived all my life with a copy of the American edition of Motherwell's *Poetical Works*, which my father bought, at twenty-one, in 1853. Alongside of it, in his bookcase, now in my dining room, stand the two volumes of the same Scot's *Minstrelsy, Ancient and Modern,* also in a Boston edition, but of seven years earlier. This *Minstrelsy* first came out in the old country nineteen years earlier. There are so many ballads in Motherwell and so much concern with Scandinavian themes that I might have considered him, with Scott, among the romantics. He is at his best, however, with "Jeanie

Morrison," in the manner of Burns. That is his one poem that counts. Cunningham is also a one-poem man, his "A wet sheet and a flowing sea" being still a favorite recitation piece in the days of my youth. Tennant is remembered for *Anster Fair* (1812) and Thom for his *Rhymes and Recollections of a Hand Loom Weaver* (1844).

CHAPTER VI

Tennyson, the Victorian Oracle

OF poets since Tennyson (1809-1892) only Kipling, in latest Victorian times, and Masefield, in Neo-Georgian times, have won the whole English-speaking world as Tennyson did during the days of his laureateship (1850-1892). Just how widely he had won it I found out on the night of his death. I was working then as a reporter on a Philadelphia newspaper, founded with the design, and successful in that design, of appealing to the least-educated elements in the community. The managing editor would come into the local room, growling over a bunch of proof in his hand: "Cut out your subtleties, you fellows, and all this culture and high art. Remember this paper is read by hod-carriers and truckmen."

These "fellows," about evenly divided in numbers between men from college and men from printing shop, telegrapher's key, and paper routes, had all been brought up on Tennyson. This we learned in the discussion that followed the receipt of the cablegram announcing his death. We had nearly all heard "The Brook" recited in dame-school. Some of us had ourselves recited "The Charge of the Light Brigade" in high school or academy. Two or three of us had plunged deep into *In Memoriam* (1850) in college. The office, however, had never before had a literary discussion in which all took part. Some of the youngsters among us had fought on to daylight about our likes in literature when we were "on late" together, or were chumming after hours in little eating places or at our homes, but poetry had been taboo as a general topic.

From what I before knew of them I was wholly unprepared

for the effect of the cablegram on those "hard-boiled" reporters and editors. The surprise came not only from the revelation that all of us knew something of Tennyson at first hand, but from the pause the news of his death gave the office. It quieted us one and all. The effect of that news was almost stunning after the first babble of conversation that followed its arrival had died down. The "write-up" was given to old Craigie, of the editorial writers, who was well known as an enthusiast over the laureate. It was the greatest moment of Craigie's life. Never before had anything so important been asked of the old Scot as to write a column on Tennyson. Think of it, a column on Tennyson for that ultra-democratic paper! An editorial and biography in one, to follow the news despatch of his death! A first-page display!

The managing editor prowled round the fifth floor all the time Craigie was busy over his column, ready to squelch any conversation should it break out anywhere in the editorial rooms. He did not find much to squelch, for we all felt Craigie must have quiet to "do" Tennyson. The old man was as important over his task as the chief mourner at a funeral. He was something better than important, too. He was rapt. He wore the look of one dedicated to a great task. He was trembly, doubtful of himself for all his familiarity with Tennyson, afraid that he would fall short of what was due the man whom he considered the greatest poet of Victorian England.

I cannot remember now what Craigie's column was like, but I can never forget the effect of that cablegram. Not even the Tennyson Cricket Club that I came on years later flourishing in a Philadelphia mill district spoke louder of the appeal of the laureate.

The very qualities, though, that made Tennyson thus popular in the days of his laureateship are those that make against his reputation to-day. If these qualities can be summed up in any one word that word is Victorianism. They are most of them qualities, however, that are aside from the main issue in the judgment of any poet. That main issue is, of course, "What of poetry is there

Why/how
he
was
a poet   — what made him good

in him?" The "honest doubt" concerning religious beliefs; the generous attitude toward the cause of woman; the acceptance of science; the liberal politics; the pleas, sometimes a little prudish, for that higher manhood which would hold under the "ape" and "tiger" in man—all these are worn or ordinary to-day.

They crowd so, these topical questions, to the forefront of much of Tennyson's verse, *The Princess* (1847) and *In Memoriam* (1850) for instance, that they somewhat obscure the poetry in these writings. So, too, did they obscure their poetry when these writings were published. Yet these topical discussions, and these deliverances on the questions of the hour, drew readers to Tennyson in Victorian times that the poetry in his writing would not alone have drawn. And, to-day, all this that is topical of yesterday gives offense to those readers who will accept poetry if it is topical of to-day, but who cannot find what is worth while in its poetical quality alone. The critics of recent years who look in all literature for what they call "the larger issues" of life find Tennyson old-fashioned, but those critics to whom sheer poetry is what is greatest in all poetry, as in all literary art, still find Tennyson one of the immortals.

Those, too, who look for quotable observations on men and things find in Tennyson more such observations than in any other body of English writing outside of Shakespeare and the King James Bible. The number and truth of such observations are what stand out as the most clearly measurable fact about Tennyson. You are a little surprised by the many passages you had to mark as you read all his six volumes from A to Z. Before sitting down to such a reading you would have said that you remembered Tennyson for that new glamour and tone and fall of words he created for English poetry, that glamour and tone and fall of words, which, developed by Rossetti and Morris and Swinburne, we now speak of as Pre-Raphaelite, the glamour and tone and fall of words of "The Lady of Shalott" (1832) and of "Sir Lancelot and Queen Guinevere" (1842). You would have said that you remembered Tennyson for a new artistry of English verse. Just what he attains to in "Morte d'Arthur" (1842) had not been in English verse before:

> So all day long the noise of battle roll'd
> Among the mountains by the winter sea;
> Until King Arthur's table, man by man,
> Had fallen in Lyonesse about their Lord,
> King Arthur: then, because his wound was deep,
> The bold Sir Bedivere uplifted him,
> Sir Bedivere, the last of all his knights,
> And bore him to a chapel nigh the field,
> A broken chancel with a broken cross,
> That stood on a dark strait of barren land.
> On one side lay the Ocean, and on one
> Lay a great water, and the moon was full.

His Talent

Paraphrase ➝ The accord here of sound with sense; the movement and change of pace; the smoothness and finish, are all Tennyson's own, gifts of his to the race that have made our blank verse capable of effects of which it was not capable before he discovered them.

You would have said that you remembered Tennyson for the rhetorical effectiveness of a number of his recitation pieces, "The Charge of the Light Brigade," "The Revenge," and "Lady Clara Vere de Vere." You would have said that you remembered him for certain poems, like "Crossing the Bar," that are now a part of the ritual of the burial service as surely as passages from the Bible. You would have said that you remembered him for pictures of landscape and country life of a still beauty that was not before he made it, for verses about Christmas cheer and New Year's Eve that are as English as holly berries and boughs of yew.

You would have said that you remembered Tennyson for the great part of Becket that he created for Irving, and for the woodsiness and idyllic charm and Old Englishness of *The Foresters*, in which, in your youth, you had seen Ada Rehan and John Drew.

There is so large a body of observations on men and things, and it is by now so wholly a part of everyday speech, that were I

many of his lines have become common sayings in America/England, english-speaking countries to list here a tenth of it, those who read would find so many old acquaintances that they would say, as the people going out of the theater after a performance of *Hamlet* always say, "What a number of familiar quotations!"

They are not usually comparable in reach and profundity to those of the Bible or Shakespeare. Some are, indeed, hardly more than catchwords of the hour, but there are discoveries about life among them, and, taken together, they constitute a fund of wisdom that is drawn upon in daily life very much as men draw on the proverbial wisdom that has been handed on by word of mouth from generation to generation.

Hardly more than phrases current, perhaps, are "large, divine and comfortable words," "Femininely fair and dissolutely pale," "The old order changeth yielding place to new," "Free love will not be bound," "Our hoards are little, but our hearts are great," "The blind hysterics of the Celt," "The grand old name of gentleman," and "His honor rooted in dishonor stood." What all may see are such lines as these: "The blue-black Irish hair and Irish eyes"; "a noble ease That graced the lowliest act in doing it"; "Man's word is God in Man"; and

> For manners are not idle, but the fruit
> Of loyal nature, and of noble mind.

There are those who will say there is a certain obviousness in all these sayings and descriptions, and the charge may be true, but it is equally true that Tennyson cast them in phrases that caught the ear of the world. The moral precepts among them are built up on the best of the Christian code of his time. Their meaning is plain. Even the man in the street can understand them on a first reading. They are easy to accept and easy to remember. Yet, with all the qualities in Tennyson that go to make a general appeal, it is not so easy to explain why so many people regarded him, for so many years, as an oracle. His optimism had something to do with such regard, for the modern world will acclaim only the cheerful prophet. His ideality increased that regard, for it was an ideality that seemed "practical," that did not demand too much at once of the world, but led steadily "onward and upward" to

> one far-off divine event
> To which the whole creation moves.

Clergymen almost to a man, and schoolmen almost to a man, quoted Tennyson on all occasions. Many who live by talk still quote him. I have heard lines from "The Higher Pantheism" in the pulpit within the year, and the last June commencement address I listened to, by a college professor of economics, ended with a quotation from "Merlin and the Gleam."

It was, of course, because Tennyson could put final form on the talk of the hour that he was so much quoted in Victorian times. Often he will condemn that talk as he phrases it. So he is doing when he writes:

> But if sin be sin, not inherited fate, as many will say,

and so he is doing, in part at least, when he speaks of

> Softness breeding scorn of simple life,
> Or Cowardice, the child of lust for gold,
> Or Labor, with a groan and not a voice,
> Or Art with poisonous honey stol'n from France.

A little nearer to statements with an oracular ring, a little nearer to "readings of life," some of them indeed almost discoveries, are: "For nothing worthy proving can be proven"; "Better not be at all Than not be noble"; "Things seen are mightier than things heard"; "Never morning wore to evening but some heart did break"; "The vow that binds too strictly snaps itself"; "Mockery is the fume of little hearts"; "Better fifty years of Europe than a cycle of Cathay"; "The thrall in person may be free in soul"; "For man is man and master of his fate";

> Kind hearts are more than coronets,
> And simple faith than Norman blood;

and

> 'Tis better to have loved and lost
> Than never to have loved at all.

There is only one line in Tennyson more often quoted than this last couplet, and this next to last. That line is inescapable in all "write-ups" of June commencements, "Sweet girl graduates in their golden hair."

Such quotations might easily be multiplied. I have avoided the more priggish among them, of which there are not a few, and the satiric, which are not all of them too happy. I wish that there were more of sayings deeply human, like "He is all fault who has no fault at all" and "For who loves me must have a touch of earth." The truth was, of course, that Tennyson's was not, humanly speaking, a rich nature, that he could not be a part of many kinds of life, that he was not easy with all sorts and conditions of men, that he could not sympathize with Tom, Dick, and Harry in their littlenesses, that he was, for all his friends and acquaintances, a man by instinct aloof from his fellows. To such is not given, as a rule, the dramatic power to know from observation of others what they cannot feel themselves. We all know the man who quiets the talk in a country store when he enters it, because those carrying that talk feel he may not approve of some of it. There may be a respect for such a man; there cannot be much of fellowship with him. So it is with Tennyson. You, reading him, do not recognize him at once as a fellow-sinner, as you do Chaucer, or Shakespeare, or Browning, or Masefield. There is something of the cleric in him, and of the not too tolerant cleric. Clerics, of course, may be of very different sorts, witness Herrick and Emerson, but it would have been easier to chum with either than with Tennyson. Tennyson was hard to gossip with, and the ability to gossip with your fellow-men is, in most cases, necessary to a deep knowledge of human nature. Hardy, for instance, for all his penetrating vision, was a fellowly soul, as ready for a word with Hodge or the Squire on ordinary things as Gay or Hudson, as Burns or Frost.

Tennyson was one with the countryside, however, if he was not one with its inhabitants. He wrote stories in verse of country people, some in the dialect of his native Lincolnshire, but none of them from "Dora" to "Owd Roa" are as intimate of country life as a hundred passages in his poetry descriptive of the countryside. It is very England that you have here. There are vignettes in "The Palace of Art" you remember as you remember places seen under unforgettable circumstances. Best of them is:

> an English home—gray twilight pour'd
> On dewy pastures, dewy trees,
> Softer than sleep—all things in order stored,
> A haunt of ancient Peace.

That, perhaps, is a memory of Lincolnshire. This proclaims itself as the southern coast:

> Green Sussex fading into blue
> With one gray glimpse of sea.

Such two-line bits are many. Some are of trees, such as:

> in the meadows tremulous aspen trees
> And poplars made a noise of falling showers.

That description is exact and vivid, with something of the wind through the trees in the words. This that follows combines picture and consonance of sound and sense:

> The broad ambrosial aisles of lofty lime
> Made noise with bees and breeze from end to end.

And this third is onomatopœia at its best:

> The moan of doves in immemorial elms,
> And murmuring of innumerable bees.

Even the Vergil that Tennyson so admired did nothing better of its kind than that.

Tennyson had always a sharp eye for the birds, and the power to describe their songs in words that reproduce them, in so far as words can reproduce bird songs. The song of the English black-bird has never been better reproduced even by that Ledwidge to whom it meant all in all than in "The mellow ouzel fluted in the elm." That line is a fellow to Emerson's of the swamp blackbird: "The redwing flutes his okalee." Just how much bird song is to him Tennyson reveals in "The Marriage of Geraint." It is in a simile the revelation comes, but it is lovingly elaborated for its own sake:

> So the sweet voice of Enid moved Geraint;
> And made him like a man abroad at morn
> When first the liquid note beloved of men
> Comes flying over many a windy wave
> To Britain, and in April suddenly
> Breaks from a coppice gemm'd with green and red,
> And he suspends his converse with a friend,
> Or it may be the labour of his hands,
> To think or say, "There is the nightingale."

Sometimes the descriptions of Tennyson, while of what he saw in England, are universal. It might have been Venus as we see her in the mountains of New Hampshire of which he was writing when he said:

> And silver-smiling Venus ere she fell
> Would often loiter in her balmy blue.

So she loiters, summer evening after summer evening, over Mt. Israel to the west.

The lack of fellowliness in Tennyson affects his characterizations as it affects his "readings of life." He attempts to create character in his realistic narratives of North-country life; in his ultra-romantic *Idylls of the King*; in his studies in Greek myth; and in his plays out of legend and history. Among the many attempted characters in these diverse sorts of writing Becket stands out lonely and masterful, a true figure against the sky. To that all will agree, but there will be differences of opinion as to whether Becket has fellows. Tennyson made a brave attempt to paint in detail Mary Tudor in *Queen Mary* (1875) and Arthur and Guinevere and Lancelot in *Idylls of the King*, but they have not for me the solidity and personality of Becket. The figures in "Aylmer's Field" (1864) never emerge into the roundness and warmth of life, and those of *Enoch Arden* (1864), for all the care Tennyson takes to have us see them clearly, are as lacking in the detail that brings people home to the reader as is the story itself in the detail of seaside life. What would Crabbe have had to say of a story of a fishing village with no smell of fish, or even of tar or salt? Clarity of outline *Enoch Arden* has; and it embodies a sacrifice so heroic, an overcoming of sexual jealousy so unusual, and so appealing to all men, that the newspaper headline writer safely assumes he may call a man in a news story an "Enoch Arden" and be understood of his readers.

It was perhaps because there was a part of himself in Becket that Tennyson was so successful with him. Or it may be that the asceticism and unworldliness that Tennyson portrayed as developing in this once so worldly and carnal man were conveyed to us so admirably by Irving that his interpretation colors our appreciation for the part. There was always in Irving something priestly and aloof, something of the man easy in an authority delegated from the Lord. Irving was so nearly Becket in his everyday nature that he hardly had to play the part.

Becket (1884) held its place on the stage as long as there was Irving to play the title rôle, but it is no longer the rival to *Richelieu* it was for a season. It is rarely played now; and *The Foresters* (1892), the only other play of Tennyson that won a measure of popularity, is fast following it into obscurity. *The Promise of May* (1882) is crude melodrama. *Harold* (1876) is largely planned, and its glorification of Saxon England, a glorification its author never lost a chance to repeat, lifts it for a while into a kind of topical eminence, but it is ill adapted to the stage, and none too easy to understand even in the leisure of the library. *Harold* is a series of scenes rather than a play, and of a period not too well known to the playgoing public. *Queen Mary* is closet-drama, too, but the tormented infatuate queen, the prey of bigotry and unrequited love, is most carefully studied, and understood, and at least partly rendered. There is little poetry in any of the plays, and only few moments of drama, but there is always eloquence and a sort of stateliness, which, though frigid, has effectiveness of a kind.

Idylls of the King is better stuff than the plays, and better as poetry than the criticism of our day will allow. In this book Tennyson has not always followed his Malory or *Mabinogion* closely, but there is enough of the old stories in his versions to give them large proportions. No man of his parts as a poet, working on material indestructible by the years, could fail to arrest the attention of his age with his versions. Tennyson, of course, did much more than that. He gave us the versions of all the Arthurian stories he essayed that were best known for at least a half-century, and that set the standard by which, even to-day, we measure all modern versions. Arnold's *Tristram and Iseult* (1852) is a better version of the old story and a finer poem than "The Last Tournament," and Swinburne's *Tristram of Lyonesse* is closer to the text and spirit of the medieval originals, but it was Tennyson's version that was best known down until the time that Wagner's *Tristan und Isolde* began to grow popular in the eighteen-nineties. It may be that Robinson's *Tristram* (1927) is accepted more widely in America to-day, but he would be a rash man who would prophesy it would long hold such a position.

Tennyson was for fifty years a parlor-table book in America, more popular here, it was often claimed, than our own Longfellow, and, as a parlor-table book, Tennyson was widely read. There are those who say, and apparently believe, that parlor-table books were not read. Such must have failed to realize that parlor-table books were commoner in households without libraries than in households with libraries, and so resorted to, perforce, for what-

ever book-reading was done in such homes. At auctions, whether
city or country, I have almost always found these parlor-table
books thumbed and worn and ready to open at this, that, or the
other place. Often they have clippings laid away in them, clippings
recording sentiments that parallel those in the book at the point of
insertion.

One parlor-table Tennyson, resplendent in cart-blue and gold,
I came upon at a sale in an old home between the Ossipees and
Lake Winnepesaukee in New Hampshire. There were books in
this home of an older generation than this Tennyson of the
eighteen-eighties, but there were not many contemporary to Tennyson. You are snowed in hereabouts now and then in winter, and
driven to the resources of the house to while away the long evenings. It may have been that this Tennyson was read in lieu of
little else to read, but read its condition showed it to have been.

Americans all over the country heard Tennyson from the pulpit
in the days when most folks went to church. The children who sat
beside their elders during the long sermons found Tennyson, too,
in their readers and books of selections for recitation. For years
and years verses of his were on Christmas cards and calendars, and
in the poet's corner in the newspapers and in the almanacs. No
other English poet of his time, not even Mrs. Browning or Coventry Patmore, had so many avenues through which to reach the
public as Tennyson, and no one at all was so easy to understand on
first reading. You can hardly overemphasize the importance of
ease of understanding of Tennyson in fixing him in the minds of
the public. That is a large part of the quarrel with poetry, that it
is hard to understand. That is a large part of the explanation of
why poor verse is so widely liked, that it is easy to understand, and
that it singsongs itself into the memory.

There was probably no one volume of Tennyson, not even
Idylls of the King, circulated so generally as Owen Meredith's
Lucile, but much more of Tennyson than one volume alone was
generally circulated.

The explanation of the allegory of *Idylls of the King*, as

given in Lord Tennyson's *Life* of his father, has hurt the reputation of the *Idylls*. The public did not like to be told that the romance of the old story was partly only a symbol of the conjugal love of Queen Victoria and the Prince Consort. So, too, does the Mid-Victorian ideal of a King, Christian and a gentleman, that Tennyson advanced, hurt the book to-day. A drawing-room king, after Du Maurier, one calls King Arthur, and another dubs him a Sunday-School King who is a far reflection of Christ. There is a desire abroad to-day to have the old kings of romance forcible beasts or heroic brutes. Such may or may not be nearer historical characters of the Dark Ages than Tennyson's pale paintings, but that such would be better suited to Tennyson's land of romance is a question.

Lancelot and Guinevere are more nearly the fated lovers of tradition than is Arthur the traditional king. Tennyson leaves the guilty pair pretty much as they are in the old romances, save that Lancelot is a little modernized toward the ideal of the Mid-Victorian gentleman. His face lived before Elaine:

> Dark-splendid, speaking in the silence, full
> Of noble things.

Tennyson tries to give us the personality of Mordred in the line that refers to his "Heart-hiding smile, and gray persistent eye." Lynette is:

> A damsel of high lineage, and a brow
> May-blossom, and a cheek of apple-blossom,
> Hawk-eyes; and lightly was her slender nose
> Tiptilted like the petal of a flower.

Hopelessly Mid-Victorian, many of the Neo-Georgian critics call such writing. We all know the talk, like all such talk representative of only one angle of criticism.

Tennyson was aware of such an attitude toward his ideals while he was writing *Idylls of the King*. Ettarre declares that Pelleas is fit only to pamper with papmeat,

> Old milky fables of the wolf and sheep,
> Such as the wholesome mothers tell their boys.

This is the only answer he deigned to make to such criticism.
Critics on the whole he found little help to him, and good critics
very few. In "Poets and Critics" he declares:

> But seldom comes the poet here,
> And the Critic's rarer still.

Tennyson would not have been in the English tradition had
he not written upon Greek themes. "Œnone" was one of *The
Poems* of 1832, and *The Death of Œnone* was the title of the last
volume he collected during his lifetime, the volume published
just after his death in 1892. From time to time, in the sixty years
between, he was writing on episodes from Greek legend. These
poems are one and all successes, and "Œnone," written when he
was a boy just out of college, is as great a poem on a Greek theme
as we have in English literature. Perhaps the Pyrenees, which he
visited with Hallam in 1830, helped him to visualize Mt. Ida,
but the Troy town one saw, as one peered with Œnone down the
gorges, had been before his mind's eye from childhood. Tennyson,
like Dunsany two generations later, looked out of his nursery
windows across the Plains of Roncesvalles to the Towers of Ilion.

There is line on line of blank verse in Tennyson that shows
his study of Milton, but it is his own music that he makes in those
opening lines of "Œnone":

> There lies a vale in Ida, lovelier
> Than all the valleys of Ionian hills.

Not Poe himself with "In the greenest of our valleys" has given
us a more liquid fall of words.

There are other passages of "Œnone" remarkable in other
ways. There is the famous deliverance of Athene:

> Self-reverence, self-knowledge, self-control,
> These three alone lead life to sovereign power.

> Yet not for power (power of herself
> Would come uncall'd for) but to live by law,
> Acting the law we live by without fear;
> And, because right is right, to follow right
> Were wisdom in the scorn of consequence.

Words like music

The blank verse of "Œnone" sings, when its maker wills it, like a lyric; it rolls, when he will have it so, with the gravity of church music; it lifts, when need is, to the eloquence of an oracle foretelling fate. Picture after picture is flashed upon you as you read, and always you have the sense of light, and height, and rare air.

"Ulysses" is another poem you remember, its restless hero, who would

> follow knowledge like a sinking star,
> Beyond the utmost bound of human thought;

the horizons it opens before you; the processional music of the lines.

"Tiresias" and "Demeter and Persephone" are other fine poems of this none too lengthy list of poems on Greek subjects. Neither his English idylls of modern life, nor his idylls of Arthurian England, are better in their kinds than these idylls of Greek life. A romantic though you would write down Tennyson, looking at his work as it unrolls before you from beginning to end, he was, by his reserved nature and clear-visioned mind, closely allied to classic ways of feeling and thought. His range is as wide in method of treatment, almost, as in subject material.

In *The Works of Alfred Lord Tennyson* (1893), the collected verse of the poet in six volumes, *The Princess* (1847), *Maud* (1855), *Enoch Arden* (1864) and *In Memoriam* (1850) make up Volume III. These four long poems, each of which when published gave title to a volume, were treasured most of all Tennyson during the middle years of the century that saw them come into being. Only *Idylls of the King* (1859), indeed, rivaled them in popularity as late as the seventies and eighties, and at the time of Tennyson's death they stood in the very forefront of his work in

These works have depreciated in value [significance] according to critics

popular estimation, and in a large part of critical opinion. Now, the pendulum has swung the other way, and the four poems are rated as not among his best. *Idylls of the King* is grouped with them, often, in depreciation. It is my judgment, as I have said, that *Idylls of the King* is wrongly belittled, but, as to the four others, I must hold with my time. *Maud,* like *Enoch Arden,* has lost savor with age; even its melodrama, which seemed more than melodrama to the mid-nineteenth century, hardly suffices to hold your attention to the end.

The Princess was very amusing to its time. Its gentle satire of women's rights was balanced by a sympathy with the cause, and, like the raccoon-trap of fable, "it caught the coon coming and going." It delighted both cons and pros. It was discussed so generally that it could not escape Gilbert, who used it for the libretto of his opera, *The Princess.* Newspapers quoted *The Princess* to satirize the women's colleges of the eighties, and its popularity was maintained until the close of the century. To-day it is one of the many long poems in English that are little read. It is more of Tennyson's age than any other of his long poems, more of his age even than *In Memoriam,* and what there is of satire in it has gone the way to inconsequence that all but the deepest satire goes.

In Memoriam was for years almost a second Bible to many people the English-speaking world over. In America it was looked to by thousands both in and out of the churches as a book of inspired counsel for right living and of solid comfort in hours of doubt. It is ostensibly the long plaint of Tennyson for the death of the friend of his youth, Arthur Hallam. It runs the gamut of the many moods in which a man may recall his dead friend. It is only partly elegiac, however, and not a real companion to "Lycidas," "Adonais," and "Thyrsis." Tennyson extends his lament for his friend into an exposition of his own faith and of his own doubts and of what of philosophy he had formulated. He accepts all he can of the established religion of his country. He is temperamentally a conformist, orthodox, at one with tradition. Yet he questions, and he is ill at ease questioning. He doubts, and he comforts himself and all doubters by declaring:

> There lives more faith in honest doubt,
> Believe me, than in half the creeds.

He advocates freedom of thought, but he is a little afraid of such freedom, and freedom of conduct he is still more afraid of:

> Hold thou the good, define it well;
> For fear divine Philosophy
> Should push beyond her mark, and be
> Procuress to the Lords of Hell.

In Memoriam is, on the whole, a heart-easing and heart-lifting poem. It makes for optimism:

> I held it truth, with him who sings
> To one clear harp in divers tones,
> That men may rise on stepping stones
> Of their dead selves to higher things.

It advocates that same holding to all that is best which he formulated more clearly and briefly in later life in "Merlin and the Gleam." I have been speaking as if *In Memoriam* were one whole. It intends to be that, but not a few of its one hundred and thirty-three parts are very loosely connected with the main theme, the regret of the poet for the loss of his friend. One such independent poem is the best known of them all, "Ring out, wild bells, to the wild sky." These verses were part of the ritual of our American Christmas in the days of my youth. They were recited in school, they were part of the service in Sunday-school, they were among those verses, to which I have referred before, that found place on Christmas cards, and they were reprinted on the editorial pages of newspapers. They seem more rhetorical now than they did forty years ago, but they are pretty good rhetoric even yet. It is only lyric poetry and narrative poetry and dramatic poetry that are not quickly outmoded. Occasional poetry, so-called, and philosophical poetry, so-called, are often found out by the years to be no poetry at all, but only verse. It is generally, of course, the lyric that lasts best, but in Tennyson certain of the narratives, like *Idylls of the King* and "Œnone" and "Ulysses," hold their own with the lyrics. The best of these lyrics are "Mariana," "The Owl," "The Lady of Shalott," "The Choric Song" from "The Lotos Eaters," "The Sleeping Palace," "Sir Launcelot and Queen Guinevere," "The Eagle," "Break, break, break," "The Higher Pantheism," "The splendor falls on castle walls," "Tears, idle tears," "Frater Ave atque Vale," and "Crossing the Bar." That is thirteen, some of them dramatic lyrics rather than pure lyrics, but a thirteen which have as great a chance of lasting as any Victorian poems. There are other lyrics one would include were one to choose them for their music and nothing more. "Claribel," of his juvenilia, is one of these, and "Sweet and low" from *The Princess* is another.

These lyrics are perfectly finished things. Were they not, they would not be to us what they are, for they do not all have the intensity of sustained emotion of many of the great lyrics of our tongue. There was an undoubted placidity about Tennyson when he took pen in hand, a decorous coldness, an evenness of tone, a condescension, which are just a little numbing. It is only in his best moments that he completely forgets himself and surrenders himself utterly to his mood. When he does so surrender himself, his ever-ready mastery of words enables him to phrase perfectly the mood that he wishes to express. The words are fitted together with an art no English poet has surpassed. We must yield to Shakespeare, with other great gifts, such a lordship over language as no other Englishman can reach; we must yield to Milton a dignity and sonorousness and epic sweep that are his alone; we must yield to Wordsworth a magic of simple words that lose no freshness with the years; we must yield to Keats his honeyed and richly colored language; we must yield to Swinburne a new music of words that goes to the head like wine; we must yield to Yeats the twilight glamour and the moony coldness that dim and chill his studied and haunting rhythms. We must yield to these masters one and all what is due them, and yet we can, at the same time, say in all justice that there is no English poet with a greater power to say what was given him to say than Tennyson, and a more perfect art of poetry in the saying of it. How masterly he is even in the expression of little things:

> ghastly thro' the drizzling rain
> On the bald street breaks the blank day!

The scope of this book prevents much detail about metrics, but I cannot pass this last line, so marvelous technically, without a word about its effects. The line has the eight syllables the meter of *In Memoriam* demands. It extends the four metrical accents that are normal for the line to five rhetorical accents that break and drag the line into the very quality of what it describes. Read it, stressing "bald," "street," "breaks," "blank" and "day"; and you have the very feel of the wan daybreak of London drizzle over the paved roadway. "On the bald street breaks the blank day" is as marvelous technically as any line of English poetry. I do not consider it a beautiful line. That it is not beautiful is one reason I took it to analyze. Some of us are distressed by a rose under the microscope.

I shall not try to analyze how it is that "The splendor falls on castle walls" and "Frater Ave atque Vale" have so musical "natural falterings" and "victorious bursts." They have been singing in the ears of many of us from an enchanted childhood in which we heard "The horns of Elfland faintly blowing." They have delighted the rapt youth in which we read that "Tenderest of Roman poets nineteen hundred years ago." Surely there were boys all over the other lands of the English-speaking world, too, who went about mouthing the "olive-silvery Sirmio" of Tennyson as lovingly as its original in Catullus.

One wonders are there to-day such boys, or girls of like enthusiasm, in America and England, in India and South Africa, in Australia and the South Seas. If there are, and I believe there are, the fame of Tennyson is secure. It is the poet's power of appealing to the youth of generation after generation that keeps him alive, that keeps poetry alive. There are hardly enough of those, men or women, of middle and old years to whom poetry is the all in all in literature to give poetry that prevalence and vigor of appeal that are necessary to the perpetuation of its appreciation. Youths who will hold to their enthusiasm for poetry on through the greying years give it its intensest life, but those youths who will later turn to less ecstatic forms of literature, or solely to affairs, are necessary, too, for a sufficiently general appreciation to give poetry a full, a robust existence. Tennyson yet holds numbers of these youths who care for poetry for a season, as well as the lesser group of the inner circle of appreciation. He is unequivocally of the "Poets whose thoughts enrich the blood of the world."

FREDERICK TENNYSON AND CHARLES TENNYSON-TURNER

There is the power of landscape painting so outstanding a characteristic of his more famous brother in Frederick Tennyson (1807-1898). There is craftsmanship that comes close to artistry. There is good breeding and pleasantness of personality in his writing. There is little more. Nearly all his sets of verses are too long. The slight material and thin lyricism of them are drawn out too finely. Each succeeding poem that you read has less effect than its predecessor. A fair sample of the work of his old age is to be found in "The Blackbird," from *Poems of the Day and Year* (1895). English country life passes by you in scene on scene as with the unrolling of a film, to the song of the blackbird. That song has been praised by a hundred poets, but Frederick Tennyson's use of it as the remembered accompaniment to the ritual of daily life is perhaps the greatest compliment paid by English poets to this most loved and familiar English bird, famed alike by Mother Goose and by Francis Ledwidge. The full pageant of English country life of yesterday is in "The Blackbird," hayfields, cottage, mill-race, village church; tavern under the elms; manor house with espaliered peaches on its garden walls, "lion-headed gates" and "mossy fountain"; the blacksmith's hammer ringing on the anvil; "the good vicar" with "long white hair," who seeks the grave of one "who grew From boyhood with him." All is very gentle, very quiet, in good taste, and at times the expression approaches felicity. All is very Victorian, and of a faint picturesqueness now in so changed times.

Frederick Tennyson came before the world as a poet in *Poems by Two Brothers* (1827), in four sets of verses so like•those of Alfred and Charles that the Laureate's son had difficulty in deciding who had written this poem and who that and who the third. Frederick Tennyson published no volume until 1854 when *Days and Hours* appeared. Then there was silence until 1890, when his *Isles of Greece* appeared. Meanwhile all the poetasters had imitated Alfred Tennyson's verse, and Frederick's, in the manner he had his share in inaugurating, seemed only a far-off echo of his greater brother's work.

There are those who hold that Charles Tennyson-Turner (1808-1879) is a better poet than his brother, Frederick. That may or may not be, but it is certain that he is a better-known one. Sir Arthur Quiller-Couch gave "Letty's Globe" its chance by including it in *The Oxford Book of English Verse* (1900), and all the English-speaking world took it to its heart on a first reading. Stedman had included it in *A Victorian Anthology* (1896), but perhaps because it was one of several there it did not become well known by that inclusion. It had been published in *Collected Sonnets* (1880), but it was not then singled out for such praise as it won twenty years later. After many readings I am not sure it is high poetry, but it is of such a humanity and universality of appeal that you can no more resist it than you can a baby's smile. Its concern with the three-year-old playing with a globe of the world endears it to all, and the happy wording of its close holds those two lines at least in memory:

> And while she hid all England with a kiss,
> Bright over Europe fell her golden hair.

That one set of verses is enough to keep green for centuries the name of Charles Tennyson-Turner. There are other sonnets to treasure, too, of his early period, that Alfred Tennyson declared had "all the tenderness of the Greek epigram." It was he who was the chief collaborator with Alfred in *Poems by Two Brothers* (1827).

CHAPTER VII

Robert Browning

ROBERT BROWNING (1812-1889) is as fully concerned with the whole of life as is Shakespeare. It is this concern that in a way justifies the superb compliment paid the later poet in the lines of Landor that all the world knows:

> Shakespeare is not our poet, but the world's,
> Therefore of him no speech! and brief for thee,
> Browning! Since Chaucer was alive and hale
> No man has walked along our roads with step
> So active, so inquiring eye, or tongue
> So varied in discourse.

That is not to say that Browning is the third poet of our literature, that the great line runs Shakespeare, Chaucer, Browning. The words are to be taken for exactly what they say, and they are true of Browning. If his lordship of language, his music of words, his art of verse, his clarity of expression, his creation of character, had been equal to his humanity, his sympathy, his knowledge of life, his familiarity with art, his insight into motive, his power of analysis, his reading of life, his intuition, his infinite curiosity as to all there is in the world and beyond the world, it might be possible to say that he was the third poet of the English tongue.

As things are, there are several other poets to be considered for the second place after Shakespeare, and, for that matter, for the first place after Shakespeare. There are many who would put Milton next to Shakespeare, and there are other poets whom proven critics would put before Browning. Spenser is spoken of, nine times out of ten, as the poet's poet, and it is true there are poet critics who would put him with Milton in the hierarchy. All the major poets, indeed, have advocates who would place them only below Shakespeare. It is safest, of course, to attempt no definite rating, as it would be safest not to attempt a list even of the major poets. One might dare, however, speaking after the fashion of the tale of Ali Baba, to say that there are Shakespeare and his forty poets, about half of them set securely above and apart from the many other true poets that make literature in English the richest in poetry in all the world, and another half of them not so surely better than another twenty that might be named.

Taking my courage in my hands, then, I divide the forty into majors and minors. For a poet to be a major, not only must he have struck a new note in poetry, made a beauty of a new kind, had a vision of life no poet had had before, but he must have dealt largely with many kinds of life, and he must have had universality of appeal. Universality of appeal, though, is not in itself a sure test, for there have been poets with universality of appeal in their own time for something else than the poetry in their verse. Some humanitarian sentiment, some at-oneness with the fashion or spirit of the hour, some echo of what people were familiar with on rostrum, in church, or in music-hall, may give currency to verse that quickly withers away. Yet it is true that no poet who has not had appeal to an audience made up of readers of other generations than his own can be surely written down a major poet. This condition makes the rating of a contemporary theoretically impossible. All that we can say of a contemporary, in an attempted rating, is that he, who has large appeal to his own generation, seems to have characteristics like those of poets who have appealed to several generations.

I have not space to attempt a justification of my rating of poets of first power as major and minor. I am, however, going to make that division for the sake of what it will suggest. These seem to me to be major poets: Shakespeare, Chaucer, Spenser, Donne, Milton, Burns, Wordsworth, Shelley, Byron, Keats, Tennyson, Browning, Whitman, Swinburne, Kipling, Yeats, Hardy, Masefield and Frost. There are poets in this list of nineteen who are not so much to me, personally, as certain of those that I list below as minor poets. I care more for Herrick and Blake and Emerson than I do for Spenser and Byron and Swinburne, but I must admit that my favored three are not cast in so large a mould as the other trio.

I list the following as poets of first power, but as minor poets, because of lack of scope, or lack of the force, not easy to define, to make their names known around the world: Sidney, Crashaw, Marvell, Herrick, Gray, Blake, Coleridge, Landor, Emerson, Poe, Arnold, Rossetti, Fitzgerald, Morris, Patmore, Meredith, Emily Dickinson, Francis Thompson, Sturge Moore, A. E. Housman, Walter De La Mare and Ralph Hodgson.

Certain time-honored names I shall be quarreled with for omitting. Two such are Dryden and Pope. Neither the one nor the other is, however, intrinsically a poet. Few satirists are, and though both were more than satirists, that more in them is most of it what is representative of their times, and not an individual quality.

These twenty-two are not all of them so surely better poets than others that might be named. I think all the twenty-two, though, better poets than Marlowe and Dekker, Ben Jonson and Drummond, Cotton and Gay, Collins and Cowper, Christina Rossetti and Austin Dobson, Robert Bridges and Sir William Watson, T. E. Brown and Henley, Stephen Phillips and Binyon, and Flecker and Abercrombie, but I admit there is no clear line of demarcation between these eighteen and some of the twenty-two I have listed as the more important minors.

Almost all the men I have listed as majors have written a great deal. Fertility and richness of imagination, largeness of mould, knowledge of life, and vision are generally qualities of major writers. Burns and Keats have not filled volumes with their verse. Burns and Keats, however, did write a good deal, considering the short years they had to write.

Almost all the nineteen majors, too, cover a rather wide range of life in their verse. Almost all are not only lyric poets, but dramatic poets or narrative poets as well, with many people in their poems. Many of them have added characters to the great portrait gallery of English literature, comparing favorably, in this respect, with the great novelists. All nineteen have given the world philosophies of life in little, what Meredith calls "readings of life." All are always, in quotation, on the lips of men. All have been men of rich experience and keen insight. To almost all, dreamers though they are called, realities have been very instant. Towering personalities, physical drive, intellectual vigor, full lives, have distinguished them almost all.

You will find all these qualities that I have listed as distinguishing major poets in Robert Browning. He has struck a new note in poetry, a note we hear as early as *Paracelsus* (1835). He has made beauty of a new kind, a beauty at its richest in *Men and Women* (1855). He has had a vision of life no poet had had before, a vision that made itself manifest fully in that "wholly unintelligible poem" *Sordello* (1840). It was, indeed, in *Sordello* that Browning first stressed what was to be for the rest of his life the chief purpose of poem after poem of his, "the development of a soul." He has dealt largely with life of all sorts and conditions, of many times and of many parts of the world, from the old Athens of *The Agamemnon* to "The Modern Athens" of "Mr. Sludge the Medium"; from the Russia of "Ivàn Ivànovich" to the Brittany of *The Two Poets of Croisic;* from the Persia of "Jochanan Hakkadosh" to the England of "Charles Avison." Most often, however, his poetry deals with the life of Italy, the country of his heart.

Browning appealed, too, and largely, to his own generation, but only toward the end of his life. Like Meredith in the novel, Browning in poetry had to create the taste by which he might be enjoyed. No other English poet, though, ever had so many agencies working for his recognition and the dissemination of his ideas as he. Browning societies were active alike in England and America. Browning has those other characteristics of the major poet, fertility, opulence, originality, largeness of mould, knowledge of man, readings of life, and a towering vitality.

Italy, which he so loved, has acclaimed him. There is a memorial tablet to him in Venice, and he has been translated into Italian, and he has a vogue in some circles. The testimony, on the whole, though, indicates that Browning is not much read in Italy. His mind is too Gothic for the Latins, too given to half-expressed analysis, too elliptical, too alien to the large and luminous day that lights their thinking. There is light and a-plenty, of course, in him, an all but blinding light. Not Turner in his landscapes or Beethoven in his symphonies has more light. Never poet cared more for sun and warmth than Browning. His love of sun and warmth and color is at the bottom of his great love of Italy. In his writing, however, the clearness of things is lost in the very excess of light. Reflected from the many facets of his genius, it fairly dazzles you reading. Often, though, all the light so characteristic of him is obscured for the moment by that mist and mirk of cold seas that shadows at times the mind of every true northerner. The shadows disperse as quickly as they gather, giving way to a glory of blown clouds and broken light, and, again, we are in the dazzling sun.

Nor is Browning one who is widely read anywhere outside of English-speaking lands. Though poems of his have been translated into many tongues, he has not made the appeal on the Continent of Shakespeare and Richardson, Macpherson and Scott, Byron and Wilde. That the most cosmopolitan of the Victorian poets should not be read generally in other countries than those of his own speech, and, particularly, that he should not be read widely in those that he has celebrated in his verse, is such an irony as Browning himself loved to turn on his tongue. No other English poet is so little insular as he, no other English poet has so little of English ways and of the landscape of England in his verse, relatively to the amount he has written. Browning loved England; "Home-Thoughts from Abroad" and "Home-Thoughts from the Sea" are proof positive of that; but he was not deeply

rooted in things English, soil, habits, culture or institutions. English love of freedom he had, of course, and he carried with him
wherever he went a picture of the English spring:

> And after April, when May follows,
> And the white-throat builds, and all the swallows!
> Hark, where my blossomed pear-tree in the hedge
> Leans to the field and scatters on the clover
> Blossoms and dewdrops—at the bent spray's edge—
> That's the wise thrush; he sings each song twice over,
> Lest you should think he never could recapture
> The first fine careless rapture!

In "De Gustibus" Browning tells us, just as forthrightly and sin-
cerely:

> What I love best in all the world
> Is a castle, precipice-encurled,
> In a gash of the wind-grieved Apennine.

He ends the poem with his adaptation of "Queen Mary's saying":

> Open my heart and you will see
> Graved inside of it, 'Italy'.

More than half of all his verse is of Italian inspiration. His
longest poem, *The Ring and the Book* (1868), is the story of a
famous murder case of seventeenth-century Rome; and of his nine
plays four are of Italy, *Pippa Passes* (1841), *King Victor and
King Charles* (1842), *A Soul's Tragedy* (1846), and *Luria*
(1846). Of his long poems half-narrative and half-analytic of
soul, many are of Italy, such as "The Statue and the Bust," "Fra
Lippo Lippi," "Andrea del Sarto," "Pacchiarotto," "Filippo Baldi-
nucci," "Pietro of Abano," and the parleyings with "Daniel Bar-
toli" and "Francis Furini." Of the shorter poems dealing with
Italy are "My Last Duchess," "A Toccata of Galuppi's," "Two in
the Campagna," "The Guardian Angel," and "In a Gondola." Of
still shorter sort are "De Gustibus" and the sonnet on Goldoni.
It is curious that of all these poems of Italian inspiration that I

have listed only two, "De Gustibus" and "Fra Lippo Lippi," are Browning at his best.

There has been a great to-do about *The Ring and the Book*, but every candid critic will admit, I am sure, that there are many parts of it that do not make for the beauty of the whole that one has a right to demand of this kind of narrative poem as surely as of the epic. What Browning himself says of "An Epistle of Karshish" is even more true of *The Ring and the Book*. It is a "long and tedious case." "This long and tedious case" has excited wonder everywhere, a wonder akin to that excited by Doughty's *Dawn in Britain* (1906) and by Hardy's *The Dynasts* (1903-1908). It awes by its very stupendousness, but it is "unduly dwelt on, prolixly set forth." The telling of the murder of Pompilia and her parents, over and over, ensures an understanding of it. You may miss certain motives in one of the tellings, but another telling, from another point of view, and another, from still another, give you a completeness of knowledge of the case that you cannot get from any other of his longer poems, *Sordello*, say.

The Ring and the Book remains a case, a most interesting case, but still a case. For all his preoccupation with the story, for all his understanding of all concerned, for all his sympathy with all that is human, Browning has been unable to make his many retellings into a thing of beauty. The lawyers, the psychologists, the students of criminology doat upon it, but it is not one of the books reread and reread by lovers of literature. I doubt if any so long and so difficult poem can be taken into the affections of average men.

There are great passages in *The Ring and the Book*, moments of tense drama, revelations of strange states of soul, analyses of characters, uncanny in their plumbing of the deeps of life, and, more rarely, flashes of dazzling poetry. On the whole, it lacks the power to keep you eager in its reading; it lacks gusto, a quality that Browning has always at his best; it lacks most of all the grand and simple outlines and the dignity of subject that a story must have to be great.

The Browning who is a great poet is the Browning of the lyrics and the dramatic monologues and *Pippa Passes*. The Browning of *The Ring and the Book* is criminologist and psychologist and all but alienist. If the poem were not Browning's, it would be no more read than *Dawn in Britain*. It is kept alive because it is by the man who wrote "Love among the Ruins," "The Last Ride Together," "Abt Vogler," "Rabbi Ben Ezra," *The Inn Album*, "In Three Days," "Meeting at Night," "The Lost Mistress," and "Round Us the Wild Creatures."

In this day of the ascendancy of the short poem, there are more critics who hold Milton greater for "Lycidas," "L'Allegro," "Il Penseroso," and the sonnets than for *Paradise Lost*. I think that I am with my time in this matter, though I belong to the generation born just after the Civil War, and I am therefore still a Puritan. To me *Paradise Lost* is a kind of second Bible. I have been trying to find a rating of some such sort for *The Ring and the Book*. Does it have a semi-psychological or a semi-philosophical standing in the minds of many people? I think it does not, that it cannot, being so little read as it is. Nor can I see it challenging comparison in any respect, except in intellectual vigor, with *The Faery Queen, Paradise Lost, The Excursion,* or *The Dynasts*. Think of *The Ring and the Book* for just a moment alongside of *The Tempest* or the sonnets of Shakespeare, and it assumes at once a place in poetry lower than the highest.

Of the ten dramatic monologues that make up Books II-XI of *The Ring and the Book*, the best as poetry are the four devoted to the principals, "Count Guido Franceschini," "Giuseppe Caponsacchi," "Pompilia," and "Guido," the second monologue of the murderer. Guido is almost always "in character"; Pompilia is seldom "in character," and Caponsacchi not only "in character," but eloquent, and largely imagined. Dowden has pointed out that the regard of the priest for Pompilia, unloving wife and unwilling mother, is very like the regard that Browning had for Elizabeth Barrett when he met her, an invalid, and unlikely ever to be a mother. At any rate Browning could understand a man's love for a woman in which sex was held in abeyance so wholly that it hardly was an element in that love.

"Giuseppe Caponsacchi" is an out-pouring, copious and almost clear, of all the welter of emotions there was in the priest's breast. He tells of her husband's efforts to involve him with Pompilia, his final going to her that he may be of help, his taking of her to Rome, his arrest with her almost at the city gates. He makes it clear that there is no sin between himself and the woman. He comes scatheless from his ordeal before the Court, a noble soldier-saint.

The trouble is, that with all its eloquence, its sincerity, its dignity, his declamation is not often poetry. The verse is almost always true dramatic speech, what such a man would say under such circumstances at that place and at that time, but it hardly ever rises above rhetoric. Always over-intellectual in his writing, over-analytic, at once elliptical and prolix, Browning hardened in all his defects with the years. He was fifty when he began *The Ring and the Book*, fifty-six when he completed it. Deeply felt by him as all the story was, Browning had no longer the sheer poetic power to transmute all the dross of the old murder trial into gold. The subject lifts toward greatness only when Caponsacchi speaks. Browning could not thrill it through and through with poetry as he could Pippa's day of days in Asolo.

All of *Pippa Passes* is life at its fullest, at its most intense, and it is all sublimated into lyric ecstasy. Browning is completely master of his material here, he has turned every life he touches, every mood of every life he touches, into poetry. How clearly they all stand out, Pippa herself in the "large mean room" splashing water as she tidies herself for this one free day of all the year. Ottima and Sebald, too, and the man they have murdered, old Luca Daddi, how they stand out, and the background, the old house, the shrub house and garden on the hill! Every word each says, every bit of description the poet puts in, is pure poetry. The contrasts are perfect—the passion of the lovers, with the cool spring song of Pippa; the horror of Jules in finding how he has been tricked into marriage with Phene, with that other song of Pippa that inspires him to face the world with the girl at his side; the controversy of Luigi and his mother, with the song of Pippa that sends him off to strike for his country; the Machiavellian fencing between Monsignor and bravo, with the song of Pippa that saved her from a horrible fate that she had no cause to suspect. Nowhere in literature are there purer lyrics than these songs of Pippa, nowhere in literature a brighter or sunnier or more radiant figure than that of the little girl of the silk-mill. Drama is here, and the sounding of the depths of life, readings of life that drive us to pondering, and a high-hearted optimism as bracing as March winds.

The Ring and the Book is a monument to the intellectuality of Browning and to his architectonic power. He has built it up as a great arch, but day and its reaches of skyey blue are not behind it and above it, or sunset and its glowing clouds, or black night and its stars. *The Ring and the Book* is a supreme accomplishment of intellectual engineering, but not great poetry. *Pippa Passes* is only a mason's arch, but it spans a run of bright water, with yellow mountain flowers by it, like those he delights in in "By the Fireside," and by it some brown bird is singing, with sunlight and the joy of height in its song.

Nor are there so many revelations by the way in *The Ring and the Book* as in *Pippa Passes*. Half a dozen sayings, at any rate, from the shorter poem, have become part of our speech. "All service ranks the same with God" is one such saying. "God's in his heaven—All's right with the world," another. "Only parents' love can last our lives," a third. "In the morning of the world, When earth was nigher heaven than now," a fourth. "Best people are not angels quite," a fifth. "There is no last or first," a sixth.

Browning wrote himself down "maker of plays"; but his plays are not great as plays, and only *Pippa Passes*, all of it, great as poetry. At least they are not great as plays as you read them. As I have seen only two on the stage, *A Blot in the 'Scutcheon* (1843) and *In a Balcony* (1855), I can say only that these two are not great in the theater. The annals of the stage record that *Strafford* (1837), written for Macready, and *A Blot in the 'Scutcheon,* written also for Macready, but played without him in the cast, were both unsuccessful on first production. Of the remaining seven *Pippa Passes* (1841), *King Victor and King Charles* (1842), *The Return of the Druses* (1843), *Colombe's Birthday* (1844), *A Soul's Tragedy* (1846), *Luria* (1846), and *In a Balcony* (1855) all win their way to the stage now and then, as often in amateur or semi-professional·productions as in professional. There has been no unequivocal success for any one of them. *In a Balcony* had a little run in America in 1901 with Mrs. Le Moyne, Miss Robson and Mr. Otis Skinner in the leading rôles. It played better than you would have expected from a reading knowledge of it. Yet it was a strain following its states of emotion, you can hardly say action, for of action there is almost none. The uncertainty of what happens at the end, if the Queen forgives the lovers, or condemns one or the other to death, or herself dies of shock, adds further obscurity to what goes before. Her final decision, if we were made aware what it was, would have thrown light on her character, as it would have told much about the judgment of Constance and Norbert.

There is a good deal of this sort of wilfulness in Browning, the refusal to explain what he means by what he says. Nor is he the only poet who so reacts to questions as to his meaning. Many of them from Donne down love to be cryptic, to have part of their writing something like the riddling of the old Irish bards. There is a sort of pride involved in it, too. They believe, often, in their hearts, that they have made themselves clear, and that it is only the stupidity of the reader that leads to the request for explanation. We are just "Dennises" and "dumb Doras" for asking what is obvious. Often obscurity is inherent in the subject, thought is tough, states of mind are hard to understand. Just as often the obscurity is the fault of the poet. He nowhere gives us the key to unlock his secrets, he shrinks from the revision that will make all clear. What he has written in the heat of creation he is loath to recast afterwards. It seems, in its difficult form, to be final, just what should be said. Browning had not the temper for thorough recasting of what he had once written. He owned that *Sordello* was "unintelligible," but he could not remould it to intelligibility.

The performance I saw of *A Blot in the 'Scutcheon* was amateur, but even at that unable wholly to kill the play. It failed to bring out much of the poetry and "good theater" that is this play's in larger measure than most of its fellows'. There is more characterization here, too, than is usual to him, Tresham and Mildred and Mertoun being possible of visualization, and their motives, even the foolish secrecy that led to the deaths of the lovers, not difficult to understand.

The Return of the Druses has a good deal of poetry in it, too, poetry that is vivid, and even gorgeous at times. The passions of its characters are Oriental, in keeping with the Lebanons from which they come. They are Druses exiled from their mountains to "an Islet of the Southern Sporades," which is garrisoned by the Knights-Hospitallers of Rhodes. The action takes place in one day, and it is carried through to its tragic close with vigor and inevitability. Djabal, the Druse leader, pretends that he is his people's Messiah, but he atones for his imposture by his suicide. The accompaniment to his leadership and to his love is war and sounding arms. It is a stirring, martial play, effective rhetorically, and with a good deal of action.

Luria harks back to *Othello*, and it presages *Monna Vanna* (1905). There is characterization in it that is something more than analysis, and brave rhetoric, and flashes of poetry. It loses dramatically by giving itself over at times to too great analysis of its hero's motives. Like Othello, Luria is a Moor. As leader of the Florentine army he has made himself too powerful and too popular to suit the masters of Florence. They plot against him, and he learns of their plotting. He refuses to meet the attack on him by going over to the enemy. In the hour of his victory he stabs himself because, mistrusted, he can be no longer of any use to Florence.

A Soul's Tragedy could never have been intended for the stage, though it eventually found its way there, in March of 1904, for once, in a performance of the Stage Society in London. Its tragedy is in the dispelling of the illusion of Chiappino, agitator of Faenza, that he is a great and a patriotic man. He is clearly rendered, as is Ogniben, the papal emissary. The lovers, Luitolfo and Eulalia, are only stock. Ogniben, indeed, is one of Browning's most individual creations, a fellow of Bishop Blougram, but distinct from him. We can catch the very tones of Ogniben's voice, so wily and tolerant and soothing. We see his smile, an unforgetable smile, the outward symbol of his worldly wisdom and of his power to penetrate a sham.

Browning is good at churchmen. Formal religion does not interest him particularly, though he has shown in *Christmas-Eve and Easter-Day* (1850), and a score places else, that he is deeply interested in the human as in the spiritual side of religion. He is curious, too, as to what religion does to those who hold to it, whether priests or laymen. Priests he loves to put under the microscope, perhaps because there was a good deal of the priest in himself. It is not only Ogniben and Blougram that we have analyzed, but the Monsignor in *Pippa Passes*, Fra Lippo Lippi in *Men and Women*, and Caponsacchi, Canon Conti, the Pope, Cardinal Acciaiuoli and Abate Panciatichi, in *The Ring and the Book*, some of them full-length portraits and some only figures in paintings of groups.

That is a striking situation with which we are presented in *Colombe's Birthday*, the lady's choice between her duchy and, perhaps, an empire; and a plebeian lover who has stood by her in her hour of trial. She chooses Valence rather than Prince Berthold, and goes back to her little castle of Ravestein. Alone of the long plays, *Colombe's Birthday* is not a tragedy. There is some external action in the play, but it is lost, as usual, in a plethora of words. The characters analyze their motives and thoughts and feelings in speech, instead of revealing these feelings and thoughts and motives in acts.

There are discoverable in *The Ring and the Book*, and in the nine dramas, only a few presentations that enable us to see the portraits and to feel the personality of the people of poem or plays. Nor are there many more to be found in all his dramatic monologues and character studies. Of how many have you a clear picture, from Pauline of *Pauline* (1833) on to the end, either body or soul? Browning was keenly aware of all things of the flesh, as keenly aware of the flesh as of the spirit. He could present a girl "Rosed from top to toe in flesh of youth." Yet he gives us so little detail in his reference to his girls, and men, too, that we wonder had he clearly visualized them to himself.

Porphyria we know for her yellow hair, but that does little more than put her in a category; it does not describe her. The "tresses" of Palma, too, are curled "Into a sumptuous swell of gold," but other details of her beauty are only a fragment of the whole, and not enough to give us a distinct picture of her. So it is, too, with Michal in *Paracelsus*. Pippa we so cherish that we make our own portrait of her from what she does and says and is. Her personality is writ large over the poem she dominates. There is a line for Phene, "of the pale-pure cheek and black bright tresses." Ottima, we are told, has "splendid shoulders," and is "magnificent in sin," but even at that we are left to visualize her from too few hints to be sure we know her as an individual and not simply recognize her as a type. Valence is a "thin sour man," with a "brow," a "pale fiery man," but again we must paint in the detail of his portrait for ourselves. Even a likeness of Mildred in her bloom is denied us. And of Pompilia all we get clearly is her smile, "the beautiful sad strange smile." Browning, by the bye, is outdone by no poet as a heaper-up of adjectives. He loves them three deep before a noun.

There is not much clear characterization of the external sort, then, anywhere in Browning. It is with the dramatic monologues as I have said, as it is with the plays and *The Ring and the Book*.

We do not see Abt Vogler, or learn much about him save his joy in his organ and his philosophy of life. What he creates and what he learns of the meaning of life are all-important, of course, in the life of any man, but there is that in us that makes us want the appearance and personality of the people that we meet in poems. In life these matters count for much, and in literature their absence puts the poem wanting them too far from our interest to mean what it otherwise might mean to us.

Nor do we see Rabbi Ben Ezra. What we learn of him is his philosophy of life, expressed over and over again, from this angle and that, in the many stanzas of the poem. In both "Abt Vogler" and "Rabbi Ben Ezra," it is the protagonist speaking. That he speaks for Browning as well as for himself is true in these two poems, as in almost all the dramatic monologues.

If the characters speaking are not clear, however, certain of the principles they hold are announced in no uncertain tones. From the monologues, and from *Pippa Passes*, we can build up an optimist's decalogue hard to match in the writing of any other poet. In "Abt Vogler" we find:

There shall never be one lost good! What was, shall live as before.

In "Rabbi Ben Ezra":

> Look thou not down but up.

In "Prospice":

> For sudden the worst turns the best to the brave.

In "The Guardian Angel":

> O, world, as God has made it! All is beauty.

In "Fra Lippo Lippi":

> The beauty and the wonder and the power,
> The shapes of things, their colours, lights and shades,
> Changes, surprises,—and God made it all.

In "Saul":

> How good is man's life, the mere living! how fit to employ
> All the heart and the soul and the senses, forever in joy.

In "Any Wife to Any Husband":

> Vainly the flesh fades; soul makes all things new.

In "Life in a Love":

> No sooner the old hope drops to ground
> Than a new one, straight to the self-same mark,
>   I shape me.

In "At the Mermaid":

> I find earth not gray but rosy,
> Heaven not grim but fair of hue.
> Do I stoop? I pluck a posy.
> Do I stand and stare? All's blue.

And in *Pippa Passes* that crowning declaration of all, that should be quoted again and again until it is as familiar as the Ten Commandments:

> God's in His heaven—
> All's right with the world!

No thinking man will hold all these declarations as possible of acceptance under all circumstances. There are, obviously, times when we will get into sore trouble if we do not look down rather than up. Like exceptions can be filed to most of them, but taken, as they should be taken, as testimony to the goodness of life, the inestimable gift of life, they constitute a ringing defiance to all powers of doubt and darkness. They are "readings of life" to remember, and some of them high poetry.

The man who formulated this creed speaks out clearly for what he is in the epilogue to *Asolando* (1889). The poet is here speaking not dramatically, but for himself, with a directness that

makes us believe that he intended it for his "Hail and Farewell."
He was, indeed, all his life:

One who never turnèd his back but marched breast forward,
Never doubted clouds would break,
Never dreamed, though right were worsted, wrong would triumph,
Held we fall to rise, are baffled to fight better, sleep to wake.

Five of the high-hearted declarations of my optimist's decalogue from Browning are from *Men and Women* (1855). That
volume is, indeed, an epitome of all Browning. There are as many
poems elsewhere in his writings that we could not do without,
but there are in no other one volume half so many as here. Among
the "fifty men and women" he refers to in "One Word More,"
the epilogue, are: Fra Lippo Lippi; Galuppi; Karshish; Childe
Roland; Bishop Blougram; Master Hugues; Shelley; Andrea del
Sarto; Saul; the "girl with eager eyes and yellow hair" of "Love
among the Ruins"; Evelyn Hope; Elizabeth Barrett Browning;
the bride of the Riccardi; Constance and the Queen of *In a
Balcony;* and the woman of "Two in the Campagna." It is in
this last-named poem that we have two lines as unforgetable as
anything in Browning:

Infinite passion, and the pain,
Of finite hearts that yearn.

It is in this *Men and Women,* in "A Grammarian's Funeral,"
that we have:

Here—here's his place, where meteors shoot, clouds form,
Lightnings are loosened,
Stars come and go.

It is here, in "One Word More," that Browning tells us: "Never
dares the man put off the prophet." And:

God be thanked, the meanest of His creatures
Boasts two soul-sides, one to face the world with,
One to show a woman when he loves her.

It is here that he paints his most notable pictures of Italy, the "woman country," in "By the Fireside," "Up at a Villa," and "De Gustibus." It is here that we have "A Pretty Woman," "The Last Ride Together," and "In Three Days," love lyrics of very differing range, but each incomparable in its way.

I do not know where in English literature, outside of Shakespeare's sonnets (1609), there is to be found a single volume of previously uncollected verse with more great poems in it than *Men and Women*. The *Lyrical Ballads* (1798) of Wordsworth and Coleridge is another such, but I am put to it to think of a fourth. The *Hesperides* (1648) of Herrick comes nearest, perhaps, to being such a fourth. The second volume of Tennyson's *Poems* of 1842, containing mostly uncollected poems, is another approximation. Still another is *The Defence of Guenevere* (1858) of Morris; and *Poems and Ballads* (1866) of Swinburne is a real rival. By such full-lunged singing as Shakespeare's and Browning's and Swinburne's the natural falterings and fresh accents, and even the flashes of vision, of a Wordsworth seem lesser excellences. They are not, of course, and no comparison can lessen the intrinsic value of the *Lyrical Ballads*. *The Wind Among the Reeds* (1899) of Yeats and *Poems* (1917) of Ralph Hodgson are other volumes that strike new notes, but each contains only a sheaf of poems as over against the high stack of Browning in *Men and Women*.

In the collected editions (1863 on) there are only eight of the original fifty-one titles of *Men and Women* preserved under that caption. Four new poems are added, and the forty-odd other poems of the original *Men and Women* scattered throughout the volumes·under various designations. It is fortunate for me that I have always read *Men and Women* as it was first printed. The original American edition was bought by my father on its publication in 1856. I came upon it in his library in youth, and made night loud with my chanting of "Love among the Ruins" and "The Last Ride Together" in my moonstruck hours.

I bought my first Browning, as is recorded in it, on V—6—

1893, an American book of selections. It is a good thing to have a Browning, in May, when one is twenty-one. It was a small volume one could easily slip in one's pocket, and thus have handy for reading when one had a few minutes to spare. Browning is not the sort of poet who has to be read only under the most favorable circumstances. He is forthright enough, burly enough, compelling enough, to hold your attention anywhere.

I often wonder if the present-day makers of big and heavy books realize that they militate against what is printed in the books by their bulky format. It is impossible to love wholly a book that you cannot carry about with you except in hand or bag. Despite its too white binding, this little Browning was a close companion of mine for years, like Arnold's selections from Wordsworth, the younger Stedman's selections from Whitman, and a Moxon Herrick. I think that a measurable part of my regard for all four of these poets was due to the intimacy with them that was possible because they could be so readily slipped into my pocket. I have read them under all sorts of conditions and in all sorts of places, in trains, in hansom cabs, on ferry-boats, in a dentist's office, and at the oculist's. I have read all four of them, too, to all sorts of people, girls and men alike, and I have argued over them in season and out. So it cannot help but be with any poetry that is worth while, granted it is printed in proportions of pocket size.

It is easy to talk about Browning to young and old, learned and unlearned, sophisticated and unsophisticated, rich man, poor man, beggarman, thief. Browning was interested in everything under the sun, and he wrote about everything in which he was interested. There are "contacts" with every sort of life and art and science in his writing, and there are descriptions of many sorts of landscape, descriptions that are almost always subordinate to some intimately human concern.

Though Browning is thus only incidentally a landscape poet, such landscapes as he gives us are more clearly rendered and more particularized in detail than his characterizations of men and women. He tells us about his people, what they think, what they feel, what they are in disposition and character, but he does not tell us, as I have said, what they look like. One feature, a distinguishing feature, is picked out, and that feature is all, in most instances, we have to suggest the portrait. Even in that poem descriptive of the beauty of· Mrs. Coventry Patmore, "A Face," we do not learn whether the lady is dark or fair, or what is the color of her eyes, or what is the outline of brow or cheek or chin, full face or in profile. His way with landscape is different. In "Up at a Villa—Down in the City":

You've the brown ploughed land before, where the oxen steam and
    wheeze,
And the hills over-smoked behind by the faint gray olive-trees.

He is not so set upon interpreting the meaning of the landscape as he is upon interpreting the meaning of the soul of man. He can content himself with just recording the look of the landscape, but he must be finding the complexities of the soul of the person considered. "Incidents in the development of a soul: little else is worth study," he declared in the preface to *Sordello*. That declaration revealed his purpose in *Sordello*, and he wrote with that same purpose on to the end. The study of the development of the soul is a legitimate end of art, but it can be overstressed, emphasized to the exclusion of nearer things, and Browning so overstressed it. This overstressing of the study of soul is responsible for much of the obscurity and prolixity of Browning. He is so much preoccupied, too, with analyses of the depths of character that he does not consider whether the character that he is analyzing is interesting in other respects than as a case. The obscurity arises, however, not only from the difficulties of his material, but because of his crab-like procedure in expressing himself. He is full of sideways and back-scuttling methods of expression. That he could be clear in his delineation of character there are only a few exhibits to show, "Fra Lippo Lippi" the most outstanding of them.

That he could be clear in his delineation of landscape there are many exhibits to show. Here is another of Italy, a city scene to put alongside the country scene quoted just above. It is from "Old Pictures in Florence":

> In the valley beneath where, white and wide,
> Washed by the morning's water-gold,
> Florence lay out on the mountain-side.

This that follows, from *Sordello,* is more detailed. It is of the countryside near Verona:

> That autumn eve was stilled:
> A last remains of sunset dimly burned
> O'er the far forests, like a torch-flame turned
> By the wind back upon its bearer's hand
> In one long flare of crimson; as a brand
> The woods beneath lay black.

And this, from *Pippa Passes,* is of the countryside near Asolo, where "Hinds drove the slow white oxen up the hills." It is Pippa herself, speaking of her holiday, who says:

> Down the grass-path gray with dew,—
> Under the pine-wood, blind with boughs,
> Where the swallow never flew.

The exotic blood that was in Browning is perhaps accountable for some part of his love of warmth and light and color, and for some part of his neglect of the northern landscape of England, so often cold and gray and blurred with rain. In *The Inn Album* (1875) is a description of what Browning calls "England's best." Two men are in a room of an inn. The younger, from the window

> leans into a living glory-bath
> Of air and light where seems to float and move
> The wooded watered country, hill and dale
> And steel-bright thread of stream, a-smoke with mist,
> A-sparkle with May morning, diamond drift
> O' the sun-touched dew. Except the red-roofed patch

Of half a dozen dwellings that, crept close
For hillside shelter, make the village-clump,
This inn is perched above to dominate—
Except such sign of human neighborhood,
'And this surmised rather than sensible'
There's nothing to disturb absolute peace,
The reign of English nature—which means art
And civilized existence.

Browning is very good at the single line of description. I never look at "the yellow half-moon large and low" without thinking that he gave us the phrase. And close-packed though the line is, I remember, at the right time of the year, "May's warm slow yellow moonlit nights." I have often wondered what bird it was he had in mind when he wrote "The white-breast of the sea-lark twitters sweet." Only the last line of "The Twa Corbies" and a couplet from "The Withering of the Boughs" of Yeats are lonelier than "Hark, the wind with its wants and its infinite wail." As heart-easing as that line is heart-chilling is:

Oh, good gigantic smile o' the brown old earth
This autumn morning!

In that neglected poem of *Men and Women*, "By the Fireside," is a more various presentation of the many phases of his love of nature than elsewhere. It is a poem of reverie, of retrospect, and it is almost always in such mood or contemplation that he enjoys most the places he has loved, rather than those places as they are before his eyes. How clear are the vignettes of Northern Italy:

In the evening-glow
How sharp the silver spear-heads charge
Where Alp meets Heaven in snow.

How he loves it all, the one-arched bridge, the charcoal-burners' huts, the bird that sings all day long, the sheep drinking at the pond, the yellow mountain flowers, the brown hawks hovering.

The west is tender, hardly bright:
How gray at once is the evening grown—
One star, the chrysolite.

It contents you, "By the Fireside," with its joy of height, with its stillness of November days, with the warm humanity of its close.

When Browning published "By the Fireside" he was forty-three. The prologue to *Asolando* was written at seventy-six, not long before his death. In it he can say:

And now a flower is just a flower:
Man, bird, beast are but beast, bird, man—
Simply themselves, uncinct by dower
Of dyes which, when life's day began,
Round each in glory ran.

That mood, sounding so strangely like that of the Hardy of twenty years later, was not, however, constant throughout *Asolando*. *Asolando* has, too, many high-hearted moments.

Though Browning here associates birds and beast with man, he is not nearly so interested in either as in his fellow-humans. When he does care greatly for birds or beasts, he cares for them because of some human attribute. There are not many references to dogs in his writing and in the most memorable of them it is to "some crushed-nosed human-hearted dog" that he refers. He would, perhaps, make up for his neglect of animals when he says, in *Pippa Passes*:

For, what are the voices of birds
—Ay, and of beasts,—but words, our words,
Only so much more sweet?

Perhaps one should not take Pippa's sentiments as Browning's, but the declaration is so typical of the extravagance that takes hold of him at times, that he may be considered as standing behind what he makes Pippa say. It is, too, of a kind with that other sweeping declaration in *Paracelsus*:

No thought which ever stirred
A human breast should be untold.

It may, indeed, be true that the "voices of birds" are "our words, Only so much more sweet," but is it true of the voices of beasts? The lowing of cattle is to me one of the most pleasing sounds in nature. The baaing of sheep is in itself not displeasing, and it has so many associations with much that was dear to man in primitive life that it is still, by association, little less pleasing than the lowing of cattle. I have seen not only traffic halted in city streets by the passing of a flock of sheep, but every man, woman and child within sight of the flock held with eyes riveted upon the flock until it had gone out of sight. Hounds' giving tongue on the scent of a fox is another sound of beasts that has long delighted man. The belling of deer is famous in literature, but less well-known to the citied life of to-day.

There is real music in the calls and cries of few wild animals. The barking of foxes at night, the wildcat's wail, the raucous whistle of the bear, the grunting of porcupines, sounds of wild beasts with which I am familiar, are far from musical. The whistle of the woodchuck-like rodents of the high sierras of the Canadian Rockies is pleasing to me in memory. As I heard it among tumbled rocks above the timber-line it had in it something of the spirit of those aloof places, as had the shriller whistling of the little hay-makers of the Sierra Nevadas. I cannot much extend the list of animals I know at first hand that have pleasing voices. The sounds one hears at zoölogical gardens and menageries are almost all not only disagreeable but menacing. No one likes better the whinnying of horses than myself, or the friendly grunting of hogs, when, full-fed and dozing, they greet the known footstep past their pens. Yet I could not conscientiously call either of these sounds, "our words, Only so much more sweet."

I can go with Browning all the way, however, in his enthusiasm over beasts and birds in "Caliban upon Setebos," and even over Caliban himself:

Yon otter, sleek-wet, black, lithe as a leech; A
Yon auk, one fire-eye in a ball of foam, ʙ
That floats and feeds; a certain badger brown ᴄ
He hath watched hunt with that slant white-wedge eye ᴅ
By moonlight; and the pie with the long tongue ᴇ
That pricks deep into oak-warts for a worm, ꜰ
And says a plain word when she finds her prize, ᴅ
But will not eat the ants; the ants themselves
That build a wall of seeds and settled stalks
About their hole.

It is sheep, however, that Browning is best with, of all animals. Why, I have no guess. There are certain people said to be born, like collies, with a way with them in the handling of sheep, and an instinctive knowledge of them. Such a man, a Scot from above Oban, was pointed out to me in Achill, off the west coast of Ireland, as a man "knowledgeable in sheep." Just what the characteristics of such a man are was not explained to me, but it proved true, when my informant and I fell into conversation with him, that the Scot knew his sheep. Browning must have been born with like instincts. He mentions sheep often, as he mentions purple light. He mentions sheep most memorably in *Saul*. I quote two stanzas of that fine poem, stanza five for what it says about sheep, and stanza six for what it says about lesser beasts:

5.

Then I tuned my harp,—took off the lilies we twine round its chords
Lest they snap 'neath the stress of the moontide—those sunbeams like
   swords!
And I first played the tune all our sheep know, as, one after one,
So docile they come to the pen-door, till folding be done.
They are white and untorn by the bushes, for lo, they have fed
Where the long grasses stifle the water within the stream's bed;
And now one after one seeks its lodging, as star follows star
Into eve and the blue far above us,—so blue and so far!

6.

—Then the tune, for which quails on the cornland will each leave his
    mate
To fly after the player; then, what makes the crickets elate,
Till for boldness they fight one another; and then, what has weight
To set the quick jerboa a-musing outside his sand house—
There are none such as he for a wonder, half bird and half mouse—
God made all the creatures and gave them our love and our fear,
To give sign, we and they are His children, one family here.

Despite its antic rats, there were reservations to my delight
as a child in "The Pied Piper of Hamelin." There were times
when it was the best of fun, and other times, when, for some
reason or other, I had to take it seriously. The readings of it I
had to take seriously were hard to bear, all the children of a great
town led out of life and engulfed in a great mountain cave! Even
the suggestion of their reappearance in Transylvania did not ma-
terially lessen the sorrow that came to me those times from their
disappearance. Often, however, "The Pied Piper" was just brave
fooling. As there were fowls always on the places where I lived
as a child, rats had been my familiars from as early as I could
remember. My elders held them as enemies, but I would have
had them, if I could, transformed into friends. One in a live-trap,
brought for me to see by a cousin, cured the worst of the many
pains-in-the-stomach of a fruit-sampling childhood. I envied the
boys that brought white rats to school in their pockets.

I have dwelt on what "The Pied Piper of Hamelin" meant to
one child, because I would stress the fact that Browning is, by this
power, a poet with an appeal for children. That is but another
proof of his universality. Browning has, indeed, poems meet for
all the ages of man. The "Cavalier Tunes" delight boyhood. "The
Last Ride Together" is a testament for youth. "By the Fireside"
is for married folks the younger side of middle years. "Bishop
Blougram's Apology" is for those of fifty. "Rabbi Ben Ezra" for

three score. *Asolando* is for old age. I have picked out only one poem for each of the seven ages of man. There are scores in Browning for each of the last five ages.

As the poems of Browning span, in their appeal, the whole life of man from childhood to old age, so, too, they span all the activities of man. Church and state, politics, all the professions, all the sciences, all the arts, all the businesses, all the trades, concern him. He is as interested in the Paris jeweler of *Red Cotton Night-Cap Country* as in Strafford, as interested in the Breton sailor of "Hervé Riel" as in Aristophanes, as interested in the Arab horseman of "Muléykeh" as in the English peer of *The Inn Album.*

No poet uses the names of more men of letters in his verses. I have jotted down at random these few in reading him through: Marlowe, Shakespeare, Jonson, Milton, Christopher Smart, Gibbon, Wordsworth, Byron, Shelley, Keats, Goethe, Heine, Dante, Ronsard, Anacreon, Homer, Euripides, Æschylus, Aristophanes and Firdusi. The names of musicians, too, dot his poems, musicians of all countries and all ages. He did not love Bach, as T. E. Brown did, but he did love Avison, Handel, and Beethoven and, strangely, Rossini. He mentions Verdi, none too approvingly, and Wagner, Liszt, Schumann, Brahms, and Dvořák. Schumann and Brahms, Browning himself has often been compared with, as with Strauss of *Thus Spake Zarathustra.* To me all three musicians speak a clearer language than Browning.

So many are the painters mentioned by Browning that his references to them have been made the material of a thesis. Michelangelo is one, of course, and Raphael another and Giotto a third. Guercino finds place in his writing, and Andrea del Sarto and Correggio. Leichton was his close friend, and Watts a stimulus. Philosophers, too, he quotes, often to quarrel with, Bruno, Kant, Schelling and Comte. Browning held them artists, too, and all artists a very part of nature, and provocative of poems as surely as people met or landscapes seen. It is Bishop Blougram who lists as things to quicken us to belief and happiness:

>   A sunset-touch,
>   A fancy from a flower-bell, some one's death,
>   A chorus-ending from Euripides.

There are many declarations throughout the writings of all
the years of Browning about theories of poetry. He sees all sides
of the question, weighs form and content, melody and thought,
the harp and the six-foot Swiss horn. Yet it is oftenest content,
thought, experience of life, that he would have as the basis of
poetry. As early as *Sordello* (1840) he had said:

>   Would you have your songs endure,
>   Build on the human heart.

Theoretically Browning does not minimize form, the laws of his
art. He says in "Abt Vogler": "It is all triumphant art, but art
in obedience to laws." As a matter of fact, though, his art often
sinks into mere ingenuity, as in those double rhymes he used in
Pacchiarotto (1876), in which he is answering his critics. In other
poems, too, of this volume, he expounds his theories. He will not
tell you exactly in what relation he stands to the principals of his
dramatic monologues. Like Hardy, he says that these are often
to be taken as dramatic, as expressing the sentiments of the speakers
and not his personal sentiments. In "At the Mermaid" he questions:

>   Which of you did I enable
>   Once to slip inside my breast,
>   There to catalogue and label
>   What I like least, what love best,
>   Hope and fear, believe and doubt of,
>   Seek and shun, respect, deride?
>   Who has right to make a rout of
>   Rarities he found inside?

The words, most un-Shakespearean, are put in Shakespeare's
mouth, but it is Robert Browning speaking. In "House" he goes
further, and declares he will not "Sonnet-sing you about myself,"
and if you, the reader, question:

Hoity-toity! a street to explore,
Your house the exception! *'With this same key
Shakespeare unlocked his heart'* once more!
Did Shakespeare? If so, the less Shakespeare he!

Browning resented, from early in his life, the charge that his
form was difficult, and that his thought was obscure. He was still
objecting in *The Inn Album* (1875), when he wrote:

That bard's a Browning; he neglects the form:
But ah, the sense, ye gods, the weighty sense!

Just why he should so resent the contrast so many critics thus
made between his form and sense is to be explained, possibly, by
the constancy of its repetition. In his heart he must have recognized that the critics were right. What they said, perhaps, was too
obvious, and the obvious Browning always particularly disliked.
He girds at the British public in Book I of *The Ring and the Book*,
and again in Book XII of that poem. At the end he hazards the
guess that the British public may like him yet. In Book I he had
put it definitely: "British Public, ye who like me not." Later, in
the epilogue to *Pacchiarotto*, written when he was more generally
accepted, he was less bitter. He has come to consider that the cup
he has to offer is of "stuff for strength," "nettle-broth," not the
"cowslip wine" so many prefer.

Browning had been able to see that Christopher Smart let
"fume obfuscate sense." He admired greatly what

Befell Smart only out of throngs between
Milton and Keats that donned the singing dress.

He called Smart's "a song where flute-breath silvers trumpet-
clang." Yet with his own weaknesses very like that he picked out
as the greatest weakness of Smart, Browning went on to the end
with his own peculiar, enigmatic, elliptical way of writing.

Even when Browning is obscure he is, in most instances, still
interesting. There is always the stuff of life in his material. "Be-

fore" and "After," the preliminaries to a duel, and the death of the man who did his fellow the wrong, are not of Browning's best, but they are a record of life. And as it is with these two sets of verses, so it is in a hundred others that are partial failures. When his writing falls short of poetry it is generally still a human document.

Though it has always this value as a human document, though it has in itself deep human interest, poem after poem of Browning is hard to remember. Though I have been reading Browning all my life, I cannot carry the content of him in my head as I can carry, for instance, the content of Chaucer, or of Shakespeare, or of Wordsworth, or of Tennyson, other poets who have written much. Nor can I carry Browning in my head as I can carry novelists who have written a great deal. I can summon up at will most of the characters and romantic situations of Scott, and of Thackeray, and of Meredith, and of Hardy. I cannot, however, so conjure up the people or the situations or the philosophical declarations of Browning. The belabored analysis of the philosophical declarations explain why it is difficult to keep them in mind. The lack of clear portraiture explains why the people are not easy to recall. The situations, too, are often involved and, so, difficult to remember. And though there are many memorable sayings in his poems, I have not nearly so many quotations from him in memory as from lesser men. He is as difficult to memorize line by line as he is to remember in general outline.

It was not a desire to be "different" from other men that drove Browning into his difficult style, but a twist in the very fiber of the man, and his inability to rewrite what he had written in simpler guise than the crabbed first expression natural to him. There are those who feel that it was with Browning very much as it is with Masefield: that his writing is a kind of improvisation, and that he succeeds, when he does succeed, by sheer creative power, and that he fails, when he does fail, by the lack of artistry in him.

There is no quarrel with the world in Browning. He accepts the world as it is, for better and for worse: "The world and its ways have a certain worth," he tells us in one place. "The flower of life is red," he tells us in another. He is for the right; he is against the wrong, stoutly, high-heartedly, all the time. But as he sees the right and the wrong about equally prevalent, and as his task is the presenting of things as they are, we have no reformer's arraignment of human nature or of God for allowing wrong to be. Browning would have joy drive out sin rather than have it driven out by duty or "unco guidness."

Browning had no feeling that he was apart from the crowd. He did believe that he was one of those God "whispers in the ear," but that belief did not make him self-righteous or hierophantic. He was just one of us, a man who read the newspapers, gossiped, went to teas, dined out, dabbled in everything that interested him.

There was nothing of the ascetic in Browning. He thought:

> God's best of beauteous and magnificent
> Revealed to earth—the naked female form.

Equally human is the picture of the lady in "A Toccata of Galuppi's":

> Was a lady such a lady, cheeks so round and lips so red,—
> On her neck the small face buoyant, like a bell-flower on its bed,
> O'er the breast's superb abundance where a man might base his head?

Wine, he held "God's gift to gladden the heart of man." He would have transposed Luther's "Wine, woman and song," though, to give woman the highest place. He knew "the value and significance of flesh." He knew the necessity of soul, but he could question, ironically, in a particular case, "What of soul was left, I wonder, when the kissing had to stop?" There is a long debate between soul and body in *Fifine at the Fair* (1872), at times quite in the medieval fashion. Fifine is a gypsy, a lively little woman, "all pink and impudence," who struts about the "spangled hips."

Fra Lippo Lippi knows the lure of spring nights whose quiet is broken by "a hurry of feet and little feet, A sweep of lute-

strings, laughs, and whiffs of song." Yet neither Browning nor his
priest believes "there's beauty with no soul at all."

> For pleasant is this flesh;
> Our soul, in its rose-mesh
> Pulled ever to the earth, still yearns for rest.

There were other Victorian poets who made as much of what
they called love as Browning did, but they none of them have his
place as a poet of love. It may be that the story of his devotion to
Elizabeth Barrett, their marriage, their happiness together, and
what their union was, in retrospect, to him, after her death in 1861,
has something to do with this position, assigned to him with little
dispute by all sorts and conditions of critics. There are those who
consider Patmore a greater love poet than Browning and there are
those who consider Swinburne a greater love poet than Browning.
I have met, too, doughty adherents of George Meredith and Wilfred Scawen Blunt as love poets, men who believed *Modern Love*
or *The Love Sonnets of Proteus* the finest Victorian love poetry.
The dissidents, though, are not many.

Browning is more forthright in speech, clearer, more intelligi-
ble in his love poetry than elsewhere. What could be more definite
than

> Let me get
> Her for myself, and what's the earth
> With all its art, verse, music, worth—
> Compared with love, found, gained, and kept?"

No young man, no old man who remembers his youth, but will
own the absolute truth of that, from "Dis Aliter Visum." Whether
the declaration that follows, of the Queen, a woman of fifty, in
In a Balcony, is as true, we had better leave to her sisters to judge.
Certainly all of us know it true in Exhibit A and Exhibit B and
Exhibit C:

> For women ....
> There is no good of life but love—but love!

What else looks good, is some shade flung from love—
Love gilds it, gives it worth. Be warned by me,
Never you cheat yourself one instant! Love,
Give love, ask only love, and leave the rest!

There is a memorable declaration upon love by Valence in
Colombe's Birthday. The Duchess asks him why it is he is sure
that Prince Berthold has no love for her. Valence answers:

Because not one of Berthold's words and looks
Had gone with love's presentment of a flower
To the beloved: because bold confidence,
Open superiority, free pride—
Love owns not, yet were all that Berthold owned:
Because where reason, even, finds no flaw,
Unerringly a lover's instinct may.

That love is the all-in-all in life is repeated so often in Browning, and from so many points of view, that we cannot help believing that it is our poet speaking for himself as well as for the characters of his monologues. Here it is expressed from the angle of
old age, in "A Death in the Desert":

For life, with all it yields of joy and woe,
And hope and fear,—believe the aged friend,—
Is just our chance o' the prize of learning love,
How love might be, hath been indeed, and is.

This exaltation of love has as its natural corollary the exaltation
of woman. He is, like Meredith, a feminist, in the right sense of
the word:

but man's best and woman's worst amount
To nearly the same thing.

That is in one mood. In another, recalling his experience of the
world, he owns that

The divinest women that have walked
Our world were scarce the saints of whom we talked.

Browning has studied love when it made for evil, as he has studied love when it made for good. Some of his longest poems are of love that made for evil, *Red Cotton Night-Cap Country* and *The Ring and the Book* for two. He knows love, indeed, in all its forms, from the wildness of passion to the tenderness of reverie. He can write of the one sort:

> How sad and bad and mad it was—
> But then, how it was sweet!

And of the other:

> And to watch you sink by the fireside now
> Back again, as you mutely sit
> Musing by firelight, that great brow
> And the spirit-small hand propping it
> Yonder, my heart knows how!

There is no summing-up possible of a man like Browning. All of life is in his poetry. There are there country things and city things, primitive things and the utmost sophistication of his day; everyday things and unusual things; all of culture; all of the seven arts. There is never a sign of lassitude in his writing. Bodily vigor, intellectual vigor, spiritual vigor, thrill his poetry through and through. A towering optimism is there always. That optimism breaks out in laughter that blows away all fog from things, and doubt, and distrust. "Whence has the man the balm that brightens all?"

Tennyson used to pity himself, that he should have the best way of saying things and the least to say of any poet of his generation. Browning would have scorned to admit that his case was the very reverse of Tennyson's, that he had more to say and less clarity of expression than any poet of his generation. Yet it is almost true that such is Browning's case. At his best, in *Pippa Passes*, and over and over again in *Men and Women*, when thought and lyrical speech are at one, Browning is as great a poet as we have in

English. At his worst he is still so interesting, for other than his poetical qualities, that we forget how far from poetry that worst is.

Man of the world, polymath, prophet, telling us of the ways of the world, the wonders of the world, the goal of the world, he bulks big among the Victorians. If Browning is not the greatest poet of his age, he is certainly its most virile thinker who used verse as his medium. There is no other philosophical poet of his time at all comparable to him save Meredith, and Meredith's verse, considerable as it is, is of small proportions set side by side with Browning's. Browning is lyric poet, of course, before he is philosophical poet, before he is dramatic poet, before he is novelist in verse. Browning is of the English Titans of all time.

ELIZABETH BARRETT BROWNING

Of all the Victorian poets time has dealt most harshly with Elizabeth Barrett Browning (1806-1861). Writing, as she did, on the very note of her time, her sentimentality and abandon were taken as true passion, and she was cried up as the first of all woman poets since Sappho's time. The story of her love affair with Browning, their flight, and the spectacle of them in their romantic Italy, fairly intoxicated a sentimental generation. She was read by the many who read usually only novels, who could not recognize her poor workmanship, who took her outpourings as a kind of gospel of love. She was still spoken of as sacrosanct when I was young. Excited ladies thought that she had "vindicated the genius" of women in poetry as George Eliot had "vindicated the genius" of women in prose.

The fates of the two have been far different. A good deal of George Eliot, the later propagandist novels in particular, have shrunk to lesser proportions than they assumed to the generation that saw their birth, but *Adam Bede* and *The Mill on the Floss* are still great novels in the estimation of those who know the English novel. No poems of Mrs. Browning have lasted as have these two great stories in prose. *Aurora Leigh* (1857) was regarded by many of its day as at once the very apotheosis of woman's love

and a tract establishing forever woman's equality and true part-
nership with man in marriage. It is a tedious and long-drawn-out
and portentously sentimental tale. There is a characterization in it,
it is true, that of Miss Leigh, Aurora's aunt, a type of Englishwoman not to be so successfully portrayed again until T. E.
Brown's Englishwoman, Lady Margaret, on the Pincian in
"Roman Women" (1895). And an insufferably arrogant man,
Romney Leigh, Aurora's cousin, is finally brought to heel by a
nobly suffering woman. It is all of it of the very essence of sentimental Mid-Victorianism. Mrs. Browning is, indeed, responsible
for a good deal of the feeling aroused among the impatient of to-
day against that unoffending time, fast growing into picturesqueness now that the twentieth century is well into its second quarter. The ideality of *Aurora Leigh* is of a sort that can exist only
among those that are protected from the realities of life by the
strong souls who are not afraid to accept things as they are. This
ideality is a sappy unhealthy growth like that sent out from the
roots of hard-wooded shrubs wintered in a greenhouse too warm
for them.

"Lady Geraldine's Courtship" and "The Lay of the Brown
Rosary" are other narrative poems that have withered with the
years. They seem poor things now, these romances in verse I
heard praised to the skies by the advanced woman of the eighteen-
eighties. *Sonnets from the Portuguese* (1847) have gone with
them. No case at all can be made out for them any longer as
making up one of the great sonnet sequences. There are interesting
correspondences between passages in them and in the much beread
letters from the poet to her poet lover. They can bear comparison
in no ways at all with the great sequences of old time, Sidney's or
Shakespeare's, or with the great sequences of her own time, Rossetti's or Meredith's. There is no revelation in them, no deep passion, no kindling lyricism. They are interesting to-day only because an interesting lady of the mid-nineteenth century wrote
them. In themselves they are obvious and ill-phrased sentimentality. "The Cry of the Children" and "Cowper's Grave" were considered as the last words in pathos by those who were young in the

days of our Civil War. I read them first in the two-volume edition published in America in 1854. I have turned to these familiar poems again and again in the forty years since I first noticed them in my father's library, but I have never been able to like them, and I carry no lines from them in my memory as I do of all poets who have ever meant anything to me. Mrs. Browning was an enthusiasm of my sister in her callow years, and I was eager to share her enthusiasms. Chopin I could like with her, and I could have even a passing enthusiasm for Arthur Hugh Clough because she took him up while she was at Bryn Mawr. Over Mrs. Browning, however, I could never be enthusiastic, and I know now that it was not simply the small boy's antipathy to sentimentality, but the reaction of the lover of poetry against sloppy work.

There is passage after passage in Mrs. Browning that reads like travesty of her own sort of writing. There are some things not so ill-said in "A Vision of Poets."

> . . . Chaucer, with his infantine
> Familiar clasp of things divine

is not half bad, and "God's prophets of the beautiful," as a phrase for all poets, is as nearly a memorable phrase as she could write. But what shall we make of this:

> An Ossian, dimly seen or guessed;
> Once counted greater than the rest,
> When mountain's winds blew out his vest.

For all her protestations that she worked hard at her art, Elizabeth Barrett Browning never knew the artist's joy in the rigors of the game, the joy in the hunt for the just word, the joy of perfection of accomplishment. Her deadly facility undid her. Her work in verse was never worthy of her life.

ARTHUR HUGH CLOUGH

It is difficult to decide how to consider a poet who has meant much to his time, but who has had a much diminished appeal to a subsequent time. Were we right, for instance, to minimize Southey, whom Byron could rank higher than Wordsworth and Coleridge, but whom our age can scarcely tolerate? What shall we say of Arthur Hugh Clough (1819-1861), who ran through edition after edition as long as men were interested in "unfaith," "honest doubt" about matters of orthodox belief, but who has only historical importance to-day? Clough's writing represents, with parts of Arnold's, and parts of Tennyson's, and parts of Kingsley's, that questioning that so agitated, not altogether unpleasantly for all its sincerity, so many Mid-Victorians. These problems, most of them, died with the nineteenth century. What were left were completely demolished by the World War. I am tempted to say that despite the pleasantness of his hexameters in *The Bothie of Tober-na-Vuolich* (1848) and *Amours de Voyage* (1849) all that is left of Clough is "Qua Cursum Ventus" and "Say not the struggle nought availeth." They have place in the anthologies and in the memories of men. Yet even these two are no more than rhetorical poetry. Clough had no new vision of the world, little passion, and infrequent music.

CHAPTER VIII

Matthew Arnold

A GENERATION ago Matthew Arnold (1822-1888) was at the
height of his reputation as a poet. Two generations ago he was at
the height of his reputation as an arbiter of social and moral values.
To some people of Victorian times he was even a minor prophet,
not a Newman, or a Carlyle, or a Ruskin, but still a leader to be
followed. To-day Matthew Arnold rates as a minor poet and as
a major critic of literature. What is best in its kind in all his many-
sided writing is his criticism of literature. There are few critics
who have been better interpreters of poets and better establishers
of values in poetry than Arnold. His "friend and aider of those
who would walk in the spirit" of Emerson almost redeems the
general tactlessness and narrowness of his essay on our poet. His
"he never spoke out" of Gray, though it is a quotation from the
Master of Pembroke, James Brown, gives you all Gray in a
phrase. His statement that if the expression of Wordsworth is
bald, "it is bald as the bare mountain tops are bald, with a bald-
ness which is full of grandeur" is at once the retort courteous in
perfection and criticism with wings.

We have found the declaration that poetry is "a criticism of
life" is at once too narrow and too broad, that poetry is a good
deal more than a criticism of life, and that other kinds of literature than poetry are a criticism of life. Many of his tests for
whether a piece of writing is literature, or, more particularly,
poetry, are, though, the tests still in use among the conservative
critics. If we have been brought up on *On Translating Homer*
(1861-1862), *The Function of Criticism at the Present Time*
(1865), *On the Study of Celtic Literature* (1867), or *The*

Study of Poetry (1880), we will still test poetry by whether it has "lyrical cry," "natural magic," and "large accent," and by whether it is in "the grand style."

Such clarity of thought and phrase, such taste and sense of perspective, and such power of analysis as these essays just named reveal, and the essays on "Wordsworth" and "Shelley" and "Byron," place Arnold on a par, as a critic, with the greatest, with Hazlitt and Lamb and Coleridge, with Dryden and Sidney. Arnold's word, indeed, was law with a greater number than the word of any of these predecessors of his. Nor has there been any one, since his day, accepted as the authority by so many readers, not Henley, not Arthur Symons, not Edward Thomas, not Abercrombie, admirable critics, in very varying ways, all of them.

It is his criticism, as I have said, that, relatively, is the best of Arnold. That is to say that Arnold, compared to other critics, bulks bigger than in any other department of letters he essayed compared with the masters in that department. As poetry, however, is a higher form of literature than criticism may be, Arnold is, absolutely, greatest as a poet. Like all but the first of poets, he is at his best in only a few poems. Arnold, all will agree, I think, is the poet of "Sohrab and Rustum," "Tristram and Iseult," "The Scholar-Gipsy," "Thyrsis," and "Dover Beach." Some, I among them, would add the two poems, "Obermann," and "Obermann Once More." Others would fight for the sonnet on Shakespeare and "A Southern Night." Very few critics would claim that he had more than ten poems of large power to his credit.

Such is the attitude of to-day, the consensus of opinion of to-day. Thirty years ago it would have been said that Arnold was the most representative poet of late Victorian times, that his verse had the very quality of that age. Agnosticism with a high seriousness, and outwardly conforming to the ritual and practice of traditional Christianity, was then a vogue. His doubt and melancholy, both of them weary and troubled and half-hearted, were shared in by thousands of his fellows of "the saving remnant," the little band of people who counted in the great welter of Barbarians and Philistines and Populace that made up the English-speaking world. Arnold was, more than any other Victorian poet, symptomatic of his time.

It is not in his best poems, however, that Arnold gives us the most of those phrases that are often on our lips. His reference to England as "The weary Titan" is in "Heine's Grave." "Who saw life steadily and saw it whole" is in an early sonnet, "To a friend." "Obermann" gives us:

> What shelter to grow ripe is ours?
> What leisure to grow wise?

From "Obermann" too, comes "unspotted by the world" and the reference to Paris as "The Capital of Pleasure"; from "The Buried Life," "The same heart beats in every human breast" and "The thousand nothings of the hour"; from "The Grande Chartreuse," "The kings of modern thought"; and from "Resignation," "His sad lucidity and soul," in which he so admirably describes an attribute of his own.

"Merope," that pedagogical and dreary masque in the Greek manner, has just one line that sticks in memory: "With women the heart argues, not the mind." In "Obermann Once More" are those two stanzas about the East that show Arnold's power of reducing to small compass moments of history or generalizations from the reading of history:

> The brooding East with awe beheld
> Her impious younger world;
> The Roman tempest swell'd and swell'd,
> And on her head was hurl'd.

> The East bow'd low before the blast,
> In patient, deep disdain.
> She let the legions thunder past,
> And plunged in thought again.

The larger part of Arnold's verse is, indeed, inspired not by life but by books. He took his three long narrative poems, "Tristram and Iseult," "Sohrab and Rustum," and "Balder Dead," respectively from Firdusi, Dunlop's *History of Fiction,* and the Prose Edda as translated by Blackwell in Mallet's *Northern Antiquities.* It is from older books, too, that his contemporaries Tennyson and Swinburne took their studies in Arthurian legend, and Morris his from Scandinavian legend. It was a habit of the time, as it had been a habit of times earlier, and as it has been a habit of times later.

Arnold, however, found not only his themes for his poems out of legend, but the themes for almost all his poetry in his reading. The poem with the quality of the elegy or the threnody, and the nature poem, seem to be almost the only kinds of poems made at first hand from life that he could handle with any largeness. "A Southern Night" took its origin from the deaths of his brother and sister-in-law. Thoughts of that Oxford student of the seventeenth century who went away from college with the gypsies, and thoughts of Clough, mingle in "The Scholar-Gipsy"; and "Thyrsis" is directly inspired by Clough's death.

The poems on Marguerite, which a latter-day biographer of Arnold made so much of, are not among Arnold's better poems. Such moments as they have are inspired, not by love of the girl, but by love of the mountains among which he met the girl. Arnold is, indeed, always good at mountains. They are a large part of more than a tenth of his poems. Sir William Watson has said of Arnold, rhetorically but not truly, that "the deep authentic mountain thrill Ne'er shook his page"; and equally rhetorically, but more truly, "Something of worldling lingered still With bard and sage." Devotion to the poetry of Wordsworth and visits to Fox Howe, the home Dr. Arnold had made for himself near Grasmere, had given Arnold the key to the charm and lift of heart there is in the mountains of Westmoreland and Cumberland. Senancour, read by Arnold in youth, had given him the key to the understanding of the freedom and sublimity of the Alps. So, in a way, even his love of mountains is, too, of literary origin. That he cared greatly for them at first hand, however, there is abundant proof in poem after poem.

In that early poem, "The Strayed Reveller" (1849), there is a mountain passage of twofold origin. Arnold is recalling an episode of Greek mythology, and he is seeing it played out against the background of a Lakeland glen which he knows:

> They see the Centaurs
> In the upper glens
> Of Pelion, in the streams
> Where red-berried ashes fringe
> The clear-brown shallow pools;
> With streaming flanks, and heads
> Rear'd proudly, snuffing
> The mountain wind.

The delight he had in such detail of nature as the rowan berries here, is again instanced in his giving of the effect of the yellow gentian, in the passage from *Empedocles on Etna* (1852), that follows:

> See how the giant spires of yellow bloom
> Of the sun-loving gentian, in the heat,
> Are shining on those naked slopes like flame.

Gentiana lutea, as he lists it in his notes, was his favorite mountain flower. He puts it into another poem, "Obermann Once More":

> The gentian-flower'd pass, its crown
> With yellow spires aflame.

All the songs of the youth Callicles in *Empedocles on Etna* have in them "the deep, authentic mountain thrill." Callicles, by the way, rode "a white mule," an image Arnold uses several times in his poetry, not, of course, in the sense the phrase has in America. It reappears as a "palfrey white" in "The Church of Brou," and, identically as in its first appearance, in "The Neckan," as the "white mule" the priest rides across the bridge close by which the transformed knight sits and makes his plaint.

Although Arnold wrote of himself to Miss Wightman, who was to be his wife, as "I who scarcely know a cow from a sheep," he bettered his knowledge of beasts and birds as time went on. Cattle group themselves so picturesquely that he could not keep them out of his mountain pictures. The hum of bees about mountain flowers was often in his ears on high pastures in Cumberland or in Alpine meadows. One of his last sets of verses was written on the death of Geist, a dachshund. Tristram's old hound is referred to kindly, and other dogs than Geist, and a pony, come pleasantly into his letters.

Birds he refers to sparingly, and generally, without identification of the species. In "Resignation," however, he writes with his eye on the object:

> The red-grouse, springing at our sound,
> Skims, now and then, the shining ground.

That is a memory of some moment on a Cumberland fell, and curiously Popean for Arnold. More characteristic is "some wet bird-haunted English lawn," and as good a line of poetry as he ever wrote. In "The Scholar-Gipsy" he recalls Godstow Bridge as a place "where black-winged swallows haunt the glittering Thames." The nightingale of "Philomela" is, I am afraid, as much a "wanderer from a Grecian shore" as an English bird he listened to at Laleham or Oxford, though he does make it sing from a "moonlit cedar" by "tranquil Thames." The old Grecian story of humans changed to birds is instant to his mind as he writes, yet he reproduces well the cry of "the evening singer old" that has sounded through English literature from Cynewulf's time to our own.

It is Arnold's insistence on high seriousness, on nobility, on grandeur, that makes him half indifferent to the little things. One feels instinctively that he could not have cared much for Herrick, that he would have failed to understand:

> Where care none is
> Small things do lightly please.

Beauty, which can reside in small things as well as large, was not
a matter of much concern to him. He was not one to care for
miniatures of any kind, even if they were etched in ivory, literally
or figuratively speaking.

This same love of nobility, of grandeur, of large accent, is one
of the elements in him that leads to his love of mountains. He is
impressed by mass in nature, if not in mankind. The majority
must be wrong, but great mountains prove themselves freeing and
uplifting to those who visit them. Height, aloofness, imperturba-
bility are theirs. From them men win peace. They passed on to
Wordsworth their "healing power," a gift so alien to all that was
Arnold he held it above all price. Mountains bring rare air, and
buoyancy of heart. Best of all are those mountains which lift bright
snow-peaks against the sky.

> Swiss chalets glitter'd on the dewy slopes,
> And from some swarded shelf, high up, there came
> Notes of wild pastoral music: over all
> Ranged, diamond bright, the eternal wall of snow.

It was not, I think, the mere chance of vacation in the autumn
that led Arnold at times to celebrate the mountains at that season.
The moods out of which he wrote his poetry were Novembry,
filled with greyness, suggestive of rain and falling leaves. Such
woods were haunted with no memories of reds and golds like
those of our American fall.

> The autumnal evening darkens round,
> The wind is up, and drives the rain;
> While, hark! far down with strangled sound,
> Doth the Dead Guier's stream complain,
> Where that wet smoke, among the woods
> Over his boiling cauldron broods.

Arnold found in all nature, as in all life, the note of the "ancient sorrow of man." It is in the *Obermann* of Sénancour and in the Alps that Sénancour taught Arnold to love:

> Yes, though the virgin mountain air
> Fresh through these pages blows,
> Though to these leaves the glaciers spare
> The soul of their white snows,
>
> Though here a mountain murmur swells
> Of many a dark-bough'd pine,
> Though, as you read, you hear the bells
> Of the high-pasturing kine—
>
> Yet, through the hum of torrent lone,
> And brooding mountain bee,
> There sobs I know not what ground tone
> Of human agony.

So, too, Arnold found an unhappiness characteristically human in the mountains of the Lake Country:

> The solemn hills around us spread,
> The stream which falls incessantly,
> The strange-scrawled rocks, the lonely sky,
> If I might lend their life a voice,
> Seem to bear rather than rejoice.

It was, of course, what Arnold read into the mountains that he here records. He carried his own sadness to the hills and colored them with it. So, too, does George Moore, who makes his Irish mountains as melancholy as Irish music. It is what they called, in the late nineteenth century, *fin de siècle* pessimism, "this strange disease of modern life" that both Irishman and Englishman take with them wherever they go.

Arnold finds, with greater justice, a like sadness in the sea. The waves on Dover Beach, as the waves everywhere in the world, "bring The eternal note of sadness in." There are Homeric echoes, often, in his descriptions of nature, nowhere more of them than when he is writing of the sea. It is "the unplumb'd, salt, estranging sea," and "The unquiet, bright Atlantic plain." Yet he finds, for once, that it is with joy that the sea "performs" "its long moon-silver'd roll." For all its moral at the close "Dover Beach" is a fine poem, with an onomatopœia as exact as that of Whitman's "With husky-haughty lips, O Sea!" Hear how the one answers the other. First Arnold:

> Listen! you hear the grating roar
> Of pebbles which the waves suck back, and fling,
> At their return, up the high strand,
> Begin, and cease, and then again begin,
> With tremulous cadence slow, and bring
> The eternal note of sadness in.

Next Whitman:

Something thou ever seek'st and seek'st, yet never gain'st,
Surely some right withheld—some voice in huge monotonous rage, of
    freedom-lover pent,
Some vast heart, like a planet's, chain'd and chafing in those breakers,
By lengthen'd swell, and spasm, and panting breath,
And rhythmic rasping of thy sands and waves,
And serpent hiss, and savage peals of laughter,
And undertones of distant lion roar.

These lines are Whitman at his best, with the surge and heave of the sea in them, and elemental passion, but Arnold stands the contrast well.

Arnold finds melancholy as native to youth as to the sea. In "Youth and Calm" he questions:

> And is the heart of youth so light,
> Its step so firm, its eye so bright,
> Because on its hot brow there blows
> A wind of promise and repose

From the far grave, to which it goes;
Because it has the hope to come,
One day, to harbour in the tomb?

How different is such an attitude from that of "the voice oracular"
of Emerson he once so admired, and in the end so belittled. Emerson, it will be remembered, said that no young man ever believed
he would die. The melancholy af Arnold, it would seem, came
partly from loss of faith, from a sense that life, which was, on the
whole, disappointing to him, ended all. It came partly, too, because he was tired, tired because of his doing more than one man's
work, his daily task as inspector of schools, and the work of poet
and critic that was nearer his heart. The melancholy of Arnold
is not the Byronic melancholy that delighted the times in which
Arnold was young, a melancholy to hug to heart and to treasure
as Tom Sawyer treasured the thought of how his folks would care
when they found him dead.

It is not a rugged pessimism, this of Arnold, like that which,
leavened with irony, occurs in Hardy, a pessimism arrived at because of insight into the real evils of life. Put this pessimism of
Arnold alongside of that of Tschaikowsky in the *Pathetique,* or
of Shakespeare in *Hamlet,* and it seems an even littler thing. It is
a vague pessimism, this of Arnold, wearily assumed. It comes
from lack of vitality as well as from loss of faith, and from the
nervous exhaustion that follows unwelcome tasks. Arnold could
not enjoy to the full the glad moments life brought him. He was
too tired to enjoy them.

No thinking man will deny that there must be much sorrow
in life, much disappointment, much disillusion, much going wrong
of things that deeply concern us. Such a one might even own that
there were necessarily more sad days than glad days, and monotonous days most of all, but no man in health and normal situation will fail to claim that the joy of the glad days lumps larger,
in retrospect, than the sorrow of the sad days. Joy is remembered
more keenly, and for longer, than sorrow. Time lessens sorrow far

faster than it lessens joy. Joy is one of the things most indestructible by the years. We recall and cherish the glad moments, and we forget, in the end, the sad moments, as we forget physical pain.

Arnold really does not know what is the matter with him when he writes:

> this strange disease of modern life,
> With its sick hurry, its divided aims,
> Its heads o'er taxed, its palsied hearts.

He may realize, for the moment, that he is tired, driven, over-worked, that the trouble with him is that he is caught by a system that he cannot control, but he does not seem to realize that there is a way of escape from it for others, if not for him. The disease, as he calls it, is curable in many instances. Men have become themselves again, by the return to "the simple life" at home, by emigration to New Zealand or British Columbia, by hobbies, by sport, by abandonment of self in some great cause.

The age that succeeded the age of Arnold is not very sympathetic to his melancholy. That melancholy has even less appeal to-day than out-and-out Byronism, and it falls far short of the effect of the numbing irony that Hardy finds whenever he looks narrowly into the constitution of things. Many things that saddened Arnold in his youth do not sadden the youth of to-day. The youth of to-day are not melancholy because of lost faith, or because injustice triumphs in the affairs of men. Nietzsche, with his comforting approval of things as they are, has been revealed to England since Arnold's day. Nietzsche is read widely in translation, and theories of disciples of his have been loud in the land. John Davidson is gone, but Phillpotts still preaches the doctrine of saying "yea" to life. If our youth are melancholy at times, as youth must needs be, and middle years, and age, they are melancholy for personal reasons, and not because of things in general. There is a good deal of high seriousness with us yet; it did not all die with Arnold. It is now, however, most often a seriousness which is directed, practically, through organization in and out of politics, toward making conditions better.

As integral a part of Arnold as is this sadness of his writing of nature, there is a good deal of Happy England in his verse. It is not the old Merry England of pre-Cromwellian days. Arnold was not the man to find what there was left of that on the Berkshire moors or in the Lake Country. It is true that in "Thyrsis" he tells us that "with the country folk acquaintance made By barn in threshing-time, by new-built rick." It may have been so, but it was more likely, I think, that Clough, his companion in his walks, about Oxford, had the way with him that won the country folk, rather than Arnold. Genial as Arnold could be with family and friends, there was a grimness about that "muffin mouth" he inherited from "pirates out of Schleswig" that made hobnobbing with him none too easy. Yet no one ever loved better the look of England, not even Masefield, who, by the bye, reëchoes, now and then, certain of the cadences of Arnold's descriptive lines. I never read "August, 1914," without thinking of these lines from "Thyrsis":

> These English fields, this upland dim,
> These brambles pale with mist engarlanded,
> That lone, sky-pointing tree.

Sometimes there is even richness in the descriptions of Arnold, a richness one would not expect in so Greek, so classic, so severe a poet. There is assuredly richness in:

> Soon will the high Midsummer pomps come on,
> Soon will the musk carnations break and swell,
> Soon shall we have gold-dusted snapdragon,
> Sweet-William with its homely cottage smell,
>   And stocks in fragrant blow;
> Roses that down the alleys shine afar,
> And open, jasmine-muffled lattices,
> And groups under the dreaming garden-trees,
> And the full moon, and the white evening-star.

"Thyrsis" has, perhaps, a fuller note than that of its earlier companion piece, "The Scholar-Gipsy," but it is a kindred note.

There is much of the Midlands in both poems, of the look of the
country about Oxford, where:

> air-swept lindens yield
> Their scent, and rustle down their perfumed showers
> Of bloom on the bent grass where I am laid,
> And bower me from the August sun with shade;
> And the eye travels down to Oxford towers.

In "The Scholar-Gipsy" we visit with him "the warm green-
muffled Cumner hills," "Bab-lock-hithe," "Wychwood bowers,"
"Fyfield Elm," "Bagley Wood," and "Hinksey and its wintry
ridge," having pleasure in the place-names as we have pleasure in
the place-names of nearer home in Emerson or Whittier or Whitman. Arnold loves these environs of Oxford, but "The Scholar-
Gipsy" ends, not with England as we know it, but on some western
beach of old time that is visited by a "Grecian coaster," which finds
there "sky traffickers, the dark Iberians." It may be only the bias
toward the Homeric simile, so deep-seated in him, that leads him
so far from his subject in the end, or it may be a failure of architectonics, a lack of power to shape a long poem through to the end.
Once Arnold so shaped a poem, "Sohrab and Rustum," though
even here he runs away from his subject in the last lines. In "Tristram and Iseult," high romance though it is, there is an inex-
plicable shift to the Merlin and Vivien story when everything
leads you to expect a quiet close, Iseult of the White Hands at
play with her children, as contrast to the stormy love-duet that
preludes the deaths of Tristram and of Iseult of Cornwall.

Loveliness in landscape, or in smaller bits of out-of-doors, such
as you find in Shakespeare, or Herrick, or Housman, is not often
Arnold's. He is never nearer it than in this passage from
"Bacchanalia":

> The evening comes, the field is still.
> The tinkle of the thirsty rill,
> Unheard all day, ascends again;
> Deserted is the new-reap'd grain,

Silent the sheaves! the singing wain,
The reaper's cry, the dogs' alarms,
All housed within the sleeping farms!
The business of the day is done,
The last belated gleaner gone.
And from the thyme upon the height,
And from the elder-blossom white
And pale dog-roses in the hedge,
And from the mint-plant in the sedge,
In puffs of balm the night-air blows
The perfume which the day forgoes.
And on the pure horizon far,
See, pulsing with the first-born star,
The liquid sky above the hill;
The evening comes, the field is still.

Like the Thackeray who puzzled him, Arnold was moved by
the spectacle of the Brontës. It was what they were to him that
took him to Yorkshire, and led to his poem "Haworth Churchyard," a poem in the unrhymed rhythm he often affects, here most
successfully. This is the picture:

Where, behind Keighley, the road
Up to the heart of the moors
Between heath-clad showery hills
Runs, and colliers' carts
Poach the deep ways coming down,
And a rough, grim'd race have their homes.

And here is another picture from the same poem; accompanied by
an invocation to the sisters to "sleep":

or only, when May,
Brought by the West Wind, returns
Back to your native heaths,
And the plover is heard on the moors,
Yearly awake, to behold
The opening summer, the sky,

The shining moorland; to hear
The drowsy bee, as of old,
Hum o'er the thyme, the grouse
Call from the heather in bloom.

More characteristic of Arnold, because more Novembry and grayer, with something of a funeral chant about it, is this passage from "Rugby Chapel," the verses in which he commemorates his father, the great headmaster:

Coldly, sadly descends
The autumn-evening. The Field
Strewn with its dank yellow drifts
Of wither'd leaves, and the elms,
Fade into dimness apace,
Silent.

It is in his prose, rather than in his verse, that Arnold has laid down such a code as he has formulated. It is not a very definite code at that. He establishes ideals, high ideals. He would have conduct, and the contacts of men, and thought, infused with "sweetness and light." He insists on the dominance of the intellect in all human affairs. If he sympathizes with aristocracy, it is an aristocracy of intellect he prefers, though his work as inspector of schools naturally led him to favor an inspired tyranny at the head of affairs. Middle-class himself in origin, he knew best the class from which he sprung, and, as is often the way in life, what he knew best irritated him most. Arnold was not broad in his sympathies, though he was tolerant of the beliefs of others. Music and painting, sport and science, meant little to him; and in literature itself, which he so loved, it was ideas and morals, rather than beauty and the pageant of life, that primarily concerned him in his writing. He was theoretically an advocate of the first best in everything, and in his criticism of literature he held rigorously to the highest standards of judgment. In his verse, however, he writes so sympathetically of the second best in "The Second Best" that

you cannot but wonder if, unconsciously, the second best was all
that he hoped for in life:

> Moderate tasks and moderate leisure,
> Quiet living, strict-kept measure
> Both in suffering and in pleasure—
> 'Tis for this thy nature yearns.

"Nature's wish" is, of course, "For that best which she discerns,"
but it is a wish that must be "strangled." He has his moments
of rebellion against this doctrine of the mean in things—one can
hardly call it the golden mean. In one such moment he com-
plains, "Calm's not life's crown, though calm is well." He had
discovered, with some bitterness, that

> He only lives with the world's life
> Who hath renounc'd his own.

Had Arnold had the luck that brought money to Browning, or the
patience to wait for the coming of money to him of Tennyson,
he might have been less melancholy, he might have been less tired.
He would undoubtedly have felt differently about many things.
He might then have had the leisure to "loaf and invite his soul,"
and from that leisure and that invitation might have come more
poetry than it was his to gather from what was left of him after
the day's work. In youth, such is the excess of vitality in man,
even the poet busy with earning his daily bread may have enough
of vitality for his writing, too. As the years go on, however, the
poet must have not only leisure to brood over his dreams, but
leisure to hoard up that experience of life without which he will
fall short of material and be wanting the stimulus to write.

Arnold was interested in his work as inspector of schools, but
it was not work which brought him stuff for poetry. He was not,
either in his daily job or out of it, part of a picturesque and romantic life, as Burns was, say, or Morris, in widely contrasting
situations. That was why even the low table-lands of the Ardennes
were so dear to Arnold, and Lakeland and Switzerland a better

world. They were, at the worst, places to escape to from the prosaic daily round. That poet is lucky who is not part of a prosaic daily round, and most of the poets that count have, somehow or other, broken their way out of such a benumbing environment. Few of them had done what they did, had they not had the power to make a new world for themselves, or the luck to win freedom. What had become of many of them had they been "long in city pent"? What had become of, in such circumstances, Spenser or Herrick, Wordsworth or Emerson, Masefield or Frost?

Arnold might not have nearly dried up as a poet at thirty-three if he could have lived in the Lake Country. He was more interested in poetry than in anything else, and had he had leisure in so romantic a place and amid so picturesque a people he might have found there, as Wordsworth found, much to write about. Arnold might have found that there were other themes for poetry than a half-hearted love affair, and Greek myths, and medieval legends, and literature, and the English countryside, and the Alps. He might have unbent, forgotten his academic reserve, been at one with his fellows in other than cultural contacts and at the table. At the table, indeed, he seems to have been a more fellowly human than at any other place. If he was not a good public lecturer, he was a good diner-out, and sometimes happy in an after-dinner speech.

The after-dinner phase of Arnold I learned of in rather surprising fashion. I was dining with a friend in the café of one of our Philadelphia hotels. It was the evening of Irving's first appearance in our city in *Becket,* an evening way back in the nineties. I had with me the two versions of the play, the library version and the one used by Irving. I gave the waiter my order, and settled down to a comparison of the two versions, side by side on the table, and propped opened by knives and forks. A program of *Becket* lay beside them. My friend habitually dined there, and soon after we were seated the headwaiter strolled around casually to see if his patron were being well taken care of. Deep in my books, I just nodded to him, as he was introduced as "Louis." Pretty soon, however, I became aware that he was looking over my shoulder at the books and theater program before me. I looked up to catch a commiserating glance from him to my friend. Joe, only too glad of a chance to jolly me, asked the Corsican if he did not approve of Tennyson. Louis gave the question due consideration, as should one of his importance—he often spoke of "me and Napoleon."

Then he replied: "Begging the gentleman's pardon, did he ever see Tennyson make an after-dinner speech? If he did, he knew well such an intelligent gentleman would never read a line he wrote." Now I had heard my share of stories about Tennyson, but never one from just this point of view. I recalled Thackeray's confession of his dread of butlers, and I wondered had Tennyson had the same dread. "Why it was this way," the headwaiter continued, "I was under-steward at the Primrose in London, and I met all the great men. The Prince of Wales he was a fine man (The Prince of Wales afterward King Edward VII). I met him and the Shah of Persia, and Meestah Arnold and Meestah Tennyson (this must have been before 1884, when Tennyson was given his peerage). Your Meestah Tennyson could make no more speech than the Shah. At a gran' dinner they would call on Meestah Tennyson to answer the toast. He would get up, he would grab the back of the chair so, and lean forward. He would say: 'Gentlemen, I am most deeply honored.' Then he would make as if he would play the piano on the back of the chair, so, so, so; then he would say once more: 'Gentlemen, I am most deeply honored, but, gentlemen, I can only say'—Play the piano some more; make motions as if he was gripping the back of the chair to jump over it, like boys in what you call—leap-frog—'that I am sensible of the deep honor you pay me, but I am not a talking man. I can only thank you for the deep honor you pay me, and sit down.'

"Then they would call on Meestah Arnold. Ah, he was a gentleman and a speaker. He would not mumble like Meestah Tennyson. He would stand up so"—Louis stood at attention and put his right hand across his breast as if inserting the fingers into a buttoned Prince Albert—"at his ease and say—what he meant, and have something to say."

Joe queried: "And Browning? Did you ever meet Browning, Louis?"

"O yes. Meestah Browning was better than Meestah Tennyson, because he knew he could not speak and never did try to make the after-dinner speech. But Meestah Arnold was the man, the greatest of the poets of my time in London."

So, too, higher circles would have said in the nineties that Arnold was the greatest of the three. He came into his own, as he prophesied, before the century's end. Now he has again subsided, in general estimation, to a place among the minors. Despite what Louis felt about Arnold the man, the trouble lay right there. There was not enough to Arnold the man. Indeed there was more to him in his verse and his essays and his criticism than in the man you met. Arnold's was not a large and deeply vital nature. All there was to him he put into his books, there was not a great reservoir of things unsaid back of what he wrote. And of that he wrote, a good deal has the tired air of which I have spoken. He was a weary poet much more truly than England was "the weary Titan." There are times in his social essays when he is "in spirits," when he banters, waxes delightfully ironic, scintillates. So he was rarely in life, except at table, at least in his public appearances.

What seemed like repression in Arnold was just as often low vitality and weariness as strait-jacketing of self. Repression there was, of course. In "Obermann" he writes:

> Some secrets may the poet tell,
> For the world loves new ways.
> To tell too deep ones is not well;
> It knows not what he says.

He seems at times to make almost a virtue of the refusal to see deeply into things. In "Resignation" he puts the words that so express his belief on the lips of Fausta, but they patently express his own belief:

> Deeply the Poet feels; but he
> Breathes, when he will, immortal air,

> Where Orpheus and where Homer are.
> In the day's life, whose iron round
> Hems us all in, he is not bound.
> He escapes thence, but we abide.
> Not deep the Poet sees, but wide.

It is a little strange that Arnold should so write, in the light of all his insistence upon ideas and criticism of life in poetry. He had himself a wide view of the world, although a great deal that fell within that view failed to interest him. But like his "poet" he did not see "deep" into things. There are not many readings of life in Arnold, for all the many phrases he made that passed into current use. Nor has Arnold always a proper sense of the values of what he saw in his wide view of things. Though poetry is the first of the arts to me, I question whether it is true that:

> Beethoven, Raphael, cannot reach
> The charm which Homer, Shakespeare, teach.

That is awkward verse, and uncertain criticism. It may indeed be true, too, that France is, though "fam'd in all the arts, in none supreme," yet many who know her painting and some who know her architecture will question it.

More that is fine comes into Arnold's poetry from his feeling than from his vision. It is his feeling from which comes the duet in "Tristram and Iseult." It was given him, somehow or other, to understand the characters of these two lovers of old legend, so utterly different from his own character. They act and speak as your imagination expects such lovers, so situated, to speak and act. There is no great power of characterization in Arnold, but, such as he has, he is master of in the waiting of Tristram for Iseult of Cornwall, and in the meeting of the lovers. There is real drama here, and drama of intense pathos. One line of Iseult's, about herself and Tristram, is as true of all life as of the little hour left the lovers, who "have now short space for being glad." And the two lines that bring Part II to a close:

> Cold, cold as those who liv'd and lov'd
> A thousand years ago

can break through the self-concern and indifference of the most
preoccupied of us, so definitely are those lines part and parcel of
the fate that awaits us all.

In "Sohrab and Rustum," too, it is the feeling of the poem
that brings it home so closely to us all. The father-and-son conflict,
the story of the father who kills his own son, is as old as life itself
and world-wide. Tale on tale of such a situation has been told;
sermon on sermon on it preached, especially from the text "My
son Absalom"; and minor phases of the conflict have been wit-
nessed in every other household. Its presentation by Arnold is,
of course, in the Homeric manner, but with not so much detachment in the telling. The full-throated close is English blank verse
at its noblest. There is so much in the poem that you cannot forget: Rustum's memories of his wife and babe,

> and all the pleasant life they led,
> They three, in that long-distant summer-time—
> The castle, and the dewy woods, and hunt
> And hound, and noon on those delightful hills
> In Ader-baijan;

and the crying of Ruksh, Rustum's horse, over Sohrab speared;
and Sohrab's death,

> Unwillingly the spirit fled away,
> Regretting the warm mansion which it left,
> And youth and bloom, and this delightful world.

There is a line in "Balder Dead" that I remember as I do
"And youth and bloom, and this delightful world." That line is
"While Twilight fell, and sacred Night came on." In this line
there is a oneness of sound and sense all too rare in poetry. Of
images that stir you in a way that is difficult to explain there is
one I treasure particularly. It is from "The Sick King in Bokhara,"

"cherries serv'd in drifts of snow." You can see so clearly the red against the white, you can savor so exactly the cool sweetness on the tongue. Other lines that haunt me are: "Cool northern fields, and grass, and flowers," "The freshness of the early world," and "In reach of sheepbells is my home." These bear out his declaration that "Poetry is nothing less than the most perfect speech of man." They have the function he would have all poetry perform, of bringing happiness to man. They, and their many fellows I have before quoted, give Matthew Arnold his place among the English poets, a place not far from the place of Gray.

CHAPTER IX

George Meredith

THERE is not much of the verse of George Meredith (1828-1909) that is poetry. What of that verse, however, is poetry, is poetry of a high order. "Love in the Valley" has more of the bloom of youth upon it than any poem of young love of its time, a time of the mid-nineteenth century when there was much poetry of young love. "Juggling Jerry" is a great poem, and of a kind that has few fellows. It is a poem of a gypsy and his death upon the open heath, a poem of out-of-doors, a pastoral without artificiality. It is, too, a summing-up of the value of life, a taking of an account of stock of what matters, a sifting of the wheat from the chaff. All of it is lightened, and buoyed up, and heartened, by wind and sun, floated in a blowing dazzle, and sweet of the earth above which it never rises far. *Modern Love* (1862) is a noble poem, a sequence of sixteen-line sonnets as great as any series of sonnets in our tongue save Shakespeare's. There is one poem in it, "We saw the swallows gathering in the sky," that has the perfection of phrase, the exact and unalterable rightness of expression, the impassioned utterance, and the music that are rarely found at one in any poem of any poet, and that are almost unique in Meredith.

These three poems, "Love in a Valley," "Juggling Jerry," and *Modern Love,* are the best of Meredith. "Grandfather Bridgeman" and "The Old Chartist" and "The Patriot Engineer" and "Archduchess Anne" and "The Nuptials of Attila" have that largeness and ease that have been all but lost to literature since Mid-Victorian times. All five poems suffer from carelessness of detail, but all have great moments. There is in them an abounding vitality, a wealth of life, a range of experience that astonish. There is a John Bullishness in "Grandfather Bridgeman" equal to that in its maker's *Rhoda Fleming* (1865). There is a sturdiness of independence and a high determination in "The Old Chartist," leavened with humor and tolerance and a sense of fair play, that instance yet again why it is that, no matter what happens, England always muddles through, worries through, bull-dogs her way to her goal.

"The Patriot Engineer" puts the man in the street over against the Alps, not altogether to the dwarfing of the man. There is something to be said for his declaration:

> A fig for scenery! what scene
> Can beat a Jackass on a green?

The keynote of "Archduchess Anne" is struck in the lines that are its finale:

> Great were her errors, but she had
> Great heart, Archduchess Anne.

"The Nuptials of Attila" spares you some of the savagery of the great scourge of Christendom, who

> Brained his horse that stumbled twice,
> On a bloody day in Gaul.

You see Attila taking Ildico to bed, and losing his life because of it. Loving another, this slight girl whose fist was only "as big As the southern summer fig," drove a knife between the great ribs of the Hun. When his followers burst in the doors they found her

> Huddled in the corner dark
> Humped and grinning like a cat,
> Teeth for lips.

A moment later she "combed her hair with quiet paws."

The outstanding quality of the poem is the suspense it breathes abroad. You feel the great horde of the Huns straining at the

leash while their lord intends his pleasure. All the rumor of the
hosts of mounted men, impatient to return to their business of
blood-letting, sounds about the quiet chamber where they do not
know that death is.

> Chargers neighed, and trappings glowed
> Brave as the bright Orient's.

And after they find him dead, that great horde of his followers
dissolves like the ice-bound Danube under "a gentle-breathing
morn" of Spring. We do not learn what became of Ildico.

> Of the Queen no more was told
> Than of leaf on Danube rolled.

Besides these five poems of large mould there are various
poems, written from young manhood to middle years, that garner
a great deal of the beauty of out-of-doors. There is the early
"South-West Wind in the Woodland," many of whose passages
are reëchoed in "Ode to the Spirit of Earth in Autumn" and
"The South-Wester." There is "By the Rosanna," which catches
the sluicing and plunge of a mountain stream as you find it in all
uplands throughout the world, whether in the Tyrol in which the
verses were written, or in the Yosemite, or in the humble Poconos,
or in Wordsworth's country. There is "The Orchard and the
Heath," in which not only the two places are contrasted, but the
children of the settled folk of the one place and the children of
the gypsies of the other.

Heaths are loved better by Meredith than any other places in
England. He cares for and writes often of woodlands, and farm-
steads, and weirs that tumble in lush meadows, but it is the heaths
that are most recurrent in his poems. In "The Beggar's Soliloquy"
his beggar speaks, I think, for Meredith, too:

> Now this, to my notion, is pleasant cheer,
>   To lie all alone on a rugged heath,
> Where your nose isn't sniffing for bones or beer,
>   But a peat-fire smells like a garden beneath.

And also in:

> You can't match the color o' these heath mounds,
> Nor better that peat-fire's agreeable smell.

There is a heath, too, in "Over the Hills":

> The sun bursts broad, and the heathery bed
> Is purple, and orange, and gray.

The hero of "The Patriot-Engineer" gives his vote for "an ale-house on a heath." A heath is the background of the poignant little poem, "The Meeting":

> The old coach-road thro' a common of furze,
>   With knolls of pine, ran white;
> Berries of autumn, with thistles, and burrs,
>   And spider-threads, drooped in the light.

One recalls, of course, passages on heaths in his prose, particularly in *Harry Richmond* (1871), in which is so much of the gypsies, who rise in mind the minute you mention a heath. All his love of heaths is summed up in "Juggling Jerry." The old gypsy is speaking:

> Yonder came smells of the gorse, so nutty,
>   Gold-like and warm: it's the prime of May.
> Better than mortar, brick and putty,
>   Is God's house on a blowing day.
> Lean me more up the mount; now I feel it:
>   All the old heath-smells!

Surrey is a county of heaths, Surrey that was his share of the world through most of his years. It is of home, then, that he is writing, when he writes of heaths. In Surrey, too, he found those pines on sandy soil that he so loves, and many other good things he might have found, too, in other quarters of England, a wind out of a yellow sunset, and wild white cherry in bloom against the black of box or cedar, and the blackbird's song.

Odes in Contribution to the Song of French History (1898)
are more valuable for their explanation of the place France holds
in the development of civilization than as literature. They are
provocative, puzzling, a challenge to your powers of interpretation, but there is not much poetry in them. Rhetoric there is in
outpouring streams, reasoned and unreasoned. "France—December
1870" dates from that month. It was written while the Germans
were besieging Paris, and printed in January, 1871. The other
odes of the series, "The Revolution," "Napoléon," and "Alsace-
Lorraine," were written very much later. All four were printed
together in 1898, "France—December 1870," a reprint from
Ballads and Poems of Tragic Life (1887).

France had long been to Meredith "the champion of the open
mind." He had dwelt much on all that she had meant to the
world, in art, in thought, in the conduct of life. He is deeply
moved as he follows in his four odes the rise and fall from the
Revolution to the loss of Alsace-Lorraine, but he never despairs
of her future. Her progress and retardation make a great spectacle
that carries with it a warning to the rest of Europe. He conceives
the France of the Revolution as a "splendid Mænad, Ravishing
as red wine in woman's form," but the surge and confusion of his
ideas about her is such that even Francis Thompson was stunned,
and wrote an abashed review in 1898. All those whom Thompson
himself had driven to desperation by his involved figures and his
flights, will read with delight that Meredith leaves him "gasping."

The onset of "Napoléon" is superb rhetoric:

> Cannon his name,
> Cannon his voice, he came.
> Who heard of him heard shaken hills,
> An earth at quake, to quiet stamped.

All through its many lines his imagination never fails him for a
moment, but the lines seldom lift to poetry. Written in his prime
as it was, you would expect "France—December 1870" to be
better poetry than the other odes, the output of the nineties, but

it is not. It is easier to understand, it expresses its philosophy of life more downrightly. Though there is not a little of this philosophy I should like to quote, it offers no such passages as those that picture the fate of the French armies in the invasion of Russia in "Napoléon":

> Titanic of all Titan tragedies!—
> That northern curtain took them, as the seas
> Gulp the great ships to give back shipmen white."

> .   .   .   .

> The snowy army rolling knoll on knoll
> Beyond horizon, under no blest Cross:
> By the vulture dotted and engarlanded.

Over against such lines as those, the lines that express his philosophy of life look, and are, barren of poetry. Here are some of them, quoted to give the sane and stout-hearted belief of the man:

> Lo, Strength is of the plain root-Virtues born:
> Strength shall ye gain by service, prove in scorn,
> Train by endurance, by devotion shape.
> Strength is not won by miracle or rape.
> It is the offspring of the modest years,
> The gift of sire to son, thro' those firm laws
> Which we name Gods; which are the righteous cause,
> The cause of man, and manhood's ministers.

"Alsace-Lorraine" is the most difficult of the four odes, and the barest of poetry. Nor has it as much of philosophy of life, understandable and acceptable, as its predecessors. In the light of what happened after the World War, happenings naturally dictated by human self-interest, it is strange to be reading of Meredith's belief in France as a peace-maker.

Meredith is a better guide in the affairs that concern the individual than in those that concern the nations. No English poet has laid down a sounder philosophy of life. It is in "The Woods of Westermain" that it comes out most effectively. "The Woods of Westermain" is a difficult poem, but certain passages speak clearly and truly about the basic things of life. It is here that he lays down the declaration that:

> Blood and brain and spirit, three
> (Say the deepest gnomes of Earth),
> Join for true felicity.

In many places in the novels, notably toward the end of *Diana of the Crossways* (1885), Meredith expresses the same thought. It seems obvious enough now, when it has entered into and become part and parcel of the tradition of the race. Man must have a sound spirit flowering up from a sound mind in a sound body.

There is good counsel as well as clear thought about things as they are in these philosophical poems. They and their like passages in the novels have given me a large part of my decalogue. I cannot, however, claim that "The Woods of Westermain," or "Earth and a Wedded Woman," or "A Faith on Trial," or "The Sage Enamoured and the Honest Lady," are great poems. They are not great poems. They have in them, though, many passages that have charted the way through the difficulties of life not only for me, but for many of my generation.

We are to accept things as they are, Meredith tells us, the ways of nature, life, and death.

> And O, green bounteous Earth!
> Bacchante Mother! stern to those
> Who live not in thy heart of mirth,
> Death shall I shrink from, loving thee?
> Into the breast that gives the rose,
> Shall I with shuddering fall?

The poems that count in Meredith belong to his years between twenty and sixty. *Poems* (1851), *Modern Love and Poems of the English Roadside* (1862), *Poems and Lyrics of the Joy of Earth* (1883), and *Ballads and Poems of Tragic Life* (1887) contain all the poetry in verse that Meredith had to give the world. There is little that matters in *A Reading of Earth* (1888), though several of its best verses date from before the collection of 1887. *Jump to Glory Jane* (1892) is only a grotesque, and *The Empty Purse* (1892) is most of it the kind of elliptical writing that got a firmer and firmer hold on Meredith as he grew older. *Odes in Contribution to the Song of French History* is, as I have said, difficult indeed, and *A Reading of Life* (1901) hardly more than distorted echoes of earlier writing.

It was *Modern Love* (1862) that won him his place among the Victorian poets. It was bitterly attacked as a painful and immoral story. Certain of his fellow-poets rallied to his support, Swinburne most stoutly, and the poem took place almost immediately as one of the great analytical love stories of our tongue. There was no defense of it, however, so potent as that made in two lines of the twenty-fifth sonnet of the sequence:

> these things are life:
> And life, some think, is worthy of the Muse.

It is the old story of the dying-out of love between once devoted lovers. A man comes into her life to take her husband's place as her lover, and a woman into his life, though less troublingly, but neither until love had already begun to die between husband and wife.

> In tragic life, God wot,
> No villain need be! Passions spin the plot:
> We are betrayed with what is false within.

The husband explains what has happened thus:

> My crime is, that the puppet of a dream,
> I plotted to be worthy of the world.
> Oh, had I with my darling helped to mince
> The facts of life, you still had seen me go
> With hindward feather and with forward toe,
> Her much-adored delightful Fairy Prince.

There is soul-searching on both sides, and half-hearted returns on the part of one and the other toward the old love, but things can never be as they were. She realizes that in the end, and finds suicide the only way out. Both are, as people go, rather fine human beings, and what happens to both wrings your heart as you read. They struggle, nobly at times, in accordance with the old code of lady and gentleman at all times, but to no purpose. The story is, of course, Meredith's own story, the separation of the poet and his first wife, Thomas Love Peacock's daughter. There is no phase of the progress of the alienation of husband and wife in *Modern Love* that does not spring from what Meredith had lived with anguish. The torture that is theirs through old memories of what they had once been to each other and of what they had enjoyed together is stressed again and again. The momentary resurgence of love that whelms one or the other of them is depicted with irony and with pity. "These two were rapid falcons in a net."

Modern Love is not so thick-sown with epigrams or proverbs as, say, "The Beggar's Soliloquy," where one or the other ends nearly every stanza, but there are many deep readings of life in the fifty sonnets. There are so many, indeed, we must have the sonnets almost by heart before we can note all such readings. Why will not knowledge of things worth while, and of the relative values of things in life, come to us in youth?

> Not till the fire is dying in the grate,
> Look we for any kinship with the stars.

That is one way of putting it. A simpler way, perhaps, is:

> Oh, wisdom never comes when it is gold.

It may not be reassuring to realize it, but we must admit that Nature is telling the truth when she says:

> I play for Seasons; not Eternities.

So it is that

> A kiss is but a kiss now! And no wave
> Of a great flood that whirls me to the sea.

And there are possibilities for endless discussion, are there not, in this:

> For woman's manly god must not exceed
> Proportions of the natural nursing size.

There is that which haunts us in

> Ah, what a dusty answer gets the soul
> When hot for certainties in this our life!

There are many phrases that stay with us; for example these three: "the violet breath of maidenhood," "the pure daylight of honest speech," "More brain, O Lord, more brain!" There are lines that say all that a line can say: "She looks the star that through the cedar shakes"; "Her tears fall fast as oak leaves after frost"; "The May-fly pleasures of a mind at ease"; "The hour became her husband and my bride." And yet, deep-thoughted as it is, full of experience, human to the core, *Modern Love* is not the thing of pure beauty that "Love in the Valley" is. There is here not only beauty, but loveliness, that soft and fresh and exquisite bloom that is quickly worn off most things in our workaday world. There is loveliness of young love, of the countryside, of language, and of music. Our tongue has never fallen in cadences more magical than in "Love in the Valley." Let three stand as sample of the score. The first is:

> Lovely are the curves of the white owl sweeping
> Wavy in the dusk lit by one large star.

The second is:

> Happy, happy time when the white star hovers
> Low over dim fields fresh with bloomy dew.

And the third is:

> Streaming like a willow grey in arrowy rain.

"Love in the Valley" has survived two generations that have lauded it to the skies. It has proven that it cannot be hurt by all the praise that has been lavished upon it, or by the searching analysis that praise has directed upon it. Whether it is a better poem in the eleven-stanza form of 1851 or in the twenty-six stanza form of later years is a question. We should be without some of the lines we love best if we had only the earlier version, but on the other hand we should be without certain stanzas that too long sustain the emotion of the poem and that add too many pictures to it. In either form, however, it is a thing of pure delight, a poem to treasure along with "The Eve of St. Agnes." There is no more praise can be said of it or of Meredith, after one has said that. All one can do is to point out certain distinctions. The poem of Keats is of indoors and colored with the warm hues of medieval romance. The poem of Meredith is of out-of-doors and colored with the cool hues of the English countryside. The one poem is the complement of the other, and each a joy forever.

CHAPTER X

Dante Gabriel Rossetti

THERE is a something alien in the poetry of Rossetti. It is a something, in fact, as wholly un-English as his name, Dante Gabriel Rossetti. Though he was born in England (1828), though he lived there practically all his life, though he died there (1882), and though he was one-fourth English in blood, he was never at one with English tradition and English ideals. A man like Joseph Conrad, born abroad, and to an outland language, made himself a part of England as Rossetti never did.

So of the fiber of Rossetti is this foreignness that you can almost say that he wrote one English poem only, English in tone, English in feeling, English in effects. That poem, of course, is "Jenny." It has in it the English kindliness, the English prudishness, the English moralizing, and, some would say, the English sentimentality. Yet it has no sentimentality. What was Latin in Rossetti saved him from sentimentality. "Jenny" is a poem about a prostitute, but with no "roses and raptures of vice" and no nonsense of reclamation. It is written in the first person, the author speaking dramatically, as if he were the hero of the sorry adventure.

The narrator tells how, after a dance, he goes with Jenny to her room. Tired out, she falls asleep sitting on the floor with her head upon his knee. He steals away, leaving gold for her to find when she wakes, that she may not be disappointed in her designs upon his purse. It is a long poem, of nearly four hundred lines, the most of it questioning why such as Jenny must be; about man's inhumanity to woman; about how, but for the grace of God, many a good girl would be in Jenny's case.

His mother liked it best of his poems. Half English herself by blood, and almost wholly English in disposition and temperament, she felt more at home with this poem, for all its distasteful subject, than with his medieval studies or his analyses of love. The characterization in "Jenny" is apt. His heroine is:

> Lazy laughing languid Jenny,
> Fond of a kiss and fond of a guinea.

The verse moves easily, without the forced rhymes that mar so much of his later work. There is none of that Lilith-like dalliance and ophidian embracing that come close to rendering loathsome passages of *The House of Life*. Here in "Jenny," Rossetti is for once the Englishman who feels that telling about kissing is bad form.

It is idle to deny that there was ground in *The House of Life* for the attack that Robert Buchanan made upon it in *The Fleshly School of Poetry* (1871-1872). That he pushed the attack too far, even to unfairness, is true, and that he recanted, in part at least. *The House of Life* is a sonnet sequence in which Rossetti declares his worship of love and beauty, and in which he broods over his beloved who is dead. There are fine sonnets in the series, "Silent Noon," "Without Her," Sonnet I of "The Choice," and "Soul's Beauty," but he descends in some of the sonnets to a lusciousness of detail, and he rhapsodizes in others in a blending of mystic and sensuous feeling wholly at odds with English tradition. You will find in Donne and certain of the seventeenth-century poets a greater detail in matters amorous than any in Rossetti, but their sensuality is not offensive in the way of his sensuality. The one is forthright, and the other sublimated. The one is frankly what it is and the other is an attempt to be something other than it is.

Let me be sure I make myself clear. There need be no quarrel with the record of passion cleanly phrased, with what in his defense against *The Fleshly School of Poetry*, he called "the passionate and just delights of the body." Here, in *The House of*

Life, in the writing-down of phases of love between man and woman ultimately husband and wife, the very conventions would sanction the record—were it cleanly phrased. What there is a quarrel with is his phrasing, and what there is a deeper quarrel with is his attempt to make what was an affair of the senses an affair of the soul.

It is pleasanter to turn to the great moments in the sonnet sequence. One of these is in "Silent Noon," which preserves a "close companioned inarticulate hour" which the lover and his beloved spent in a sunny pasture, when all out-of-doors was "visible silence, still as the hour-glass." "Without Her" is extravagant, perhaps, but with a poignancy that many of its fellows lack. For all their passion certain of these sonnets read curiously like exercises. Sonnet I of "The Choice" tolls the knell, "Eat, drink and be merry for tomorrow ye die." The sonnet on the sonnet that introduces the sequence is a carved perfect thing, and a summing-up once and for all of what the sonnet is at its best.

The House of Life has no such story to tell as *Astrophel and Stella* or *Modern Love.* There is a record of love scenes, not too clearly rendered. There is a chronicle of regrets for the beloved, and of self-reproachments as to his treatment of her, who can no longer feel his neglect, being dead. Or so it would seem, but the interpretation of many of the later sonnets is not by any means easy. Though the sonnets of *The House of Life* are some of them of his youth, and some of them of his older years they have all been so worked over that they have as a whole the cast of his later work. They are studied, full of artifice, dominated by their rhymes which force him often to say what those rhymes dictate rather than what was in his mind to say when he sat down to write. They prove that, great as was his power over verse, he was never a master of rhyme, that he seldom could bend the sonnet wholly to his will.

I first read *The House of Life* in youth, but few of its lines remained with me, became then and there part of those many lines of poetry that I have carried for years in my head from

men as different as Shakespeare and Donne, Milton and Pope,
Wordsworth and Keats, Browning and Tennyson, Emerson and
Poe, Whitman and Emily Dickinson, Yeats and Kipling. Indeed,
I think such remembered lines are only three from all *The House
of Life,* those last three from Sonnet IV:

> How then should sound upon Life's darkening slope
> The ground-whirl of the perished leaves of Hope,
> The wind of Death's imperishable wing?

And as to these I am far from certain that there is more of poetry
than of rhetoric in them. As I read the sonnets through now, for
whatth time shall I say, I do not find many more lines to put
beside these three. What of "Thy mastering music walks the sun-
lit sea"? What of

> As the cloud-foaming firmamental blue
> Rests on the blue line of a foamless sea . . .?

What of

> Alas for hourly change! Alas for all
> The loves that from his hand proud Youth lets fall,
> Even as the beads of a told rosary . . .?

Is there not more of rhetoric in the first and last of these than
of poetry, and is the cameo-like hardness of the second more than
perfect artifice? As I read the series over slowly, and many lines
aloud, I begin to wonder, Am I losing my joy in poetry, am I no
longer able to tell poetry when I see it? I cannot find much of
first significance and yet many of the elect of criticism praise the
sonnets to the skies. I turn to the sonnets of Shakespeare, and I
am comforted. They speak out with all the old inevitability, with
all the old power, with all the old divination. They are, my chosen
ones among them, what they have always been, "truth with beauty
dyed."

For the forty years since my first reading of *The House of
Life* I have been driven to it many times by the exigencies of

teaching. I have never been able, however, to make it a part of me as I have the sequence of Sidney, and the sequence of Meredith. I must own that there are only a few poems of Rossetti that I have turned to for the joy of reading them, as I turn, say, to much of Herrick and of Wordsworth, of Emerson and of Frost. "The Blessed Damozel" has held me captive since I was a boy, and "Sister Helen" almost as long. Once I liked greatly the irony of "The Woodspurge," and the music of "The Stream's Secret," but neither poem is to me now what it was in youth.

There are more arresting lines in "The Blessed Damozel" than in any other poem of Rossetti. Its form, too, is arresting. Ballad-like in a way, it has, instead of the refrain of the ballad, four parenthetical passages or interpolations by another than the story-teller. These interpolations are stanzas four, eleven, seventeen, and twenty-four. The story of "The Blessed Damozel," a story of a girl who has died and who is now in heaven, is told in the third person by the poet, but from the point of view of the girl. The interpolations, which quicken the dramatic effect, are by the lover of the girl, who, though she has been now ten years in "Heaven, across the flood Of ether," is as much in love with her as when he had her on earth to cherish and serve.

"The Blessed Damozel" is not, somehow, for all its dramatic effect, a very poignant poem. The detachment of it all; the lowliness of spirit of the girl; the absence of rebelliousness in her attitude; the inevitability of her fate: all tend to reconcile you to her situation. The very decorativeness of the poem adds to the aloofness of it, as the ritual of the funeral, sometimes, takes away from the poignancy of death. "The gold bar of Heaven," her eyes that were "deeper than the depth Of waters stilled at even," the lilies in her hand, and the stars in her hair that was "yellow like ripe corn" mitigate the pathos of her loneliness. Some of the decoration, too, gives you a sense of distance, of far-offness, of objectivity, that diminishes its instancy. How remote is

> The light thrilled towards her, fill'd
> With angels in strong level flight,

as remote as some time-dimmed painting high in the vaulted ceiling of a great cathedral.

Image after image of power enhances the decorativeness of the poem, and image after image by its very beauty takes your mind off the sad plight of the girl, so patient in her waiting for the coming of her lover. One of these images gives you as great a sense of space, of the infinity of the reaches of world beyond world, as any image in English literature. It is the image in stanza six. Earth is so far away from the high heaven from which she looks that it but "Spins like a fretful midge." Fine, too, is stanza nine:

> From the fixed place of Heaven she saw
> Time like a pulse shake fierce
> Through all the worlds.

Rossetti is good at rendering distance and space and the outlands of the world that lie "forlorn of light." An instance of this power may be noted in "Love's Nocturne" in

> Darkness and the breath of space
> Like loud waters everywhere.

At the opposite pole from the Puritan though Rossetti is, he is, like the Puritan, deeply concerned with death. He thinks of those who "Follow the desultory feet of death"; he is haunted by "wild images of Death"; he identifies death and love in "Death-in-Love"; he finds "Songs of Death" as heaven to his soul; he sees death as an "infant child" in "Newborn Death"; he believes death no bar to his love of his beloved. Death broods over his ballads, too, "The Staff and Scrip," "Sister Helen," "Rosemary," "The White Ship," and "The King's Tragedy." "A Last Confession" is dark with its shadow, and "The Blessed Damozel" is all but all of it a vision of death. There are lyrics of his, too, about death, "My Sister's Sleep," "Down Stream," "A Death-Parting" the most distinguished of their class. Only Stephen Phillips, indeed, a Puritan of Puritans, among the poets of the century shows a greater preoccupation of death.

Rossetti is at one with the Puritans in this concern with death because, perhaps, he has, like them, the dark medieval mind, so far removed from the sunny mind of the Greeks, on the one hand, and from the sharply lighted mind of the modern man, on the other. Rossetti is, of course, basically the medievalist, but in *The House of Life* he tried to be modernist, too. Power of analysis he undoubtedly has, and the cold clarity of vision of the Latin, but the mind that lies behind the clarity of sight is dark. It was dark from his boyhood, and his sluggish way of living and his narrow interests and his addiction in later years to the use of chloral all conspired to deepen this native darkness of mind.

Watts-Dunton said of Rossetti that he was interested in only four things, poetry, painting, medieval mysticism, and woman. It is strange, indeed, that his father's son had so restricted a range of interests. The father, Gabriele Rossetti, was Italian patriot and popular poet, in his younger years a man at ease among his fellows and able to meet any man upon his own ground. The son was artist and lover, and not much else. There was, of course, the compensation in his case of intense concentration on what appealed to him in these narrow interests and restricted sympathies. He was completely absorbed in writing a poem when the fit was on him. Everything else was excluded. His whole life was in what he was shaping. And as they absorbed him in their creation so his best poems absorb you in your reading of them.

"Sister Helen" centers all your interest on itself, blots out all the world save this little corner of Scotland with which it is concerned, and compels such complete attention to its action that it is all your life for the time you are reading it. You feel, somehow, that your subconscious self is preoccupied with it, as well as the conscious self you have forgotten in your preoccupation. Its dialogue marks an advance upon the half-hearted use of a second speaker in "The Blessed Damozel." When Helen is done melting her waxen image she sends her little brother up into the balcony of her castle to see what portends. "The moon flies face to face with me," he tells her from up in the balcony. She is expecting the kin of the man she is killing by witchcraft. He is all the while growing more and more ill, she is sure, as she melts the wax image that represents him. He had been her lover, this Keith of Ewern, but he had deserted her, and three days before the day of the action of the poem he had wedded another. It was that day that Helen began her melting of the image. First comes before her castle, as her little brother reports, Keith of Eastholm, her lover's brother. Then, Keith of Westholm, his other brother. Then his father, and his bride. They one after another humble themselves to her, but she turns a deaf ear to all their pleas, and there is nothing for them to do but to go home. After they leave she waits the passing of her lover's soul. The forty-second and last stanza of the poem records that passing:

> "Ah! what white thing at the door has cross'd,
> > Sister Helen?
> Ah! what is this that sighs in the frost?"
> "A soul that's lost as mine is lost,
> > Little brother!"
> (*O Mother, Mary Mother,*
> *Lost, lost, all lost, between Hell and Heaven*).

The italicized words are the refrain, recited by the ministrel who is giving the dialogue between Helen and her brother. The minstrel is playing two parts, and acting as chorus, too.

After "Sister Helen," "The Bride's Prelude" is the most dramatic of the ballads of Rossetti. It tells how a girl about to be married confides in her sister a shameful secret. The ballad is unfinished, so we do not learn why she told the secret, or what came of the telling, or if the marriage was made. The bridegroom is the partner of her sin, a sin of several years before, when she hardly knew the world. It is a hot noon, this of the telling of the secret, a hot noon and still in the arrased room of the old castle. The heavy atmosphere and the stifling heat make harder the telling to Aloyse, and harder the enduring of the telling to Amelotte. The conditions add to the menace of we know not what that threatens the frail girl.

The detail is worked in in the way characteristic of the Pre-

Raphaelites, the way they borrowed almost wholly from the early manner of Tennyson. The Pre-Raphaelitism that informed the painting of Rossetti may well have owed something to the simplicities and to the faithfulness to detail of Italian painters before Raphael. The Pre-Raphaelitism of his poetry owes nearly all to Tennyson, and what not to Tennyson, to Coleridge and Chatterton. There is reference to the founding of the Pre-Raphaelite Brotherhood in Chapter IV of this book, and to *The Germ*, the organ of the Brotherhood that was published in 1850. As is there pointed out, Rossetti was the dominant force in the Brotherhood. He used it as a means of exerting his influence over others, so it was not nearly so important in his life as in that of men who were in part his disciples, Morris and Swinburne for two.

"Rose Mary" is another ballad in the Pre-Raphaelite manner, full of detail, rich in color, medieval in feeling. It has all the usual accoutrements, it runs true to form, and it gets the usual effects. It is appealing, though, conventional as it is. Rose Mary looks into the beryl-stone to forewarn her lover, Sir James of Heronhaye, of what peril is before him on the road to Holy Cross. Unfortunately her mother does not make it clear to her that only a maiden may see the future in the beryl-stone. Rose Mary has given herself to her lover. She cannot see what is hidden in the mist that lies in a hollow of the hills by one of the roads to Holy Cross. Armed men are there, and they kill her lover. Rose Mary's mother goes to the castle of Heronhaye, and finds a tell-tale packet of letters on Sir James that proves him untrue to Rose Mary. He has wooed, too, Jocelind, "the warden's sister of Holycleugh." It was that warden who led the men that killed Sir James. The end is Rose Mary's death as she cleaves the beryl-stone with her father's sword.

There are other ballads quite a few, but none other comparable to "Sister Helen," "The Bride's Prelude," and "Rose Mary." "The King's Tragedy" is but another version of the barring of the way to the conspirators against King James I of Scotland by Catherine Douglas, who was thereafter called Barlass. It is a better ballad than "The White Ship," or "Stratton Water," but it is not of his best. "The Staff and Scrip" has a certain distinction because of its pictures of medieval life. Such a one as

> The Queen sat idle by her loom:
> She heard the arras stir,
> And looked up sadly: through the room
> The sweetness sickened her
> Of musk and myrrh

is just the sort of picture that Rossetti loved to paint, and which he could paint. "Troy Town" and "Eden Bower" are somewhat like "Sister Helen" in form. Both have moments of beauty, but they are lacking in incisiveness and intensity. "A Last Confession" is a far better poem than these last-mentioned ballads. It is, however, not so wholly Rossetti's own as the ballads. It is in the very vein of Browning. It tells how an Italian patriot, dying, tries to tell a priest how he killed the girl he had raised from a child, when in her bloom she turned from him. It is of sterner stuff than most of Rossetti, with felicities simpler than his are usually. It holds you spellbound through all its twenty-five pages. This that I quote is beautiful, but it does not sound like Rossetti speaking:

> Life all past
> Is like the sky when the sun sets in it,
> Clearest where furthest off.

And this description of the girl's eyes is simpler than Rossetti's wont:

> eyes
> As of the sky and sea on a gray day.

He wins to something like his own manner in:

> Bright wings and water winnowed the bright air,

but the poem is, on the whole, the most un-Rossettian in manner of all he wrote.

"Dante at Verona" is another narrative, but it is hardly worthy of its subject. It is uncertain, blurred, and wandering. What the poet intended to be a thing of fine scorn and noble suffering is just good writing with a high purpose which it does not attain. There is his translation of the *Vita Nuova*, too, to attest to his regard for Dante. It is of good texture, and those who should know say that it is a good translation. As it is translation, though, and not re-creation, it does not add to the stature of Rossetti as a poet. Nor are his other translations, from Italian, or French, or German, particularly important. Best among them all is his "Beauty," "a combination from Sappho," as he so justly calls it.

"The Portrait" is hardly what you would expect a poem of its title by Rossetti would be. It tells you

> This is her picture as she was:

but there are no details of hair and eyes such as you would think to come on in the author of "The Blessed Damozel," a poem of the greatest detail. There is an insistence on background and memories of places visited by himself and his beloved.

> In painting her I shrined her face
> 　'Mid mystic trees, where light falls in
> Hardly at all; a covert place
> 　Where you might think to find a din
> Of doubtful talk, and a live flame
> Wandering, and many a shape whose name
> 　Not itself knoweth, and old dew,
> 　And your own footsteps meeting you,
> And all things going as they came.

Is that easy to visualize, or to feel in your marrow without visualizing? Or does it remain cloudy, obscure, out of focus? It has, of course, the eeriness so characteristic of the man, and there is none of that "lewdness swathed in sentiment" which he inveighed against, but which he fell into unawares in *The House of Life* when he intended a glorification of body and soul at one.

There are passages in "The Portrait" as memorable as any
in all Rossetti. One of them is:

> Yet memory
> Saddens those hours, as when the moon
> Looks upon daylight.

And another is:

> I came upon
> Those glades where once she walked with me:
> And as I stood there suddenly,
> All wan with traversing the night,
> Upon the desolate verge of light
> Yearned loud the iron-bosomed sea.

The lyrics of Rossetti are not so good on the whole as his
ballads or other narratives, or as the best of the sonnets of *The
House of Life*. "Down Stream," a dramatic lyric, is written out
of outings at Kelmscott, the home of William Morris on the
Thames. "The Sea-Limits" is very studied and involved, but it
has in it one line that is surely great. This is the line in which
it is said of the noise of the sea on the beach:

> Time's self it is, made audible.

There is the pathos of little things noticed at a time of trouble,
and of death in festival season, in "My Sister's Sleep." It is a
highly accomplished poem, of most artful simplicity and of perfection of phrase.

"Sunset Wings" has something of England in it, of the look
of the sky, and of trees in the sunset glow. It was seldom that
Rossetti wrote with his eye and ear so intent on the object as
he did in:

> And now the mustering rooks innumerable
>   Together sail and soar,
> While for the day's death, like a tolling knell,
> Unto the heart they seem to cry, Farewell,
>   No more, farewell, no more!

That Rossetti could appreciate simple things is evident now and then, as here. More often they stirred him strongly, but in a way that he could not quite make out, and that he failed in trying to explain. So it is when he writes

> Work and play,
> Things common to the course of day,
> Awed thee with meanings unfulfilled.

Rossetti has no poem that can be written down his credo, but what he holds to he writes down more clearly in "Soothsay" than in any other poem:

> To have brought true birth of Song to be
> And to have won hearts to Poesy,
> Or anywhere in the sun or rain
> To have loved and been beloved again,
> Is loftiest reach of Hope's bright wings.

This poem is far from either of the two veins characteristic of him. It is not in his medieval vein, the vein of "Sister Helen," or in his modern vein, the vein of *The House of Life.* "Soothsay" is, curiously, Emersonian, awakening memories of "Each and All" and "To Rhea." This, surely, is cryptic in the fashion of Emerson:

> Let no man ask thee of anything
> Not yearborn between Spring and Spring.
> More of all worlds than he can know,
> Each day the single sun doth show.

The appeal to Nature for the explanation of things as they are is not usual in Rossetti. Nor, for that matter, any attempt to explain things. Rossetti was as incurious as to whys and wherefores as any man that ever lived. A little part of the pageant of things was what interested him. Woman's beauty, and love, and old sorrow, and the making of pictures and poetry out of these, were sufficient to content him.

At times in his life his friends mattered too. One cannot help but wonder, though, if many of them were not tolerated because they were interested in what interested him, or for what they could do for him. No man was ever helped more by his friends than was Rossetti. Ruskin advertised him by friendly criticism of his pictures, and Morris and Swinburne wrote very favorable reviews of his *Poems* of 1870. They log-rolled for him with so loud a noise that you do not wonder they provoked such an attack as *The Fleshly School of Poetry*. Yet almost all who were devoted to him fell off one by one, until Theodore Watts-Dunton remained almost the only one of long standing at the time of his death. Rossetti's was too dominant a nature for friendship. It is interesting to find him acknowledging as much in "Soothsay":

> Let thy soul strive that still the same
> Be early friendship's sacred flame.
> The affinities have strongest part
> In youth, and draw men heart to heart:
> As life wears on and finds no rest,
> The individual in each breast
> Is tyrannous to sunder them.

That last line is interesting, too, as one of the many illustrations of his curiously un-English way of using English. "Is tyrannous to sunder them" is as indirect a way of saying that the years wear out friendship as the ingenuity of man has hit upon. His faint rhymes, which are really something less than rhymes, if something more than assonance, have also an un-English quality. The way of our tongue is to emphasis in rhyme, and emphasis in rhyme can be attained only when the accent falls on rhyme words that correspond exactly in sound with one another. It is a tortured English that we have in:

> Or may the soul at once in a green plain
> Stoop through the spray of some sweet life-fountain
> And cull the dew-drenched flowering amulet.

Here, of course, the word-accent is not on the syllable of "fountain" that rhymes with "plain." And it cannot be pleaded that the phenomenon here presented is an avoidance of monotony, an imperfect rhyme to prevent a too regularly recurrent chiming of words. In the following instance, the accents fall on the words that should rhyme with each other, but the rhyme "Man's" and "glance" is not a perfect rhyme:

> The day when he, Pride's lord and Man's,
> Showed all the kingdoms at a glance
> To Him before whose countenance
> The years recede, the years advance.

The truth is that Rossetti, as I have said before, is not a master of technique. He has chosen here in "The Burden of Nineveh" a difficult rhyme-scheme, and he is driven by it to use words that would not be his choice to express his meaning and to carry forward the thought of the poem were it not for that rhyme-scheme.

A worse instance of the kind is to be found further on in the same poem. In this instance he is so weak as to let pass:

> And as I turned, my sense half shut
> Still saw the crowds of kerb and rut
> Go past as marshalled to the strut
> Of ranks in gypsum quaintly cut.

That "crowds of kerb and rut" is very forced. There is such a thing, of course, as the rhyme-scheme helping a poem. John Davidson points out an instance of this in the seventy-third sonnet of Shakespeare. Here the rhymes lead to images that would not be suggested were it not for the rhymes, but that unquestionably add to the effectiveness of the sonnet. The rhymes do not so help Rossetti. The "naked" and "ached" rhyme of "Eden Bower," and the "pleasaunce" and "swans" rhyme of "The Bride's Prelude" show unquestionable uncertainty of hand. They are a result of poor craftsmanship. That Rossetti should have fallen into such imperfections when the art of poetry was the half of life to him is ironical indeed. So much was it to him, so wholly was he absorbed into his writing that it shut him out from all else in the world, and prostrated him from the agony of composition.

It was with Rossetti, I think, as with many a poet and painter and composer—there was not enough else in his life to balance his art, and the resultant instability not only made him unhappy but brought about a nervous condition that prevented him from bringing many of his plans to fruition and that impaired what he did write and paint in his later years. To say this is to say that Rossetti is not of the major poets. He made a few poems of high beauty, "Sister Helen," "The Blessed Damozel," "The Bride's Prelude" in the one vein; "A Sonnet Is a Moment's Monument," "Silent Noon," Sonnet I of "The Choice," and "Soul's Beauty" in the other. He was, as the last-named sonnet reveals, a devoted servant to beauty. It is true of him that "though her gaze struck awe" he "drew it in as simply" as his breath. It is true of him, as he further claims in this same sonnet, that in her praise his "voice and hand" shook. Had the man but matched the artist in him Rossetti might have been of the greatest. As it is he ranks with Marlowe and Crashaw, with Blake and Coleridge, with Francis Thompson and Ralph Hodgson—a goodly company.

CHRISTINA ROSSETTI

It is sometimes forgotten how much reading there was of contemporary English poetry in America in the days just after our Civil War. We all know of copies of Milton that found their way to New England in the late seventeenth century; of verses of Pope circulating in Pennsylvania shortly after he paid his respects to a couple of Philadelphia poetasters in *The Dunciad* (1728); of Thomson's *Seasons* (1730), and Young's *Night Thoughts* (1746), and Gray's *Elegy in a Country Churchyard* (1750), handed down as family heirlooms from the mid-eighteenth century; of Macpherson's *Ossian* (1762) brought over before the Revolution, or reprinted in Lancaster, Pennsylvania, or Morristown, New Jersey, in the early nineteenth century; of Burns finding a welcome among the Scotch and Scotch-Irish of our frontiers even in his own lifetime; and of Tennyson rivaling Longfellow among his own people. Not so many of us realize that the Brownings and the Pre-Raphaelites and Coventry Patmore sold about as well in America as in England and were as much discussed in the press and on the rostrum.

It has surprised some people to find that the first two volumes of Christina Rossetti (1830-1894) were republished in Boston in 1866, were bought widely, were talked about, and were quoted in the newspapers. I picked up, before 1900, *Poems* (1866), containing both *The Goblin Market* (1862) and *The Prince's Progress* (1866), in a reprint of 1896; and at the same time *A Pageant and Other Poems* (1881) in the original American edition. I had heard in childhood of the Rossettis, as of Ruskin, at home, as well as at dame-school, but not so favorably at home as at school. "Uphill" and "The Goblin Market" were read to us in class, before 1882 I know, because it was in 1882 I left that dame-school. The school-mistress gave them great praise. She was a disciple of Fröbel, and an advocate of woman suffrage and all that went with it. She was delighted to have some other woman poet than Elizabeth Barrett Browning to put over against the many men among the Victorian poets in England. Among American women poets we heard a good deal about Julia Ward Howe, and we were told of Celia Thaxter, of Alice and Phoebe Carey, and of Lucy Larcom, with values, so far as I can recall them now, pretty accurately placed.

In later years I was to come upon appreciative criticism of Christina Rossetti in places of high authority, but, after many rereadings, she remains to me a poet of one poem, "The Goblin Market." "The Goblin Market" is an achievement in the kind of poetry of which "The Ancient Mariner" is the type poem in English. "The Goblin Market" is a poem of evening, of an evening long ago, on a streamside in a wood not far from a farmstead. The poem is medieval in material, sinister in tone, glowing with color, with much in it of the menace of oncoming night and of the prevalence of the powers of darkness. Evening after evening two sisters go to the stream for water. They hear the goblins crying their wares, "plump unpecked cherries."

> Grapes fresh from the vine,
> Pomegranates full and fine,
> Dates and sharp bullaces,
> Rare pears and greengages,
> Damsons and bilberries.

Lizzie knew what had happened to their elder sister Jeanie, so she urged Laura to run home with her and to turn a deaf ear to the pleadings of the goblin-men. Jeanie had bought their fruits and had gone into a decline, and had wasted away, and had died:

> While to this day no grass will grow
> Where she lies low.

But Laura, curious, had bought fruits of the goblins with a golden curl she had snipped off. She, too, pined away, but she was won back to health by the sharp restorative power of fruit juices the goblins crowded on to Lizzie's face when she went to buy from them but refused to eat what she bought. Lizzie's cool head and stout heart saved her sister, and they both lived to be mothers with many children at their knees.

There are passages of several kinds of beauty in "The Goblin Market." It has Keatsian lusciousness in the opening descriptions of fruits and berries. It has catchings of that suggestion of evil that we meet in "Christabel," and that Watts-Dunton tells us is so close to the very heart of romance. There are vignettes of Laura, and of the countryside, that prove Christina the sister of the painter Dante Gabriel.

> Laura stretched her gleaming neck
> Like a rush-embedded swan,
> Like a lily from the beck,
> Like a moonlit poplar branch,
> Like a vessel at the launch
> When its last restraint is gone.

The very air of Chaucer's England is in

early in the morning

When the first cock crowed his warning,
Neat like bees, as sweet and busy,
Laura rose with Lizzie:
Fetched in honey, milked the cows,
Aired and set to rights the house,
Kneaded cakes of whitest wheat,
Cakes for dainty mouths to eat;
Next churned butter, whipped up cream,
Fed their poultry, sat and sewed;
Talked as modest maidens should.

And in this that follows is the quality of that later England whose kindness of countryside is the envy of the world:

But when the first birds chirped about their eaves,
And early reapers plodded to the place
Of golden sheaves,
And dew-wet grass
Bowed in the morning winds so brisk to pass,
And new buds with new day
Opened of cup-like lilies on the stream.

It is for such pictures of

pleasant days long gone
Of not-returning time

that I value "The Goblin Market" as much as for the stir and writhing of the goblins, cat-faced, rat-faced, and owl-faced; its suggestion of the evils of darkness; its glints and glows of lights "that never were on sea or land." It may be that old readings of it in school so long ago have something to do with my great preference for this one poem, or that I like it partly for the painting by Dante Gabriel Rossetti, "Buy from us with a golden curl," delighted in and pored over so many times in childhood.

Outside of "The Goblin Market" I can find no other poem of

sustained beauty of the first order. There are other poems I like,
"Maiden Song," "An Old-World Thicket," "Twilight Calm,"
"A Pageant," and "Sœur Louise de la Miséricorde," but I would
choose no one of them for an anthology of the best in English
poetry. They might do for a "silver treasury" but not for a
"golden treasury." In many other poems than these mentioned
there are lines of quiet beauty. Nearly all her verse is, technically,
good verse, well written and finished, but there are few poems
that rise above tepid or lukewarm feeling. This woman who had,
in her human relations, the great gift of caring about people,
could not often get her intensity of feeling into her verses. And
when she was able to express intensity of feeling, it was generally
sprung of her fear for the salvation of her soul.

There is little poignancy, for instance, in "The Lambs of
Grasmere," that poem of 1860 about the ewes dying in the late
winter and wet spring from the failure of pasture. Miss Rossetti
must have known of the conditions at first hand; she must have
been deeply moved; but the expression in the poem is so calm,
so lacking in the tears of things, that she makes you care scarcely
at all. That she loved animals must be true, she writes of them
so much, and with such observation of detail. Sheep were her
favorites among beasts, as swallows among birds. Yet she brings
no sudden sympathy about your heart for the hardships or deaths
of any bird or animal, as a Wordsworth can, or a Sturge Moore.

Miss Rossetti is better, indeed, in those portions of her verses
in which she is purely descriptive. I treasure this, for instance,
only less than I treasure "Homecoming of the Sheep" of Ledwidge:

And filing peacefully between the trees,
     Having the moon behind them, and the sun
Full in their meek mild faces, walked at ease
     A homeward flock, at peace
With one another and with everyone.

A patriarchal ram with tinkling bell
     Led all his kin; sometimes one browsing sheep

> Hung back a moment, or one lamb would leap
>   And frolic in a dell;
> Yet still they kept together, journeying well,
>
> And bleating, one or other, many or few,
> Journeying together toward the sunlit west;
> Mild face by face, and woolly breast by breast,
>   Patient, sun-brightened too,
> Still journeying toward the sunset and their rest.

That is from "An Old-World Thicket," a poem that in its third stanza has a description of birds that would do admirably for a warbler migration at the height of our American spring:

> Such birds they seemed as challenged each desire;
>   Like spots of azure heaven upon the wing,
>   Like downy emeralds that alight and sing,
>   Like actual coals on fire.

In "Twilight Calm" we have again that old picture of cattle coming home at evening of which the world will never tire:

> From far the lowings come
> Of cattle driven home.

In this poem we have, too, squirrel and dormouse, hare and deer, bat and owl, stock-dove and nightingale, the fall of night and the gathering stars. It is not a companion piece to the "Ode to Evening" or "Elegy in a Country Churchyard," but it is an achievement in its minor way.

"The Months," whose sub-title, "A Pageant," gives title to the fifth collection of verse of Miss Rossetti, *A Pageant and Other Poems* (1881), brings us, too, those beasts and birds, flowers and fruits, those natural phenomena, that she most affects. She celebrates snow and Robin Redbreast; snowdrops and lambs; catkins and violets; nestlings and blossoms of the may; cuckoos and nightingales; roses and strawberries; yellow flags and peaches

and thunder-storms; wheat and oats and barley; plums and figs
and browning leaves; hops and nuts and logs on the hearth; pine-
cones and shooting stars; hips and haws and mistletoe and that
hellebore called the Christmas rose.

Her knowledge of nature, for a city-woman's, is fairly accu-
rate. She lays it down that

> one day in the country
> Is worth a month in town.

That is all well enough as a slogan or as a passing fancy, but you
cannot help wondering if she would not have thought otherwise
after being snowed in for a week. There is almost always a doubt,
as you read her references to country things, if she really knew
more about them than an end-of-the-century summer boarder with
bird list and plant book.

Christina Rossetti is at her happiest when she is writing, not
of the English countryside, but of romantic lands out of place
and out of time, which all the Pre-Raphaelites find so close to
London. She is sure of her effects here. There is no fellow to
"The Goblin Market" among her poems of this class, but
"Maiden-Song" is a good specimen of the genre. The heroines of
this poem are delectable maidens all three, the sisters Meggan
and May and Margaret. Margaret was

> Like a blush-rose, like the moon
>   In her heavenly sheen,
> Fragrant-breathed as milky cow
>   Or field of blossoming bean,
> Graceful as an ivy bough
>   Born to cling and lean.

Its lilt is always as easy and free as this, with a fall that Hodgson
was to echo in later days.

It was not to be expected of one with so limited an experience
of life as Miss Rossetti, and with a mind so set on the next world,
that she should give us in her verse much of the realities of

things. She does not. Readings of life are few. We find, indeed, a saying such as: "Nothing was ever beautiful in vain." That has some hold on the memory, but there are scarcely a half-dozen of the like. One, perhaps, is:

> Better by far you should forget and smile
> Than that you should remember and be sad.

Poignant emotional experience Christina Rossetti had in two defeated love-affairs. That she allowed her religion to be a bar between herself and one lover, and years later, between herself and another, shows that her sense of duty rather than her emotions ruled her. She did not generally reveal her own emotions directly in her verse, but expressed them in what appear to be poems about other people. Thus in "Sœur Louise de la Miséricorde" she wrote:

> I have desired, and I have been desired:
> But now the days are over of desire,
> Now dust and dying embers mock my fire;
> Where is the hire for which my life was hired?
> Oh vanity of vanities, desire!

This has the sound of satiety, the very note on which Ernest Dowson was in later years to write many of his poems. It is not satiety, I think, in Christina Rossetti, but merely that hushed expression that subdues so much of her verse. There are those who believe that the hushed expression covers fire within. I think not. Family affection and religion, I believe, were her strongest emotions, and what others were in her life did not often rise to intensity.

That she denied herself much, I think is true, but I do not believe it was at a very great sacrifice. It was of herself, I believe, at least in part, that she wrote in "A Portrait," although her brother, William Michael Rossetti, makes Lady Isabella Howard the original of the poem. It was, no doubt, a composite, but certainly it was true of Christina Rossetti that:

> She gave up beauty in her tender youth,
> Gave all her hope and joy and pleasant ways;
> She covered up her eyes lest they should gaze
> On vanity, and chose the bitter truth.

In "Sweet Death" she can write:

> And youth and beauty die.
> So be it, O my God, Thou God of truth:
> Better than beauty and than youth
> Are Saints and Angels, a glad company.

These are strange sentiments to find in the daughter of the free-thinker Gabriele Rossetti, and in the sister of the apostle of sensuousness, Dante Gabriel Rossetti. It would seem that the blood of her maternal grandmother, who was wholly English and devoutly Church of England, was dominant in her over the three-quarters of her blood that was Italian. Christina's religion was an evangelical Christianity, unwontedly blended with High Church enthusiasms. She was orthodox through and through. She was convinced of her own unworthiness. She was afraid of the hereafter, she, the soul of goodness.

The religious troubles that she went through were the religious troubles of the average Mid-Victorian Protestant in America as well as in England. Her record of these troubles in her devotional poetry was eagerly read by the many who shared them. Her books of verse were widely distributed in America, and at the time of her death no writer of religious verse worthy of the name of poetry had so large a following. Without its artistry, her religious verse would have long since gone the way to oblivion most religious verse so quickly goes. She was no Herbert, or Vaughan, or Crashaw, or Patmore, or Francis Thompson. There are few moments of large luminousness or kindling rapture in her devotional poems. In "Christian and Jew" she surpasses herself, seeing

> White-winged the cherubim,
> Yet whiter seraphim,
> Glow white with intense fire of love.

Such intensity is very exceptional in Christina Rossetti. Most often you find her self-abasing, as in "The Lowest Place," uncertain of her way, doubtful of the fate of one so full of shortcomings as herself. In her love poetry, repressed as most of it is, there are moments of insight. One is that in which she saw the truth which each one of us has observed in a score of instances, the truth that: "Love pardons the unpardonable past." I can find in her writing no insight into spiritual things comparable to this of earthly love. She contents herself in the devotional verse with paraphrases of the Bible, as in "A Testimony," or by setting down her thoughts on some holy day of the Church, as in "Good Friday."

With a large body of well-written devotional verse to her credit, Christina Rossetti is of importance as a religious poet largely because most religious verse of the past hundred years is so decidedly inferior to verse inspired by love and delight in beauty, by the strangeness of life and by the wonders of widening horizons, by discoveries of truth, of the constitution of things. Her real forte was in rendering episodes of life, half-medieval, half out of time, in the Pre-Raphaelite fashion, one of which, "The Goblin Market," is a poem as full of romantic enchantment as any English poem, whether of Spenser or Coleridge, Tennyson or Hodgson.

CHAPTER XI

William Morris

WILLIAM MORRIS (1834-1896) is not a poet for all moods. He has not the power to force you to pay heed to him, if you are your ordinary prosaic self, as a Donne has, or a Masefield. You must come to Morris a little removed from the workaday world, if you are to come under his spell. You must be willing to surrender yourself to yesterday, to a life that is simple, to places that are aloof, to a pageantry like that of some medieval arras, to a music dreamy and languorous, if you are to be carried away by his songs and dramatic lyrics and stories in verse.

They are not all of a kind, his writings in these several forms. His true lyrics are few, but one of them is best known of all his work, the song beginning "In the white-flowered hawthorne brake" and having for the refrain of each of its four verses:

> Kiss me, love! for who knoweth
> What thing cometh after death.

The strong bias toward drama there was in the man turns even this poem of sixteen lines into a dialogue of "she" and "he." The dramatic lyrics have tense moments in them, "The Haystack in the Floods" the most tense. "The Haystack in the Floods" is, indeed, the most notable poem of Morris, and one of the most notable dramatic lyrics in all English literature. All is seen with the eyes of Jehane, the lady of the knight who is riding to his death. What passes before her as she rides in the rain with him is chronicled, her Robert's distraction in the knowledge that he is a doomed man, his watchfulness acquired in his short life of danger, the meeting with Godmar near "that rain-soaked hay," her man's courage against great odds, the treachery of Robert's men, his capture, Godmar's offer of his life on terms that she could not accept, what was before her as the paramour of Godmar, the infamy with which he threatens her, the butchery of Robert, and the taking captive of herself. There is an intimation at the end that she has been driven mad by what she has gone through. We hope she has, or that, like Deirdre, she can win her way out by death.

The dialogue with Godmar after Robert is taken prisoner occupies more of the one hundred and sixty lines of the poem than any other part of its action. It is real drama. Here, as in "Sir Peter Harpdon's End," there is no typical Morrisian haze about the writing. All is clear, sharp-cut, with an anguish that leaves its marks on you reading you cannot rid yourself of. You see all that happens so distinctly, and somehow it brings to your mind a realization of the many such scenes there must have been in those bad old times of chivalry. Both "The Haystack in the Floods" and "Sir Peter Harpdon's End" are far more dramatic than that series of scenes within scenes that Morris calls *Love Is Enough: A Morality* (1873).

It was *The Life and Death of Jason* (1867) that brought him his first popularity, but *The Earthly Paradise* (1868) has displaced it now as his representative work in narrative verse. It is, I suppose, his introductory verses to these tales, the verses in which he dubs himself "The idle singer of an empty day," as well as the very bulk of the three volumes, that have centered attention on *The Earthly Paradise*. It is not a book to sit down to and read through. It is a book to turn to and read for an hour when you wish to forget this world or to be transported to one still in the Golden Age. Its prologue tells us of a band of sea-rovers, Norsemen mostly, wandering westward, in the fourteenth century, to some Atlantis or idyllic El Dorado inhabited by descendants of Greek folk. One of the principal men of the group served as a soldier in Byzantium, long, long before. He is now three score and ten, like his companions, and like them, too, he is willing to settle down at least half-contentedly to last days of Indian summer ease.

The wanderers and the Greek folk tell tales as the Canterbury pilgrims did. Two tales are repeated for every month of the year. There are short verses, descriptive of the months, and other short verses, of the nature of prologues and epilogues, between the long tales. Most of the tales are of Greek origin, but a few are medieval and another few of Scandinavian origin, and just one Arabic. All are medievalized, as are their counterparts the prose romances, all are re-told with the glamour and remoteness characteristic of Malory, save the Scandinavian tales, whose stark Northerners break through the haze with which Morris loves to invest his figures, and are revealed large-limbed and heavy-thewed like their originals in the sagas.

I had often read at *The Earthly Paradise* before I read it through, all but all of it, during three months of sorrow and strain. One time I had read "Atalanta's Race," another time "Ogier the Dane," another time "The Hill of Venus," and another time "The Lovers of Gudrun." There had been other times when I had read the lyrics descriptive of the months, or had hunted through the tales for the songs incidental to them. Oftener still I had just idled away a sleepy hour looking through the three volumes for the pleasure of recalling the lines and passages I had marked on previous readings. There came the time when the long illness of my mother made most reading impossible to me. I turned to *The Earthly Paradise* then and found it an anodyne. It alleviated, more than any other book, the sorrow that had to be borne. I read Parts I and II and IV and about half of Part III from March to June that unhappy spring. It so happens that I have come upon several others who found *The Earthly Paradise* a help in similar times of trouble. There is a great deal of sorrow in its tales, but that sorrow is not of any poignancy. The haze about the poems, their effects as of a something pushed into the background, the sense that all in them happened long, long ago, results in a deadening of your feelings as you read. It is almost as if you had taken an opiate.

It may be only because of the moods in which I have read it, but somehow or other *The Life and Death of Jason* has never meant so much to me as the best stories in *The Earthly Paradise*, the stories that I have named. Like all who went to school in the seventies and the eighties, I was brought up on the story of the Argonauts, and so there were few surprises for me in *The Life and Death of Jason*. Perhaps because it was not a thing of strangeness and wonder, as "Ogier the Dane" was, and "The Hill of Venus," and "The Lovers of Gudrun," the Greek story was of less appeal than these. Its treatment by Morris is, of course, romantic rather than classic. In so far as it is Greek in feeling it is Greek in the manner of *The Odyssey* rather than of *The Iliad*. There are times when Morris forgets his countryside should be that of the Eastern Mediterranean or a countryside out of place and time. Then he makes the look of the land the very look of England. English vanes swing over English churches, when he should be describing Thessaly. Chiron the Centaur is like some English squire, grown wise with the years, and benign and gentle. Medea is now a girl of the English country set and now a witch-wife out of English fable. The lyrics by the way that break the long narratives have always a setting of southern England. Some of them are haunting, "I know a little garden close" for one, and "O surely, now the fisherman" for another.

Morris often calls Chaucer his master, but the atmosphere of his poems is almost always that of Malory. There is, too, often a tired air about Morris, which is as far as can be from the freshness and heartiness of Chaucer. It is afternoon in September with Morris and morning in May with Chaucer. There is never any suggestion of humor in the verse of Morris; there is no raciness there, though there is sensuousness; there is ruggedness and red blood only in his Scandinavian figures, the rest being flat and faintly glowing, like stained-glass figures seen against the after-glow. Morris was himself of a towering temper and alive to the fingertips, but when he took pen in hand dream fell on him, and he could not, for all his will to do so, fashion his men and women after Chaucer's. No doubt he tried hard enough. There is a patent sincerity in his tributes to his master. Most keenly felt is that at the opening of the last book of *The Life and Death of Jason,* Book XVII of that long poem:

> Would that I
> Had but some portion of that mastery
> That from the rose-hung lanes of woody Kent
> Through these five hundred years such songs have sent
> To us, who, meshed within this smoky net
> Of unrejoicing labor, love them yet.
> And thou, O Master!—Yea, my Master still,
> Whatever feet have scaled Parnassus' hill,
> Since, like thy measures, clear, and sweet, and strong
> Thames' stream scarce fettered bore the bream along
> Unto the bastioned bridge, his only chain.
> O Master, pardon me, if yet in vain
> Thou art my Master, and I fail to bring
> Before men's eyes the image of the thing
> My heart is filled with: thou whose dreamy eyes
> Beheld the flush in Cressid's cheeks arise,
> When Troilus rode up the praising street,
> As clearly as they saw thy townsmen meet
> Those who in vineyards of Poictu withstood
> The glittering horror of the steel-topped wood.

Save that Chaucer is made by Morris to have his own "dreamy eyes," this seems to me a true presentation.

There are those who say that the best poems of Morris are to be found in *Poems by the Way* (1891). Such critics are generally fellow-Socialists of Morris, men who hold him a greater figure in the public life of his time than in literature. They point to his creation of the Morris chair; to his theories and practice of interior decoration; to his weaving; to his Kelmscott press; to his revelation of Old Norse literature to his day and generation; to his lectures on economics; to his political speeches; to his street preaching; to his advocacy, through every channel open to him, of Ruskin's belief that beauty is necessary to every life that is lived, and that "art is man's expression of his joy in labor." This work for humanity is greater, such critics believe, than any accomplishment in literature, and they believe, too, that only that literature is of much importance which furthers what they regard as the advancement of humanity. Such critics think "The Voice of Toil," "The Day Is Coming," and "The Message of the March Wind" are great poems. As a matter of fact, they are just well-written propaganda, in no way comparable to his best work. Morris himself rather minimized such writing when he said of himself:

> Dreamer of dreams, born out of my due time,
> Why should I strive to set the crooked straight?

He did so strive, of course, and with much of his might, but this is not the only moment in which he doubted whether all his labor for the uplift of his fellow-man was worth while.

Another group of critics thinks that the best of Morris is to be found in his first book of poems, *The Defence of Guenevere* (1858). There is a great deal to be said for the point of view of this group. There is more strangeness, more wonder, more color, more glamour, more music, and more romance in these early verses than in the later work. There is not in them, though, the sense of largeness there is in "The Lovers of Gudrun" or *Sigurd the Volsung*, or characters at once of such heroic proportions and such essential humanness, but in the respects I have named the Greek and medieval poems stand first among his tales in verse. There is less, too, of Morris in these Scandinavian tales. He follows *The Laxdaela Saga* and *The Volsunga Saga* more closely than in his renderings of the more Southern stories. The Northern tales have not the qualities of decoration of the more familiar stories. They are not so Pre-Raphaelitish, so veiled, so glowing. He leaves his Norse stories, indeed, more as they were in their originals than any other of the artists of his time who used them.

He had, by the bye, nothing but blame for Wagner's versions, but this was perhaps largely due to his hatred of Wagner's music.

The dramatic lyrics of *The Defence of Guenevere* are most of them lacking in the clarity and sureness of outline that distinguished the Northern tales. In these dramatic lyrics there is not only a lack of clarity, but sometimes a doubt as to the meaning, or a downright obscurity that even long familiarity cannot dispel. There are no such difficulties with the best of them. In "The Defence of Guenevere" itself you can follow all the drama of the trial of Guenevere at Carlisle, her defiance of Gauwaine and her rescue by Launcelot. The only weakness of the poem is that it is too long. You cannot sustain your interest and attention at so high a pitch as the poem demands for so long. But almost all the poems of Morris are too long, all, indeed, save the simplest songs and lyrics.

Morris wrote very easily. And writing so easily, he held that all verse was merely craftsmanship. "If a chap," he said, "can't compose an epic poem while he's weaving tapestry, he had better shut up, he'll never do any good at all." Morris was a good craftsman when he had elbow room, but he had no power of saying much in little space. And his utterance was not a full and rich utterance. His voice, like that of the "chief priest" of the Western land in which the wanderers of his *Earthly Paradise* came to rest, was a "thin voice."

There was little of the seer in Morris. His thought is often on death, as it is often on the emptiness of life, but he seldom hazards a guess at what is beyond. He adjures each one of us:

> Look not before thee! the road left behind,
> Let that be to thee as a tale well told
> To make thee merry when thou growest old.

And again he tells us:

> All stories end with this,
> Whatever was the midway gain and bliss:
> He died, and in his place was set his son;

> He died, and in a few days everyone
> Went on their way as though he had not been.

These passages are close to "readings of life," but such are infrequent in Morris. Nor is the pregnant phrase common. Ogier the Dane was a man "To whom all life, however hard, was good." Atalanta was "Too fair to let the world live free of war." And Gudrun, speaking of her lovers, said of Kiartan, "I did the worst to him I loved the most." Such lines are rare in Morris. Plentier are bits of landscape caught in a line, or two, or three. One is "Beneath thy gold-hung, grey-leaved apple-trees." Another is:

> Or in the birchwoods watch the screaming jay
> Shoot up betwixt the tall trunks, smooth and grey.

And a third is:

> For to my grey tower back I go
> High-raised above the heathy hills
> Where the great erne the swift hare kills.

Morris, like Rossetti, was very fond of the refrain. They both borrowed it, of course, from the old ballads of the border. You often remember a poem by its refrain. *"When the Sword went out to sea"*; *"Two red roses across the moon,"* and *"Hah! hah! la belle jaune giroflée"* bring back the stories they symbolize. Even more momentous are the variations on bells in "The Blue Closet." I am not quite sure why the knight whom the four ladies sing to came to his death, or how he returned from the dead, but I like to read "The Blue Closet" for its picture of the castle and its immured princesses, and for the tolling bells. It comes to a close on this deep note:

> And ever the great bell overhead,
> And the tumbling seas mourn'd for the dead;
> For their song ceased, and they were dead.

It is years now that "Golden Wings" has been haunting me. Not even our own Poe has a music more otherworldly. And what a picture is that of the old castle that stood:

> Midways of a walled garden,
> In the happy poplar land.

And poor Jehane du Castle beau! What is her story? And what the story of her lover who failed to come? And of what "slain man" were the "stiffened feet" in the punt in the castle moat?

Yet it does not hurt us much as we read—that is the recurrent thought—all this sadness in "The Blue Closet" and "Golden Wings," and in "The Lovers of Gudrun" and *Sigurd the Volsung*. It was so long ago all this sadness was. One feels like reiterating the words again and again, "It was all so long ago! It was all so long ago!" That is the burden of Morris, "It was all so long ago!" And often there is added to this burden that other only less prevalent, "It was all so far away!" Much of this which happened so long ago and so far away happened out of the world we know, in Arcady or Avalon or Broceliande or other country "beyond wave." The little touches of English landscape so unconsciously introduced in his descriptions of remote countries are not many enough to make these outlands homey places. The beauty in the poetry of Morris is a beauty of away off and enchanted and dreamy things. There is little in it that is instant to the daily life of men.

CHAPTER XII

Algernon Charles Swinburne

IT IS rather the vogue to say that Swinburne (1837-1909) is only music and a manner. That "music and a manner" is really, though, a large concession. He is great surely just for his music and his manner. There may be little revelation of the realities of life in Swinburne, but his is the distinction of having achieved such a music of English words as was never before he made it. His manner, too, is new, his frank paganism, his rapture of sense, his unabashed candor of fleshliness resulting in passage after passage among the most surprising and unforgettable moments of English poetry. He is always long drawn out, nearly always wordy, too constantly echoing Tom Paine in his denunciation of kings and priests, over-insistent on "the raptures and roses of vice." He has given us, however, ten lyrics parts of which are among the greatest poetry of our tongue, and two cantos of an epical romance that are better sustained than any of the lyrics, that are enkindling and passionate poetry of the highest order.

"Hymn to Proserpine," "Ilicet," "The Garden of Proserpine," "Hesperia," "The Sundew," "August," "The Last Oracle," "A Forsaken Garden," "At a Month's End," and "The Hounds of Spring" are the ten lyrics, and "The Sailing of the Swallow" and "The Queen's Pleasance" from *Tristram of Lyonesse* (1882) the two dramatic lyrics masquerading as narrative. The ten poems are from *Poems and Ballads* (1866), *Poems and Ballads; Second Series* (1878), and *Atalanta in Calydon* (1865). They are all the product of the years between youth and middle age.

Swinburne never grew old in mind or heart or spirit. He was at seventy what he had been at seventeen, the public-school boy of good family. He learned little by any experiences save those of boyhood and youth. He inherited a tradition of conduct and of cultivation. He was brought up on those sound essentials of education, the Bible and the Greek and Latin classics. In boyhood the code of the public school was added to the family code, and youth brought him loves in plenty. He tells us that some of the experiences he records in his love verse are dramatic rather than personal, but he who reads will not doubt that there are known girls of flesh and blood responsible for "Fragoletta," "Faustine," "Félise," and "Dolores."

These love affairs are all those of a very young man. No dreamless middle age succeeded this dreamy youth, so troubled and passionate. Youth went on and on. That was one of the tragedies of his life. The usual experiences of maturer years were not his. There were in his life only love and mating, relationships with the family to which he was born, literary friendships, wanderings by the seashore, swimming, gallops over moors, gloatings over babies, and writing. And writing was the greatest of these. Even his sentimentalities over babies that he met on Wimbleton Common were turned into song. All his life was but material for his art. And that life was a painfully narrow life, and not fully lived in its narrowness. For all his devotion to babies and rhyming of them, there is no fatherhood in his attitude. He was just a poor devil of a bachelor man. There was no nest-building in his life, nothing domestic, no chores about house or place, no haggling with butcher and baker and candlestick-maker. Theodore Watts-Dunton seized upon Swinburne in 1879 and carried him off from London across the Thames to Putney. Thereafter he was looked after, guarded from the world, taken care of almost as if he were in a nursing home. Perhaps it was well that he was, perhaps it was necessary to a continuance of his work, of his life even. But this coddling had its inevitable effect upon him, just as the coddling of George Eliot by Lewes had upon her. It removed Swinburne even further from the workaday world and pinched his life into the severest limits, strait-jacketed his spirit, kept from him the friends not approved by his super-friend. No English poet of them all was more sequestered from the world, and no English poet of parts ever knew so little of it. Books and youth, books and memories of youth, were his stock-in-trade his life through. Had he had real troubles of a personal sort he had never so lost himself in worship of poets and apostles of freedom, in Landor and Mazzini and Hugo.

So it is there are few readings of life in his writing. Such as there are are mostly discoveries about love. He found out that "desire is a respite from love, and the flesh not the heart is her fuel." There are a few discoveries about the brevity of life, the menace of death. "They have the night," he says nobly, "They have the night, who had like us the day." Almost as final are "What love was ever as deep as a grave?" and "There are worse things waiting for men than death." Lines that last in memory are: "Though all the stars made gold of all the air"; "Thick darkness and the insuperable sea"; "A land of sand and ruin and gold"; "I shall never again be friends with roses"; "The thunder of the trumpets of the night"; "A place beyond all pain in Avalon"; "The hidden harvest of luxurious time"; "Under wan skies and waste white light"; "Far windy Russian places fabulous"; "The whin is frankincense and flame"; "Sing while he may, man hath no long delight"; and "The mystery of the cruelty of things." There are descriptions of nature here, some of them romance-haunted; phrases that take us to the world's end; and reflections on time and fate that set us brooding.

There is no poet since Keats in whom there is more that is glamorous than Swinburne. "Hesperia" is full of such glamour, flashed to us from a new music of words:

Out of the golden remote wild west where the sea without shore is,
Full of the sunset, and sad, if at all, with the fulness of joy,
As a wind sets in with the autumn that blows from the region of stories,
Blows with a perfume of songs and of memories beloved from a boy.

"The Garden of Proserpine" offers us several such passages, of which that most often recurrent to me is:

> Pale, beyond porch and portal,
> Crowned with calm leaves, she stands,
> Who gathers all things mortal
> With cold immortal hands.

It is perhaps the cup of the love draught that Tristram and Iseult were fated to drink together that gathers to itself the greatest glamour, that

> strange thing
> That might be spoil of some dim Asian king,
> By starlight stolen from some waste place of sand.

My excuse for these many quotations is that they can quint-essentialize Swinburne as could no words of mine. They give his music and his dominant manners. Manners, I say, for he has, as a matter of fact, several manners. There is his pagan manner, the manner of his frank poems about his loves, listed above, "Fragoletta," "Faustine," "Félice," and "Dolores"; and of "Laus Veneris," of "Anactoria," of "At a Month's End," and of "On the Cliffs." From the poems of this class are culled the quotations common in everyday speech, the phrases on the lips of men or in the newspapers: "Sleek supple soul and splendid skin"; "No soul she hath, we see, to outlive her; Hath she for that no lips to kiss"; "The print and perfume of old passion"; and "But thy bosom is warm for my face and profound as a manifold flower." It is in these poems that we have, too, the sharp cameos of women loved, of Fragoletta, whom he thus questions:

> Thy sweet low bosom, thy close hair,
> Thy straight soft flanks and slenderer feet,
> Thy virginal air,
> Are they not over fair
> For love to greet?

Of Faustine, of well-remembered charms:

> That clear hair heavily bound back;
> The lights wherein
> Shift from dead blue to burnt-up black;
> Your throat, Faustine,

> Strong, heavy, throwing out the face
> And hard bright chin
> And shameful scornful lips that grace
> Their shame, Faustine.

Equally sharp are the portraits of Dolores, who had a "Red mouth like a venomous flower," and of Félise, his snake "with bright bland eyes."

There is his Pre-Raphaelite manner, met with in "August," "The Masque of Queen Bersabe," "The King's Daughter," "The Sea Swallows," "The Weary Wedding," and a score others. In these Swinburne is as true a member of the brotherhood as Rossetti or Morris. He adopts the medieval convention, the simplicity and earnestness of the painters who came before Raphael, the insistence on detail, the naïveté of composition, the freshness of imagery, the spring light and—it must be confessed—the wavering artificiality of tone that are so characteristic of all who followed the ideals of Rossetti.

> The warm smell of the fruit was good
> To feed on

might have been written by Morris, as might, too:

> That August time it was delight
> To watch the red moons wane to white
> 'Twixt grey-seamed stems of apple-trees.

There is a clear critical manner far simpler than that of his usual prose criticism, in his sonnets on the Elizabethan dramatic poets. These are not particularly good as sonnets, or as criticism either. They are rhetorical, and with a curiously hard rhetoric. None of them is of higher intention than that on John Webster, but it undoes itself with hyperbole. That to Thomas Heywood is better, but there is more imagination in Lamb's phrase, "a prose Shakespeare," and truer praise of him than in all the fourteen lines of Swinburne.

There is the manner of his *Songs Before Sunrise* (1871). This manner is, in most of the poems, ardently rhetorical, and sometimes it abandons itself to a kind of orgiac fury. Even in "To Walt Whitman in America" he can work himself into such a state as to speak of

> carrion
> That makes time foul for us here,

the "here," I suppose, referring to all Europe, rather than to England alone. He goes on to say:

> Chains are here, and a prison,
> Kings, and subjects, and shame.
>
> . . . . .
>
> God is buried and dead to us.

One cannot help wondering how he would feel to-day about things in Europe, with Russia and Italy and Germany as they are, and most kings in the discard.

There is his manner in his Greek poems other than those inspired by Sappho, "Phædra," "At Eleusis," *Atalanta in Calydon*, and *Erechtheus* (1876). The blank verse he uses for the most part in these poems does not encourage him to the extravagances of some of his rhymed poems, and the feeling of kinship with Greek life he has while writing them seems, too, to hold him in check. Greek history and mythology, he tells Edmund Clarence Stedman in a letter of 1875, he feels "much nearer to us even yet than those of the Jews, alien from us in blood and character." Yet Swinburne himself has the abandon of the Oriental rather than the restraint of the Greek. In "Aholibah" he follows the story told us in "Ezekiel," but the love plaints have the words and the accent of "The Song of Solomon." In "A Litany," too, the language is Biblical, and "Super Flumina Babylonis" owes its being to Psalm CXXXVII. In another sense than Arnold meant it of Milton, Swinburne is, too, a compound of Hebraism and Hellenism. On the whole, the romantic triumphs over the classic in Swinburne. Just how much of this romanticism comes out of the East, however, is a problem. At times it seems as if Victor Hugo were its chief source, but at other times it is out of the Bible, with paraphrases startling in their closeness to the original.

There is a manner that Swinburne follows in his dramas, those of them that are chronicle histories, that is, and that are written in contempt of the conditions of the stage of his day. His first publication, in 1860, was of two plays, *The Queen Mother* and *Rosamund*. These are, of course, mere 'prentice-work. The one is about Catharine de' Medici, in whose court was brought up Mary Stuart, the heroine of three of his later dramas. The other was about that Rosamund who was the mistress of Henry II. All in all, Swinburne was to write a round dozen of plays, of varying merit, of varying length, of varying purposes. The two plays on Greek subjects are as much masques as plays. The trilogy on Mary Stuart, chronicle histories, is his most important work in drama. They are *Chastelard* (1865), *Bothwell* (1874), and *Mary Stuart* (1881).

In *Chastelard* Mary is presented in her first years in Scotland, still light-hearted despite impending tragedy. In *Bothwell*, she is presented in her infatuation with Bothwell, the analysis of her unhappy passion being as frank as that in the much more circumstantial study by Maurice Hewlett in *The Queen's Quair* (1904). In the play, however, Mary is not so broken, so demeaned, so muddied as she is in the novel. Her craftiness, her subtilty, her hardness, stand her in good stead with Bothwell, warring against her infatuation.

In *Mary Stuart* she is presented drifting to the scaffold. Her sentence is brought about, according to Swinburne, through the agency of Mary Beaton, who sends to Queen Elizabeth her mistress's treasonable letter, which Mary had written but had not despatched. Mary Beaton sent the letter because Queen Mary forgot a song her maid of honor sang to her was a song of Chastelard. Chastelard, the French minstrel who had loved Mary, was executed by the Queen's order because he had presumed too much and dared too much in his love of her. Mary Beaton had loved him in life and in memory all the years since his death, and she had not forgiven her mistress his death. The forgetting by Queen Mary of the song fired her long-smoldering hatred. Her accomplishment of her revenge after twenty-five years is one of the unforgettable exhibitions in literature of an unforgiving hate.

Locrine (1887) is based on what its maker calls a "wan legend" of early Britain. Its story, too, is of an unforgetting hate, the hate of Queen Guendolen against her husband who has preferred to her his mistress Estrild. It was played by the Elizabethan Stage Society in London in 1899, but, despite a sympathetic reception by a discriminating audience, it failed to win itself a place on the stage. Its writing is tortured by a scheme of changing rhymes.

Rosamund, Queen of the Lombards (1899) is still a third play of a woman's hate. It is the old story of the queen forced by her husband to drink out of a cup made from her father's skull. She tricks into her arms Almachildes, the lover of her maid of honor, and uses him to kill the husband who has made her dishonor her father. She drinks poison after Almachildes stabs Albovine. Like the earlier chronicle plays, *Rosamund, Queen of the Lombards* is written in blank verse, a blank verse the simplest and least adorned he ever wrote.

It is little likely that these plays, or their fellows, *Mariano Falerio* (1885), *The Sisters* (1892), or the incomplete *Duke of Gandia* (1908), will ever take a place on the stage. *Bothwell*, for instance, is a stupendous affair, an epic drama of one hundred and sixty thousand lines apportioned among sixty-four characters. To read it is a task comparable only to the conquest of *The Faery Queen*, or of *The Ring and the Book*, or of *The Dynasts*. My complete reading of it, a reading after many samplings, occupied me for four hours a day for eight successive days of a hot August. Finished at last, it left me with a visualization of Mary's court and courtiers such as I have gained from no other play or novel, whether by Scott or Schiller or Hewlett.

I would emphasize the fundamental brainwork of these plays about Mary, Queen of Scots. It is a quality too often overlooked in the consideration of Swinburne, as is also the great number of lines he has written that open vistas into regions of romance. There is so much of his writing, so huge a mass of it, and so much of that mass empty of all but sound, that human patience is exhausted in the attempt to read him. The needles are lost in the haystack. There are so many places in his writing that need rewriting, that he has not reworked as he should, to get out what is redundant, inconsequential, and, too often, mere filling. He has little of that right hardness of texture that poetry must have to endure.

Nor has Swinburne been given full credit for the power of characterization that is his. Three great queens, certainly, he has given us, Mary, Guendolen and Rosamund. All are fated, destined to sorrow and tragic ends, all have poise and an accent of greatness. For Swinburne at any rate, tragedy is not only the overthrow of the individual by fate, but the overthrow of something great. Rosamund is as inflexible in her purpose as Lady Macbeth, but she has a passionate loftiness of demeanor that is nearer that of the heroines of Greek tragedy. Rosamund feels that her revenge is holy, and her personal debasement in attaining it of no consequence at all in comparison to the end attained. There are none of the men of his plays limned so largely as these three women. King Mark, though, is clearly painted, Locrine a full-length portrait, and Bothwell given us in detail, in all his works and ways. Here is Iseult's husband:

> On the mid stairs, between the light and dark,
> Before the main tower's portal stood King Mark,
> Crowned: and his face was as the face of one
> Long time athirst and hungering for the sun
> In barren thrall of bitter bonds, who now
> Thinks here to feel its blessing on his brow.
> A swart lean man, but kinglike, still of guise,
> With black streaked beard and cold unquiet eyes,

Close-mouthed, gaunt-cheeked, wan as a morning moon,
Though hardly time on his worn hair had strewn
The thin first ashes from a sparing hand:
Yet little fire there burnt upon the brand,
And way-worn seemed he with life's wayfaring.

There is yet another manner in Swinburne, his manner when
he relaxes and deigns to be familiar, to play, to fuss with little
things. It is in such verses that his words for words sake, for filling, for padding, are most easily discernible. The lines "To a Cat,"
which run to eleven stanzas, have stuff in them for no more than
five, and would be all the better for being reduced to three.
Stanzas 1, 2, 3, 8, and 9 exhaust what he has to say, and the last
two really develop a thought additional to that of the first three.
There are "soft places" in stanzas 1 and 2, the "love's lustrous
meed" in stanza 1 being impossible of justification, mere filling.
It is pleasant, of course, to see the little gentleman unbending, and
to find him writing with his eye on the object:

> Stately, kindly, lordly friend,
>   Condescend
> Here to sit by me and turn
> Glorious eyes that smile and burn,
> Golden eyes, love's lustrous meed,
> On the golden page I read.

Stanza 3 is wholly of good texture:

> Dogs may fawn on all and some
>   As they come;
> You, a friend of loftier mind,
> Answer friends alone in kind.
> Just your foot upon my hand
> Softly bids it understand.

That last couplet is the little thing perfectly done, and revelation,
too, if of a little kind.

All of these manners owe a good deal of their qualities to the subject material. Yet Swinburne has no distinct manner when he writes of the sea, of which he writes more than of anything out-of-doors. He writes of the sea, indeed, in most of the manners I have instanced, but always exultantly. "For song I have loved with second love," he says in "The Garden of Cymodoce," "but thee, Thee first, thee, mother." The onset of this poem has the out-at-sea quality of the Channel island of Sark that inspired it:

> Sea, and bright wind, and heaven of ardent air,
> More dear than all things earthborn.

Her association with Lesbos, with its encircling sea and white cliffs, is one of the reasons he so admires Sappho.

A strong swimmer and sure-footed climber of cliffs, the sea and its shore gave him much of the delight of his life. It was perhaps at his father's place on the Isle of Wight that he knew best the meeting of sea and land, but his Northumbrian ancestry inclined him to make more, sentimentally, of the coast near his grand-father's seat at Capheaton. A good rider, Swinburne loved the moors along the sea, where he had had many a sharp gallop. *The Tale of Balen* (1896) gave him a chance to revel in description of the north country, for it was there, along the Tyne, that Sir Balen grew to manhood. He pictures it in winter, under "the bright Northumbrian snows." He pictures it "in linden-time," when

> the heart is high
> For pride of summer passing by.

One wonders, whether it was with Swinburne, when he lay dying of pneumonia in Putney, as it was with his knight who again

> saw the moorland shine,
> The rioting rapids of the Tyne,
> The woods, the cliffs, the sea?

The sea, certainly, must have been before his mind's eye to the end. He had sought it again and again, all his life long, and it was always instant to him, even in the London suburb to which Watts-

Dunton restricted him for most of the year. Swinburne knew every mood of the sea, and he caught mood on mood in his verse:

> Came a light wind fast hardening forth of the east
> And blackening till its might had marred the skies;
> And the sea thrilled as with heart-sundering sighs
> One after one drawn, with each breath it drew,
> And the green hardened into iron blue,
> And the soft light went out of all its face.

The South Downs along the Channel he loved, as he loved the cliffs of Northumberland, but more than cliffs or downs he loved the sea below them:

> And on the lip's edge of the down,
> Here where the bent-grass burns to brown
>   In the dry sea-wind, and the heath
> Crawls to the cliffside and looks down
>   I watch, and hear beneath
>   The low tide breathe.

At times, when he writes about the sea, it is with echoes of the Bible in his ears, and in the very intonation that Kipling caught from him:

> Will ye bridle the deep sea with reins, will ye chasten the high sea with rods?
> Will ye take her to chain her with chains, who is older than all ye Gods?
> All ye as a wind shall go by, as a fire shall ye pass and be past;
> Ye are Gods, and behold, ye shall die, and the waves be upon you at last.

On another note again, and reverberant with echoes from Milton, is this sea-piece:

> And the night spake, and thundered on the sea,
> Ravening aloud for ruin of lives; and all
> The bastions of the main cliff's northward wall

> Rang response out from all their deepening length,
> As the east wind girded up his godlike strength
> And hurled in hard against that high-towered hold
> The fleeces of the flock that knows no fold,
> The rent white shreds of shattering storm.

Next to the sea, Swinburne loved poetry, and the great poets.
The names of Sappho and Catullus, Shakespeare and Marlowe,
Shelley and Hugo are always on his lips. There are many references to other poets, Chaucer, Milton, and Baudelaire for three,
and he has a kind word for little people, like Sydney Dobell. In
the "dedicatory epistle" to Theodore Watts-Dunton prefixed to
his *Collected Poems* (1904), Swinburne writes: "The half-brained
creature to whom books are other than living things may see with
the eyes of a bat and draw with the fingers of a mole his dullard's
distinction between books and life: those who live the fuller life
of a higher animal than he know that books are to poets as much
part of that life as pictures to painters or as music is to musicians."
His practice accords with his preaching. He has written more lines
that take as their point of departure the verses or lives of other
poets than any English poet, though there are not so many of the
lines sound criticism as of the critical lines of Sir William Watson.
    What Swinburne was to himself is revealed in what he reveals
of Tristram as poet. After using the phrase "warm wine of amorous words," which fits so closely so much of his own writing, Swinburne goes on to say of Tristram:

> Full well he wist all subtle ways of song,
> And in his soul the secret eye was strong
> That burns in meditation, till bright words
> Break flamelike forth as notes from fledgling birds
> That feel the soul speak through them of the spring.

These, too, are words equally applicable to himself. In "A Ballad
of Life" his lady may be Lucrezia Borgia, but it is to one trans-
figured to his muse that he refers when he writes:

> My lady is perfect, and transfigureth
> All sin and sorrow and death.

That, at any rate, was the way he felt, that poetry could transfigure Lust and Shame and Fear, and make them admirable.

So great was his preoccupation with the poets who have written of England that he can hardly see the countryside with his own eyes. Thus when he would describe a country road in late spring when the lime is in blossom, he is more intent on Chaucer than on the bit of landscape he remembers. "Each year," he writes, "Each year that England clothes herself with May She takes thy likeness on her."

Swinburne knows his flowering plants fairly well, as he does his flowering trees. He sets sundew before you as you have seen it in a score of swamps when he addresses it as "O red-lipped mouth of marsh-flower," though it is, of course, the leaf and not the flower to which he refers. He does not describe the diminutive plant, however, for its own sake, but to say "I have a secret halved with thee," his meeting with his beloved where the sundew grew. He gives you the very essence of the scent of white lauristine when he calls it "This flower that smells of honey and the sea." He gives you the tang of remembered woodland in:

> The savour and the shade of oldworld pine-forests
> Where the wet hill-winds weep.

He has not, however, the detailed knowledge of out-of-doors of a Tennyson or a Wordsworth.

In a letter to Edmund Clarence Stedman Swinburne gives something of his belief as to what poetry is. Speaking of Bryant's "Thanatopsis" and Lowell's "Commemoration Ode" he says: "I cannot say that either of them leaves in my ear the echo of a single note of song. It is excellent good speech, but if given us as song its first and last duty is to sing. The one is most august meditation, the other a noble expression of deep and grave patriotic feeling on a supreme national occasion; but the thing more necessary, though it may be less noble than these, is the pulse, the fire, the passion of music—the quality of a singer, not of a solitary philosopher or a patriotic orator. Now, when Whitman is not speaking bad prose he sings well. . . . It is a poor thing to have nothing but melody, and be unable to rise above it into harmony, but one or the other, the less if not the greater, you must have."

Again, in a later letter to Stedman Swinburne writes: "The fusion of lyric with dramatic form gives the highest type of poetry I know." It was this fusion that makes the earlier parts of *Tristram of Lyonesse* so great. In "The Sailing of the Swallow" and "The Queen's Pleasance," what we have is really dramatic situation presented lyrically. The two poems are narrative only in form. The scenes of the storm and of the fated pledging of the lovers are nobly passionate. Equally passionate are the scenes of the lovers' abandon in their season of freedom in the forest. There is no love poetry more forthright than this in Victorian times, but it is free from offense. What might have seemed only a depicting of lust is lifted into a description of great passion by the intensity of the poet's feeling.

After "The Queen's Pleasance" the poem lessens in intensity, and it gutters out unconsequentially in the end. The death scene of the fated lovers falls far short of its presentation in both Arnold and Binyon, and comes to a close of unpardonable banality. The rebelliousness of Swinburne, his revolt against the conventions, his outspokenness on topics Mrs. Grundy disapproves, have all been traced to his paternal grandfather. From all his ancestry, however, he inherited a very real patriotism, at which those who regarded his sympathy with republicanism as a form of cosmopolitanism were very much surprised. You didn't really have to scratch him very deep to discover John Bull. He was English, English Conservative, in many of his prejudices and points of view. He was not always aware of England as a nation, as one of the great powers, but when he was so aware of it no Tory of them all could be more patriotic. Here is the proof of this insular patriotism:

> Calm as she stands alone, what nation
> Hath lacked an alms from English hands?
> What exiles from what stricken lands
> Have lacked the shelter of the station
> Where higher than all she stands?

This, of course, is even further from poetry than the fulminations of *Songs Before Sunrise*. No man was ever of qualifications further from those necessary to a laureate than Swinburne. He is as poor in praise of English science as in praise of English bounty. He is ill at ease, indeed, when he questions:

> What Newton's might could not make clear
> Hath Darwin's might not made?

Such philosophy of life as there is in Swinburne is that of a world-wearied man. Two gifts only, he tells us in "Félise," God

> has given us yet,
> Though sad things stay and glad things fly;
> Two gifts he has given us, to forget
> All glad and sad things that go by,
> And then to die.

If there is any good on earth it is love, of what sort this speaks plainly enough:

> Let come what will, there is one thing worth,
> To have had fair love in the life on earth:
> To have held love safe till the day grew night
> While skies had color and lips were red.

And yet love is not wholly good:

> I have loved overmuch in my life. . . .
> Too soon did I love it, and lost life's rose; and I cared not for glory's!
> Only the blossoms of sleep and of pleasure were mixed in my hair.
> Was it myrtle or poppy thy garland was woven with, O my Dolores?
> Was it pallor of slumber, or blush as of blood that I found in thee fair?

Sounding, as this does, of the satiety of the voluptuary, it is at odds with the inexhaustible energy of the man. This was dominantly, perhaps, an energy of the emotions, of the nerves, rather than of the intellect, but there was intellectual energy in him, too. The great trilogy of Mary Stuart proves that, and many a flash in the poems. He cultivated his senses; he allowed his powers of analysis to be dormant; he explored life very little; all the intellectual side of him was subordinated to his feelings and his urge toward sounding rhythms.

Perhaps, after all, Swinburne knew best what brought out what he had to give English poetry, incomparable rhythms and moments of glamorous delight.

The proof of the greatness of Swinburne lies in this: that you may put his name and your memory of his verses beside the names and your memory of their verses of the great men of English poetry, and feel sure that he holds his own with them, with what they have written. His "August" is not so great a poem as "To Autumn" of Keats, but its beauty is a real beauty, and a great beauty. "The Garden of Proserpine" is not so surely a great poem as "The Lotus Eaters" of Tennyson, but it is not lessened by comparison with "The Lotus Eaters." "On the Eve of Revolution" has not the thunders of "Avenge, O Lord, Thy slaughtered saints," but it storms along mightily for all that. Keats and Tennyson and Milton are masters of harmonies, but the music of no one of them is more overpowering than the music of Swinburne. His music remains, when all has been said, his greatest and distinguishing gift. So strange and full of wonder is this music when you first hear it, that you can hardly believe it is your childhood's language out of which it is made. For his music alone he would have place among the great, even if he had created no Guendolen, or Rosamund, or Mary; if he had not fashioned "The Sailing of the Swallow" and "The Queen's Pleasance"; even if he had not written twenty lines as memorable as "They have the night, who had like us the day."

CHAPTER XIII

Of Fitzgerald and the East

"AND it's all deuced pleasant." So Edward Fitzgerald (1809-1883) wrote to Bernard Barton from Bedford on July 24, 1839, of the place at which he was staying on the edge of town, and of the time he was having there. The rustle of poplars was in his ears, a fishing expedition only half an hour off, and the prospect after that of "tea in a pot-house," and a good walk home. In a score places else in his letters a similar contentment is voiced, but it is not always summed up in a phrase, as it is here: "And it's all deuced pleasant." So it might be written of his *Rubaiyat* (1859), at least outwardly; so it might be written of his correspondence; so it might be written of his life in toto.

Edward Fitzgerald had an even greater genius for friendship than Charles Lamb. Many elements went to the make-up of this genius for friendship. Luck in his birth was one. He came of good Irish stock, with an Earl of Kildare among his ancestors, and geniality and an interest in his fellows as part of his inheritance. Means were another element. He had the wherewithal to be nice to friends and neighbors.

School-fellows that counted were another element. With him, at Bury St. Edmunds, were James Spedding, who was to be the biographer of Bacon; W. Bodham Donne, already the classical scholar in the making; and J. M. Kemble, the son of Charles Kemble, and the brother of Fanny Kemble, one of Fitzgerald's correspondents of later years. J. M. Kemble lived to become, not an actor like his father and sister, but "Anglo-Saxon Kemble." College mates as congenial and as sharpening to his wits and as helpful to his development added, too, to his training for friendship. Two of them, indeed, were of the school group, Spedding and Kemble. With Fitzgerald at Cambridge were also Monckton Milnes; Frank Edgeworth, the brother of Maria, the novelist; and Thackeray. The Tennysons, Charles, Frederick, and Alfred, were at Cambridge while Fitzgerald was there, but it was later that they became, all three, intimate friends of his. It is curious to find Fitzgerald writing years afterwards of feeling, in the presence of Alfred, "a sense of depression at times from the overshadowing of a so much more lofty intellect than my own." He did not so feel about Thackeray, or about Carlyle, both of whom the world holds men of loftier intellect than Alfred Tennyson.

I have written of Fitzgerald's friends because they were so large a part of his life, and because his letters to them are, after his *Omar Khayyam,* his greatest contribution to literature. W. Kenworthy Browne, of Bedford, was another of his intimates; and Bernard Barton, the Quaker poet, and the Rev. George Crabbe, son of Crabbe the poet, his neighbors at Woodbridge. Major Edward Moor, another neighbor, was a retired East Indian, who interested Fitzgerald in the East even before he met Professor Cowell and took up the reading of Persian. Moor was the author of *Oriental Fragments,* which Fitzgerald calls "an almost worthless book." It was the man, not the writer, who mattered to him. From a boy Fitzgerald had been fond of the old man, his talk of the East, and his Shiraz wine, carefully preserved from his Asian days.

Fitzgerald's life in the flat Suffolk of the seacoast was a continual delight to him. Here he "heard the Language of Queen Elizabeth's, or King Harry's Court . . . better a great deal than that spoken in London Societies, whether Fashionable or Literary: and the homely strength of which has made Shakespeare, Dryden, South and Swift what they could not have been without it."

Yet Fitzgerald found picturesque speech in London, too: "Now the black Trees in the Regent's Park opposite are beginning to show green Buds; and Men come by with great baskets of Flowers: Primroses, Hepaticas, Crocuses, Great Daisies, etc., calling as they go 'Growing, Growing! All the Glory going!' "

All that Fitzgerald wrote about was of the very texture of his life, a part of his daily living. The aconites that bloomed in February in his garden, the roses that bloomed there in May and June, his red-legged doves that Tennyson celebrated, his books, his yachting with "Posh," his singing of old songs, his memories of Madame Vestris, his translations, and his writing of all sorts, are at one in his letters with gossip about neighbors and friends. So he was in youth, and so he was in age. In 1839 he wrote to John Allen from Geldstone Hall, Beccles, in North Suffolk: "Here I live with tolerable content: perhaps with as much as most people arrive at, and what if one were properly grateful one would perhaps call perfect happiness. Here is a glorious sunshiny day: all the morning I read about Nero in Tacitus lying at full length on a bench in the garden: a nightingale singing, and some red anemones eyeing the sun manfully not far off. A funny mixture all this: Nero, and the delicacy of Spring: all very human however. Then at half-past one lunch on Cambridge cream cheese: then a ride over hill and dale: then spudding up some weeds from the grass: and then coming in, I sit down to write to you, my sister winding red worsted from the back of a chair, and the most delightful little girl in the world chattering incessantly. So runs the world away. You think I live in Epicurean ease: but this happens to be a jolly day: one isn't always well, or tolerably good, the weather is not always clear, nor nightingales singing, nor Tacitus full of pleasant atrocity. But such as life is, I believe I have got hold of a good end of it."

It was this sort of living that made Carlyle think Fitzgerald little more than an idler. The strenuous sage wrote to Charles Eliot Norton of Fitzgerald's "innocent *far niente* life." Now, in the little more than half-century that has passed since Carlyle's letter was written, there are some of us wondering if not only the *Rubaiyat* but the *Letters* have not an equal chance of survival with *The French Revolution* and *Cromwell*. It is difficult for the men of the Carlyle type of mind, for the weighty-thoughted and seriously intentioned people, to realize that it is beauty and joy that keep writing alive, and dear to men, and sought after and savorsome to the palate, and not the higher purposes and the higher morality.

Writing to Cowell, his mentor in all things Spanish and Persian, and his adviser in many things else, on May 7, 1857, of Omar and Æschylus, with both of whom he was then working, Fitzgerald says: "I think I shall become a bore . . . by all this Translation: but it amuses me without any labour, and I really think I have the faculty of making some things readable which others have hitherto left unreadable." A little later we have a delightful picture of Fitzgerald at the work of translation out-of-doors. He was never so happy as when lolling about with a book in sunny weather.

"When in Bedfordshire I put away almost all Books except Omar Khayyam!, which I could not help looking over in a Paddock covered with Buttercups and brushed by a delicious Breeze, while a dainty racing Filly of W. Browne's came startling up to wonder and snuff about me. . . . You would be sorry, too, to think that Omar breathes a sort of Consolation to me! Poor Fellow; I think of him, and Oliver Basselin, and Anacreon; lighter Shadows among the Shades, perhaps, over which Lucretius presides so grimly."

Under a later date, July 1, in this same letter, he writes what he well might have put in a quatrain:

"June over! A thing I think of with Omar-like Sorrow. And the Roses here are blowing—and going—as abundantly as even in Persia."

By November of 1858 Fitzgerald is speaking to Cowell of his *Omar* as an "Epicurean Eclogue in a Persian Garden." He justifies his freedom of adaptation by saying: "But at all Cost a Thing must live; with a Transfusion of one's own worse Life if one can't retain the Original's better. Better a live Sparrow than a stuffed Eagle."

When the *Rubaiyat of Omar Khayyam* was finally published by Quaritch in 1859 no author's name appeared on the title-page. The book won scant response from reviewers or public, and it was finally disposed of only when it was put into a penny bin before Quaritch's door. Rossetti and Swinburne were among those who bought copies, led to the bin by Whitley Stokes, the Irish scholar. These men did what they could for the book, but it could be helped along only to the slowest sort of a recognition. There was a reprinting in 1862, but no second edition until 1868. The *Rubaiyat* was hardly more warmly welcomed in its second edition than in its first. In America Charles Eliot Norton gave it the pleasantest sort of a review, and began an appreciation of it here that has become as great as that aroused in England. *Omar Khayyam* had its influence on the poets from its first publication, but it never made Fitzgerald a celebrity in his life-time. That he became after his death, with a constantly increasing sale of the *Rubaiyat,* and the formation of Omar Khayyam Clubs in England (1892) and in America (1900). It is curious that Fitzgerald should be the other poet of his generation than Browning to be honored by a society devoted to his praise. There was an antipathy between the two, shared in equally by both. "In Browning," writes Fitzgerald, "I could see little but Cockney Sublime, Cockney Energy, etc." Browning responded in kind, and even after Fitzgerald's death he took occasion to speak of the "vague" and "slipshod" translation his *bête noire* had made of Æschylus.

Despite the perfect clarity of it all, it is not possible to take quickly to heart and mind and inner consciousness all the meaning, all the beauty, all the desperate pathos of the *Rubaiyat*. It is, indeed, so close-packed with all sorts of good things that it takes many readings for you to realize what a reading of life it is, what a collection of images, what a treasure-house of finely phrased lines.

In intent gnomic poetry, it breaks into lyricism again and again. On the whole, though, the gnomic element dominates. When you have said that, you have said the *Rubaiyat* does not attempt to be the highest sort of poetry. Many of its excellences, indeed, are of the deliberately low-flighted sort preferred by the eighteenth century. Here is a couplet intentionally Popean:

> One thing is certain and the rest is Lies;
> The Flower that once has blown for ever dies.

And here a single line of like sort:

> Unborn To-morrow and dead Yesterday.

Of his own time, and destined, I had almost dared to say, for all time, is that marvelous phrase of "And then and then came Spring." Remember its like in Shelley, and you will still say it is a fellow of that. Fitzgerald's line has uncertainty and hesitation in it; it has pain in it, the pain that is so close to rapture; and it has longing, and heart's cry:

> And then and then came Spring, and Rose-in-hand
> My thread-bare Penitence apieces tore.

There is passion, and a kind of despair in:

> Ah Love! could you and I with Him conspire
> To grasp this sorry Scheme of Things entire,
> Would not we shatter it to bits—and then
> Remould it nearer to the Heart's desire!

There are wine and woman and song perfectly wedded in quatrain XII, the best known of all the *Rubaiyat*, and for two generations now the summing-up of heart's desire for the literary-minded youth of our race:

> A Book of Verses underneath the Bough,
> A Jug of Wine, a Loaf of Bread—and Thou
> Beside me singing in the Wilderness—
> Oh, Wilderness were Paradise enow!

There is lyricism there, and out-of-doors, and food, and love, and the leisure which makes all these good things even better than their normal selves. There is here celebration of that plain living and high thinking which Fitzgerald held to be the best of life—

that is from one point of view there is such celebration. From another, this quatrain may be held the very reverse of the code of
Concord, and, instead, the celebration of plain thinking and high
living. In interpretation, as in other matters, it may be, as Fitzgerald says, that "A Hair perhaps divides the False and True."

There was a finer image in the first version of *Omar* that Fitzgerald printed in 1859 than in any of its successors of 1868, 1872,
and 1879. It is that of the very first quatrain, the image of morning throwing the stone in "the Bowl of Night":

> Awake! for Morning in the Bowl of Night
> Has flung the Stone that puts the Stars to Flight:
> And Lo! the Hunter of the East has caught
> The Sultan's Turret in a Noose of Light.

That is more arresting than the more familiar lines:

> Wake! For the Sun, who scatter'd into flight
> The Stars before him from the Field of Night,
> Drives Night along with them from Heav'n and strikes
> The Sultan's Turret with a Shaft of Light.

There is here just an inkling of the freedom of adaptation
of his original that Fitzgerald allowed himself. There has been
entirely too much writing, though, about the relation of Omar the
Persian poet to Fitzgerald the English poet. As a matter of fact
Fitzgerald, in the *Rubaiyat*, has now transferred the Persian faithfully into English; now followed a suggestion in the Persian,
made it, in Hewlett's phrase, the springboard from which he
leaped; now done mosaic work from several originals; now made
entirely new poems for which no suggestion even is to be found
in the original. Those who are curious in the matter can consult
editions in which literal translation from the Persian is put over
against Fitzgerald's version. That of Edward Heron-Allen is the
best. The relation of Omar and Fitzgerald is no more important than that of the Henry plays of Shakespeare and their originals, or of Burns's "O my luve is like a red, red rose" and its

originals. The finished poem of Fitzgerald is what matters, and it matters a great deal.

There are few other four hundred and four lines of an English poet of a greater wholeness of good tissue. There are no other four hundred and four lines of an English minor poet that have meant more to the last half-century than these four hundred and four lines. There were three hundred lines, or seventy-five quatrains, in the first edition of 1859; four hundred and forty lines, or one hundred and ten quatrains, in the second edition of 1868; and four hundred and four lines, or one hundred and one quatrains, alike in the third edition of 1872, and in the fourth edition of 1879.

It is not, I think, fanciful to assume that the hundred and one quatrains Fitzgerald chose for the final form of the *Rubaiyat* have a relation to the thousand and one stories of *The Arabian Nights*. There are many more quatrains assigned to Omar Khayyam in existence, perhaps a thousand and one. There may not have been quite so many known at the time of Fitzgerald's translation, but he could have greatly enlarged his chosen number had he wished to.

He was a great believer in exclusion, in condensation, in all forms of brevity. He advised Bernard Barton and Frederick Tennyson, poets his friends, to cut down the number of verses they had at hand to print for collections of their poems. He tried his hand at abridging *Clarissa Harlow* of Richardson, and certain tales of Crabbe he reduced considerably for his *Readings in Crabbe* (1879).

Their brevity and compression are virtues of the *Rubaiyat*. Nearly each quatrain is a creation in little itself. Now and then the thought, and less often the sentence structure, carries over from one quatrain to another. Quatrains XXVII-XXX make a poem of four stanzas on the uselessness of philosophers, and there is a close relationship running through nine stanzas in which figures symbolism of pots and potters.

There are certain recurrent themes that hold the whole

Rubaiyat together. The dominant one is that of the brevity of life, the dropping of rose-leaves, the quick passing of youth and spring and all that is good. Again and again the burden returns. Thus we meet it first:

> You know how little while we have to stay,
> And, once departed, may return no more.

Thus it recurs:

> The Bird of Time has but a little way
> To flutter—and the Bird is on the Wing.

And thus:

> The Wine of Life keeps oozing drop by drop,
> The Leaves of Life keep falling one by one.

And thus:

> Ah, make the most of what we yet may spend,
> Before we too into the Dust descend.

And thus:

> I came like Water, and like Wind I go.

The old doctrine of "eat, drink, and be merry" sounds next oftenest in Fitzgerald. It follows naturally on his plaint over the brevity of life. What right the Persian scholars have to interpret the references to Wine and the Grape as spiritual things in Omar himself, I do not know, but just about such right, I suspect, as the Biblical scholars have to interpret spiritually the "Song of Solomon." There is no symbolism of this sort in Fitzgerald. He means Wine when he says Wine. There is no more uncertainty about that than about the fact that he liked his grog hot. He did not believe Omar spoke symbolically about Wine. Cowell did so believe, as became so pious a man. The two disputed much over this and allied matters as they worked together over the Persian. Fitzgerald means just what Herrick would have meant by the words had he, and not Fitzgerald written:

> Better be jocund with the fruitful Grape
> Than sadden after none, or bitter, fruit.

The Grape, Fitzgerald holds, is "the sovereign Alchemist" who can

> in a trice
> Life's leaden metal into Gold transmute.

Most forthright is the command:

> Drink! for you know not whence you came, nor why:
> Drink! for you know not why you go, nor where.

There are other thoughts and realizations, of the inevitability of fate for one, the inability of man to change what has happened. So it sounds, slow as a funeral bell, and as final:

> The Moving Finger writes; and, having writ,
> Moves on: nor all your Piety nor Wit
> Shall lure it back to cancel half a Line,
> Nor all your Tears wash out a Word of it.

Many aspects of mortality, indeed, are instant to Fitzgerald's thought. He fancies:

> that never blows so red
> The Rose as where some buried Cæsar bled.

So, too, it seems to Masefield, who gives utterance to the thought in his sonnets, obsessed by the beauty of roses and by the constant nearness of death.

There is some of the usual paraphernalia of Persian poetry in the *Rubaiyat*, rose-gardens, Sultans, caravans, deserts, and "cypress-slender ministers of wine," but there is little sumptuousness.

> The Seas that mourn
> In flowing Purple

has few parallels in Fitzgerald anywhere. He felt somewhat as did the eighteenth century, and as did his friend Thackeray,

toward excess of any kind. There is a peacock in *The Bird Parlia-*
ment (1889), but none in the *Rubaiyat,* and only one tulip there,
which is, next to pomegranate and peacock, the commonest decorative motive in Persian art.

A large part of the effect of Fitzgerald comes from the putting
by him of one sort of thing over against another, from parallels,
comparisons, contrasts, opposites. Such are of the very nature of
the epigram. It would be wrong, though, to consider the *Rubaiyat*
as nothing more than a series of epigrams. Epigrams are generally
closely allied to wit; they are offspring of the head. There is too
much heart in the quatrains for them to be written down only as
epigrams. Head and heart are at one in them.

In these couples, or opposites, or contrasts of Fitzgerald, it is
usually the weaker of the two, the more human, the more everyday that he approves, not saint but sinner, not soul but body, not
temple but tavern. So it is he makes his choice between day and
night, wine and water, sweet and bitter, rose-garden and desert,
mirth and sorrow, here and there, now and to-morrow, earth and
heaven, summer and winter, sun and rain, eating and fasting,
known and unknown, life and death. He approves, of course, the
first of each pair, day, wine, sweet, rose-garden, mirth, here, now,
earth, summer, sun, eating, known, life.

There are those who believe such a preference alien to the
English mind. It is not alien to the English mind, or to the American mind. It is just common human the world over. Nor can this
attitude be gotten around by saying that Fitzgerald had the Irish
point of view. He had not. He always spoke of himself as a
"Paddy," but he was not tolerant of the weaknesses of "Paddy."
It is true, of course, that there are certain affinities between the
Irish mind and the Eastern mind, affinities perhaps unduly stressed
because of the old pseudo-etymology that made Erin and Iran the
same word. It is just a natural weakness of the flesh that leads to
such preference.

Let it not be forgotten that there was talk in America, from
early days, of Persian seers and poets, as well as of poets and seers

from further East. This talk was nowhere more prevalent than in Concord by Musketaquid, among a stock almost wholly English. Emerson the prophet paid heed to Zoroaster, and Emerson the poet wrote verses that were appreciative of Saadi and Hafiz. More than that, the Epicurean Persians won him to moods not unlike their own. In the verses "To J. W." Emerson even adjures us to "Hear what wine and roses say." Such a sentiment in a Puritan is surprising only to those who do not realize that being a Puritan does not necessarily exclude from life any of "the just delights of the body."

Even earlier than Emerson the interest aroused by Sir William Jones's translation of Hafiz (1770), and by his writing about Eastern literature, had led to compositions in English in what was thought to be the Persian manner, or manners akin to it, Indian or what not. *Lalla Rookh* (1817) of Moore was the most popular of these, but Mangan tried his hand, too, at various Eastern manners, saying bitterly that the public preferred his Hafiz to his Mangan. The vogue of Eastern themes had lessened somewhat by the mid-nineteenth century, when Fitzgerald was busy with the Persian poets. Yet Matthew Arnold's *Poems* of 1853 contained his "Sohrab and Rustum," from the *Shah-Nameh* of Firdusi. It was in the seventies that Sir Edwin Arnold began his interpretations of Eastern life and thought. *The Light of Asia*, appearing in 1879, gave his verse a wide currency, coming as it did when the English-speaking world was having one of its periodic fits of Indomania.

Sir Edwin Arnold's *With Sa'di in the Garden* (1888) is just as much a re-creation of a Persian poet as Fitzgerald's *Omar Khayyam*, but nothing more than facile stuff. Nor is *The Kasidah of Haji Abdu-El-Yezdi* (1880) of much better quality. It is all Burton's own, a compound of the Eastern life Sir Francis knew so well, set to the usual accompaniment of camel bells and desert glow.

It is the Arab, too, that Wilfred Scawen Blunt celebrates, both in his own verse and in his translations. *The Seven Golden Odes of Pagan Arabia* (1903) is his triumph in its catching of the spirit of pre-Mohammedan Bedouins. Sir Alfred Lyall has, too, his little niche for *Verses Written in India* (1889).

The East came to Yeats and "A. E." not only directly, through the translations and talk of Charles Johnston, but indirectly, through Emerson. Xenophon in the schools kept Persia before the imagination of English youth, as did the Bible in Church the Semitic East. It is not strange, then, to find the East making so decided an appeal to Lawrence Binyon, and James Elroy Flecker and Lascelles Abercrombie. *Porphyrion* (1898), and *Hassan* (1922), and "Vashti" (1912) must all be placed high in the accomplishment of the poets.

It is Dunsany, however, who has given us, of all poets since Fitzgerald, the most memorable rendering of the East. Dunsany has used the East for his own ends even more freely than Fitzgerald. It is as an English poem inspired by the poetry of an old Persian that the *Rubaiyat* takes its place. It is as an Englishman's dream of beauty that we welcome the fantastic world of Dunsany, its landscapes and ruined cities and strange figures. Its colors are warmly Oriental, more glowing than the hues of rose and tulip, purple sea and flashing sun, rising moon and scattered stars, that are woven together into the quieter tapestry of Fitzgerald.

All the range of Islam, from Morocco on the Atlantic, eastward through Persia and India and Indo-China, to the Malay lands in the Pacific, affords material to "Laurence Hope." There are only faint echoes of Fitzgerald in her work, and the loose structure and cheap sentiment of her verse are far from his careful art and deep sense of the tears of things. The admirers of Tagore resent comparison of their idol with Fitzgerald. Fitzgerald, they say, is hardly even a shadow of a Sufi. Fitzgerald is hopelessly Western, materialistic, of the earth. It remains a fact, however, that without Fitzgerald to break the way for it, all English poetry of the East would have come into its own more slowly, even the spiritual poetry of Tagore.

Sarojini Naidu calls one of her volumes *The Bird of Time* (1912). That alone shows that she, or her literary advisers, went to school to Fitzgerald. I can see little relation of her art to his, though she can write of "The rapture of your Sufi wine," and call certain of her verses "From the Persian." Nor do I find much of *Omar Khayyam* in the delicate verses of Toru Dutt a generation earlier. Just as the West has attracted the East, bringing Mrs. Naidu and Tagore to England, so the East has called poets from Great Britain. The verse of James H. Cousins has suffered a change since he went to India in 1918. "A. E." had led him to Eastern wisdom in Dublin, but it was not until he became resident in India that his verse took on Eastern color. *Above the Rainbow* (1926) has something of the lift that sight of the Himalayas gave to his heart.

A book, then, might be written of the influence of Fitzgerald on the poetry in English of late Victorian and Neo-Georgian times. From Swinburne to Kipling, from Kipling to Flecker, it is all pervasive. You note the influence in writers of all groups, in such decadents as Symons and Dowson, as well as in the poets of Empire. It is at times the influence of the thought of the *Rubaiyat*, its philosophy of life, its Epicureanism, and at times the influence of its Eastern color and images. There is an element of travesty in "The Rupaiyat of Omar Kal'vin," but Kipling in other poems reveals that he has studied Fitzgerald as carefully as he has studied Fitzgerald's foe, Browning. There are no English-speaking lands, indeed, but show the influence of Fitzgerald. You will find it potent in writers, Australian, Indian, South African, American. With us in America, indeed, *Omar Khayyam* is part of the man in the street. Drummer and cowboy and college professor have the hundred and one quatrains by heart. Schoolboy, advertising writer, and minister quote it to their several purposes.

Omar Khayyam is one of the miracles of English literature. That is, it is a work of art of high power written by a man who has, in that department of art, poetry, written no other book, and for that matter no other single poem, of high power. It is true, of course, that as a letter-writer Fitzgerald takes a first place, a place by Lamb and Cowper. There are, too, passages in the letters of

Fitzgerald that are lyrical, with a good deal of the lift of poetry. Yet even these best passages are not of the perfection of form, the inevitability of phrase, the heart's-cry of the *Rubaiyat*.

It is easy to say that Fitzgerald made a success of the adaptation of Omar because he was in sympathy with his original. That he was in sympathy with Omar is true, but he was just as sympathetic, through other sides of his nature, with Calderón and Æschylus and Sophocles, plays of all of whom he adapted. Yet neither *Six Dramas of Calderón* (1853), nor *Two Dramas from Calderón* (1865), was a success; nor the *Agamemnon* (1865) from Æschylus, nor *The Downfall and Death of King Œdipus* (1880-1881) from Sophocles.

The *Rubaiyat* is a miracle on a par with the miracle of Walton's *Compleat Angler*, of White's *Natural History of Selborne*, of Clare's asylum poems. That is, it is the work of a man who was slow coming to any power at all in literature, who was not from his youth destined for success in literature, who was not looked upon by those who knew him as sure, by the quality of him, to one day amount to something as a writer, who suddenly achieved by a visitation of power that can only be described as miraculous.

The greatest miracle of all in English literature is, of course, the King James Bible. That, however, was made what it is by a visitation of style to a group of men not studied writers with a life-long intention to find beauty. The Bible, too, was translated at a time when use had not worn our language thin, or strait-jacketed it into phrases too readily serviceable for any one of a group of allied meanings. A part of the picturesqueness of the Bible derives from the picturesqueness of the everyday speech of the time of its translation.

There is no parallel, of course, between the case of the Bible and the case of Fitzgerald. It is true that, though born and brought up in England as he was and never long out of it, Fitzgerald must have heard something of the picturesqueness of Irish speech from his father and mother, Irish-born both of them. It is true, too, that, later in life, he became very much interested in the speech of the fishermen he met along the Suffolk coast, and sailed with on the German Ocean. Yet he did not use the picturesqueness of Irish English, or the picturesqueness of sea-faring English, in his writing. The diction and phrasing of his writing, its style in all its phases, is from books; or from the talk of cultivated people. It harks back to the eighteenth century in its clarity and ease and urbanity. There is nothing archaic, though, about it, as there is nothing of the spasmodic, or of the Wardour Street, or of the pseudo-classical.

Fitzgerald was of a very individual cast of mind, with a style as individual. He was weightier perhaps in his verse than in his prose, more aware of the brevity of life and of all that is sweet in life. The prose, like the verse, has much in it that is Anacreontic, Epicurean, Horatian, Omarian. Prose and verse both are of the marrow of the man who made them. They are the man as his friends knew him transmuted into art. They are the very essence of him. Their outward show is of taking things lightly, of shrugging the shoulders at life, and letting it go at that. Inwardly, quatrains and letters alike reëcho with the world-old plaint of man over the little time he has to know the beauty of the world. They are original, their like was not before they were. The quatrains of *Omar Khayyam* are not only the first things of their kind in English poetry, but in all the poetry of the West. Minor though they are, the verses of the *Rubaiyat* mark the beginning of a mode in English poetry. Best of all they are in themselves things of beauty, building up into a "golden Eastern lay," as Tennyson called it, such as men will find pleasant and easy to the mind as long as men are human.

CHAPTER XIV

Coventry Patmore

THERE are two Coventry Patmores, the Coventry Patmore of *The Angel in the House* (1854-1863) and the Coventry Patmore of *The Unknown Eros* (1868-1877). The Coventry Patmore of *The Angel in the House* was known to the million and more who bought copies of that poem, the Coventry Patmore of *The Unknown Eros* is known to the little band who care for the abstract and rhapsodic poetry that descends from Crashaw. There is, of course, a relation between the two manifestations of the poet. The underlying motive of all the earlier narratives is man's love of woman. The underlying motive of many of the later odes is God's love of man. In Coventry Patmore's (1823-1896) own mind all his work is one, for to him there is a parallelism between the love of man for woman and the love of God for man. As he puts it in *The Victories of Love* (1863), the fourth part of *The Angel in the House:*

> Image and glory of the man,
> As he of God, is woman.

Patmore thought there had been left for him by good luck the subject of all subjects,

> The hymn for which the whole world longs,
> A worthy hymn in woman's praise,

the subject of wedded love, a greater theme than "The Life of Arthur, and Jerusalem's fall." It was inspired by his first wife, Emily Andrews, whom he married in 1847, and who died in 1862. It was not only her husband who thought her a notable woman.

Browning found inspiration in her for "A Face" of *Dramatis Personæ* (1864). Millais did a portrait of her and Woolner a medallion.

It is a usual tale, this of *The Angel in the House*. The course of true love flows smoothly for Felix and Honoria through *The Betrothal* (1854), *The Espousals* (1856), *Faithful for Ever* (1860), and *The Victories of Love* (1863). After three hundred pages and the recital of twenty years of marriage it comes to a quiet and contented close. Such sorrow as it chronicles is in the life of Honoria's cousin and suitor Frederick. The story, and the incidental episodes, do not much matter, however. What matters is a few of the lyrical asides. Defending it indirectly in "Olympus," Patmore refers to

> Some dish more highly spiced than this
> Milk-soup men call domestic bliss.

"Domestic bliss" does all but inspire him in preludes and lyrics by the way, but it is hardly a subject to furnish forth so long a poem. There is no denying that *The Angel in the House* is tiresome, that it drags and palls and surfeits. There is no denying, on the other hand, that there are passages of high poetry in it, and one part of it that is a lyric to remember. "The Revelation" is a perfect thing of its kind, a discovery about life in inevitable phrases—

> An idle poet, here and there,
> Looks round him; but, for all the rest,
> The world, unfathomably fair,
> Is duller than a witling's jest.
> Love wakes men, once a lifetime each;
> They lift their heavy lids and look;
> And, lo, what one sweet page can teach,
> They read with joy, then shut the book.
> And some give thanks, and some blaspheme,
> And most forget; but, either way,
> That and the Child's unheeded dream
> Is all the light of all their day.

That is the only lyric in all *The Angel in the House*, however, that is worthy of a place with "Saint Valentine's Day," "The Azalea," "Departure," "The Toys," and "Amelia," the best of his later work.

Patmore was prouder of "Amelia" than of any other of his poems, but he thought all of a high level of accomplishment. "I have written little," he said in the preface to the two volumes of his collected verse he called *Poems* (1886), "but it is all my best; I have never spoken when I had nothing to say, nor spared time or labor to make my words true. I have respected posterity; and, should there be a posterity which cares for letters, I dare to hope that it will respect me."

With so high a standard as this it is hard to understand why Patmore included "The River" and "The Falcon," from *Poems* (1844), in *Poems* (1886). The edition of this first *Poems*, published when he was twenty-one, he called in and destroyed after one hundred and forty-seven copies were sold. And wisely. *Tamerton Church Towers* (1853) marks an advance on his juvenilia, but not much of an advance. *The Angel in the House* itself, for all its celebrity and its value as a record of Mid-Victorian society, is not one of the great English narrative poems. It has its moments, as I have said, but they are brief, and few and far between. It would ill serve the fame of Patmore to overpraise it, and send readers to it only to have them disappointed. I have my father's copy of *The Betrothal*, in the American edition of 1856. The marked passages are not many, either my father's or my own. One is the memorable two lines:

> And round her happy footsteps blow
> The authentic airs of Paradise.

Another is:

> She near, I, grateful, felt as might
> A blind man sitting in the sun.

And a third is:

> The foolish, fashionable air
> Of knowing all, and feeling naught.

These lines have long been on the lips of men, if not so often as the "lonely watcher of the skies" that is his most quoted line. Printed in "Tired Memory," it persists even though it is not to be found in the revised version of the poem in his *Poems* of 1886.

In the later parts of *The Angel in the House* are other lines that have made a place for themselves among the memorable sayings of our tongue. Such is:

> His only love and she is wed!
> His fondness comes about his heart,
> As milk comes, when the babe is dead.

And such another is these four lines his quizzical turn of mind makes him put on the lips of a woman:

> We know, however wise by rule,
> Woman is still by nature fool;
> And men have sense to like her all
> The more when she is natural.

As the husband of three wives and as the father of three daughters it must be admitted Patmore had unusual opportunities for knowing "The Sex." Woman was, of course, the chief concern of his poetry, but he was far from a feminist in the later sense of the word. He was, indeed, hopelessly old-fashioned and patriarchal in his attitude toward her. He held that "If there is anything that God hates utterly it is a clever woman." He spends a great deal of serious thought and a great deal of humor upon woman. And he is guilty of woeful lapses from a sense of humor, sometimes, in writing of woman. "Amelia" is one of his best poems, but no one, man or woman, can read it without a shrug at his complacency in taking Beloved-Number-Two to the grave of Beloved-Number-One as a part of her wooing. One has a more serious objection to "Departure." In this poem Patmore upbraids his wife for dying without saying good-by at the last. One understands, of course, that his querulousness is largely figurative, but there is an unhappy literalness always in the background. It reminds me, every time I read it, of my neighbor who found fault with his wife for dying without telling him where she had put away his winter under-clothing. One can still appreciate, however, the uncanny power of that death scene, with this lady of "great and gracious ways" going

> With huddled, unintelligible phrase,
> And frighten'd eye,

upon her "journey of all days."

The "Proem" to *The Unknown Eros* has many fine lines, and its first ode, "Saint Valentine's Day," the light and lift of spring about it. "The Azalea" is another experience of his love for Emily Andrews sublimed into a perfect poem. He tells us in bald prose, under date of August 23, 1862, "Last night I dreamt that she was dying: awoke with unspeakable relief to find that it was a dream; but a moment after to remember that she was dead." That was a record jotted down as a suggestion for a poem. The poem made from it has a poignancy of feeling and beauty of imagery and a perfection of execution that go far toward establishing it as the best he has done.

The great compliment to his beloved with which "Amelia" opens,

> Whene'er mine eyes do my Amelia greet
> It is with such emotion
> As when, in childhood, turning a dim street,
> I first beheld the ocean

is on too high a level to be sustained throughout so long a poem.

Only "The Toys" approaches "The Azalea" in poignancy. It is a universal experience he records here, a punished child's attempt "to comfort his sad heart" by arranging his favorite toys and trinkets on a table by his bedside before he cried himself to sleep.

In writing of most of our poets of real power one can assume a familiarity not only with their poems that have made their way to general recognition, but with their most memorable sayings.

One cannot assume such a familiarity in the case of Patmore. Because of the dismissal of *The Angel in the House* as lawn-party poetry, its important passages have been obscured and the really great poetry of the later odes passed by as just some more stuff by "that namby-pamby Patmore." I am driven, then, to a stringing of quotations to sustain my contention that Patmore has as great moments as any of the Victorian poets. I have not the space to present adequately proof of his many-sidedness. This poet of "domestic bliss" was, for instance, a satirist of power, who could see, from his aristocratic standpoint, the tendencies of democracy in England only as "The amorous and vehement drift of man's herd to hell."

Patmore was, in everyday affairs, a man who got things done. He had a good deal to do with the formation of the "volunteers" who were the basis of England's militia. He managed well his Sussex estate of Heron's Ghyll. He dealt in gems. He wrote many articles for magazines and on a wide range of subjects. There are many circumstances in his career that have led those who have written about him to center what they have to say on something else than the beauty of his poetry. Certain critics are interested in his conversion to Catholicism, and in the philosophy of his religious verse. Others drift into anecdotage about his vagaries and prejudices. Others lose themselves in a discussion of *The Angel in the House* as social history. And still others are so absorbed in the metric of his odes they miss all else in them. What needs to be emphasized is the sheer poetic power of the man. It is nowhere more strikingly revealed than in the "jottings for poems" and other extracts from his notebooks printed by Champneys in *Memoirs and Correspondence of Coventry Patmore* (1900).

Here are bits of verse that are in themselves perfect accomplishments of two or three lines, but some of which might well have been the culminating passages of poems of considerable length. Perhaps, had he lived longer, certain of these would have been developed, and others printed, as Drummond of Hawthornden printed similar snatches among his madrigals and epigrams.

These bits are of all sorts, readings of life, cameos, fragments of lyrics. His conservatism comes out strongly in:

> Save by the Old Road none attain the new,
> And from the Ancient Hills alone we catch the view.

His faith dictates this declaration:

> When the soul owns herself sincerely to be nought
> The whole of heaven flows in as freely as a thought.

His many days discovered for him that "Hours are long but years are short." There is surprise after surprise as you read these bits in Chapters V and VI of Champneys. How did the stern old ascetic who believed in "the genial laws of natural sense" stumble on:

> What little, laughing Goddess comes this way
> Round as an O and simple as Good-day,
> Bearing upon the full breast of a Mother
> One Cupid whom she does with kisses smother,
> And, I should say,
> Within her breast another?

He refers to primroses "that touched mine eyes like kisses cool" and to daisies as "so lowly and so like the sun." A thing seen with absolute clearness, and perfectly put, is "Under the lily leaf lie the red tench." This that follows is, no doubt, a memory of a sight familiar to him as he looked out to sea from the Sussex downs:

> Sad as a ship far off at fall of day,
> Alone upon the wide sea-way.

And this a memory of a day, perhaps, when he looked up to the downs from Hastings or some other seaside town:

> As seen from smoky street, the thymy head
> Of some high hill alone with the sweet sun.

There are many fellows to these in Champneys, and more in the odes. I have quoted enough, perhaps, to show that Patmore could, to use his own words in speaking of England, greatly say, and truly sing

> in the bird voice and the blast
> Of her omniloquent tongue.

CHAPTER XV

The Victorian Minors

THE spectacle of Robert Stephen Hawker (1803-1875) is so romantic it has compelled the world to put a higher value on his verses than their intrinsic value warrants. Back of them, back of the stout figure of the Vicar of Morwenstow their maker, you see, down a break in bare cliffs, the sea he so loved, the great Atlantic, and Lundy Island against the sky. You think of all the strange stories about him. You are interested in the clergyman who was followed into his church at service by five cats, who directed his horse by voice instead of reins, who was the friend and aider of shipwrecked sailors. A kind of Cornish Scott, he was a collector of folklore and a forerunner of the Celtic Revival. He ministered to the people of his windswept parish a full forty years, composing much of his verse orally as he went about his daily work. That parish work was always first, his writing second. Yet he was able to harvest a fair sheaf of it from *Records of the Western Shore* (1836) to *The Quest of the Sangraal* (1863).

I have been interested in him ever since I heard him first spoken of by my history teacher in college over forty years ago. I have bought a first edition of *Ecclesia* (1840) with his autograph in it. I have again and again tried to read him through, but I never succeeded until it became my duty so to read him. It was in *Cornish Ballads*, his complete works collected by his son-in-law, C. E. Byles, in 1904, that I so read him. It was a reading brought me only infrequently anything better than rhetoric. The glamour about the man does not extend to his verse. Two sets of verses alone have claim to a place in English poetry, "The Song of the Western Men" and "The Quest of the Sangraal." The one is based on a fragment of an old ballad about a Trelawney:

> And shall Trelawney die?
> Here's twenty thousand Cornish men
> Will know the reason why!

It is said to have deceived Macaulay, Scott, and Dickens into thinking it a genuinely old ballad. It is spirited declamation, with but a glimmer of poetry in it. You can hardly say more of "The Quest of the Sangraal." Even his love of Cornwall can inspire him to nothing better than:

> Ah! native Cornwall! throned upon the hills,
> Thy moorland pathways worn by angel feet,
> Thy streams that march in music to the sea,
> 'Mid Ocean's merry noise, his billowy laugh!

I can read his verse with interest if my mind is on something in it other than its poetry. He is full of odds and ends of folklore and local tradition. Red-legged choughs are told him by the people about Tintagel to be "King Arthur's birds." He writes informative foot-notes. "My glebe occupies a position of wild and singular beauty. Its western boundary is the sea, skirted by tall and tremendous cliffs; and near their brink, with the exquisite taste of Ecclesiastical Antiquity, is placed the church." Yet he cannot put into his verse his feeling of beauty vanished from our modern world or his deep-felt joy in his place "Mid all things fierce, and wild, and strange, alone!" Nor does he expand upon that theme that might be so fruitful, "the exquisite taste" of ecclesiastical antiquity. For some reason or other the man could not realize what he was potentially.

THOMAS BABINGTON MACAULAY

It is ungrateful for one who had joy in declaiming "Horatius at the Bridge" in boyhood to have to own, come to years of discretion, he can find no poetry in Thomas Babington Macaulay (1800-1859). In certain "selections" from English literature he is not even mentioned as a writer of verse, and yet time was his *Lays of Ancient Rome* (1842) was all the vogue. Nor is he one of those whose prose is nearer poetry than his verse. He was the rhetorician in all he wrote. His verse is emphatic, clear, swinging, with never a lyric note. The closest to poetry it ever came is in "A Jacobite's Epitaph," which has certain excellences of an eighteenth-century sort.

WILLIAM BARNES

No two writers could be more different in tone and in outlook on life than those two poets of Dorsetshire, William Barnes (1801-1886) and Thomas Hardy (1840-1928). Barnes was the idyllist, the man determined to find only pleasantness and gentle pathos in his countryside. Hardy, knowing that same countryside no better, put down all its moods from lively to severe, and all its range of stories, from broad comedy to desolating tragedy. Hardy seldom writes in the dialect of Dorset, contenting himself, when he wishes to suggest rusticity, with a local word or a local phrase or a bit of dialogue in the patois. Dorset speech was a dialect to Hardy, to be resorted to only at times. Dorset speech was his language to Barnes, though he had begun with what he afterward called "national English."

It cannot be questioned that the Doric lends a kind of quaintness to the verses of Barnes, removes them from the workaday world, breathes about them airs from Arcady. If you read them again and again, however, you come to find that the chief function of the dialect is to cover mediocrity of thought and obviousness of expression. Taken out of the dialect, the verses go as flat as do most of our American dialect verses when similarly treated.

Barnes is, in fact, in most of his verses little more than a rhymer. He records many picturesque aspects of country life, rural customs, the troubles of humble folk from enclosed commons, from stray horses, and from movings-away from homes lived in long years. It is the Arcadian quality of his writing, its sunniness, its quick pathos, that have won it its many readers since it broke upon England in 1858 in *Hwomely Rhymes*. This collection had been preceded by *Poems in the Dorset Dialect* in 1844, but that book had won only a few admirers. His verses written in ordinary English as *Poems of Rural Life* (1868) failed both in England and America.

Barnes was an old man when, in 1879, he collected all his dialect verse in *Poems of Rural Life in the Dorset Dialect*. This collection gave him a definite place as a picturesque phenomenon in English letters. Hardy's praise had its influence in bringing the book before the public. It is a mistake to let Hardy's praise, either of this book, or of all Barnes after his death, make you expect too much of the man. Barnes should be taken for what he is, a pleasant rhymer whose verses preserve Wessex speech and Wessex ways. Read Hardy's description of him in cloak and knee-breeches and buckled shoes, and followed by his little grey dog. Rejoice in it as a picture of old England gone forever; but discount "a lyric writer of a high order of genius" as the enthusiasm of an old friend. There is little of the verse of Barnes poetry at all. There are none of the verses written out of passionate longing, and only a few out of really deep feeling. In most of them the mood is, "This, that, and the other thing out of doors is pleasant: let us rhyme of it."

There are neat pictures of what Hardy calls the Dutch school.

> An' the miller's man
> Do zit down at his ease
> On the seat that is under the cluster o' trees,
> Wi' his pipe an' his cider can.

There are pastoral bits, some in eclogue form, and more simply descriptive, that jog it happily:

> where elems high, in steatly ranks,
> Do rise vrom yellow cowslip-banks,
> An' birds do twitter vrom the spray

O' bushes deck'd wi' snow-white may;
An' gil'cups, wi' the deaisy bed,
Be under ev'ry step you tread.

De La Mare finds Barnes good, including six poems of his in *Come Hither* (1923). Of these three have about them a pathos of childhood that De La Mare can no more resist than those born sobbers, T. E. Brown and Dickens. There is a love poem "Wull ye come in early Spring?" and that song that echoes Herrick, but is wholly unsophisticated: "The air to gi'e your cheaks a hue." There is more feeling in "Woak Hill," though, than in any of these. It is, almost surely, his lament for the wife he lost, and about his best poem.

I packed up my goods all a-sheenèn
Wi' long years o' handlèn,
On dousty red wheels ov a waggon,
To ride at Woak Hill.

The brown thatchen ruf o' the dwellèn,
I then wer a-leävèn,
Had shelter'd the sleek head o' Meäry,
My bride at Woak Hill.

But now vor zome years, her light voot-vall
's a-lost vrom the vloorèn.
Too soon vor my jaÿ an' my childern,
She died at Woak Hill.

That is more like Hardy, and thereby better, than most of the verses of Barnes.

MANGAN: THE IRISH POE

Twice "Twenty golden years ago" an Irishman told his college class—a class in history—the story of James Clarence Mangan (1803-1849). That was the first time I had heard the poet's name, though not the first time I had heard his poetry. I can hardly remember the time when bits of "My Dark Rosaleen" were not in my memory, along with "Brian O'Llyn Had an Old Gray Mare" and stories of Dean Swift, all learnt from the old gardener who began my education in things Irish. My Wexford County friend, innocent of reading and writing, had the lines of "My Dark Rosaleen" almost accurately, and another "unlearned" Irish peasant, a farm-hand over in Jersey, dictated them thrice "twenty golden years ago" to a friend of mine almost word for word, though he changed the order of the stanzas and omitted one.

It falls to the lot of few poets, even in a country like Ireland, where so much literature persists in oral tradition, to write verses that are remembered and loved by learned and unlearned alike. It is the one poem that all know, and its popularity is, of course, based on its patriotism. To-day in Ireland, among the younger generation, Mangan's name, like his "Dark Rosaleen," is a household word. Young Irishmen who have formal praise only for Allingham and Ferguson and DeVere will insist that Mangan is a great poet, contending that his weaknesses of technique are only those of his day. They will resurrect the old quarrel as to whether he learnt his trick of refrain from Poe, or Poe from him; declaring lustily that our own poet was the imitator, as indeed the dates of publication of the poems of the two men may be made to show.

It seems to me that of everything Mangan has written it must be said, as Matthew Arnold said of Celtic poetry in general, that it is not great poetry but "poetry with an air of greatness investing it." There is the "large accent" about "O'Hussey's Ode to the Maguire," by far the finest poem of Mangan's, and its every stanza is plangent with "lyric cry." Only now and then, however, are its lines in the "grand style," and its general execution is not well sustained. Go to quote it, you find that the lines, separated from the context, lose strength, color, and even music. With all its ups and downs, you can best get a sense of its power, a very real and a great power, by reading it through aloud.

The first stanza of "Rury and Darvorgilla" gives you the verse of Mangan in its strength and weakness. There is music like Poe's in the first three lines, a music that is broken by the heavy syllables where light syllables should be in beginning of the anapæst of the third foot of the last line. As out of place rhetorically, as this "reckless" is musically, is the "pen" of the third line.

> Know ye the tale of the Prince of Oriel,
> Of Rury, last of his line of Kings?
> I pen it here as a sad memorial
> Of how much woe reckless folly brings.

As with De Quincey and Poe, we are apt to read into Mangan's writing the tragedy of his life. It was a life that sounded the deeps of humiliation and despair, "The gulf and grave of Maginn and Burns." Mangan tells us in "The Nameless One":

> how, with genius wasted,
> Betrayed in friendship, befooled in love,
> With spirit shipwrecked, and young hopes blasted,
> He still, still strove.

"The Karamanian Exile" sounds again the note of despair that is never absent from his writing. Living in Dublin all his days, James Clarence Mangan felt none the less vividly, although only imaginatively, all the sorrow of exile; and he must have been sadly lonely, intellectually and spiritually, although he had more than enough company in the scrivener's and attorney's offices of his 'prentice years, and in the library where those of his latter years, of which we know anything definite, were spent. Those two notes of lamentation, the lament for exile and the lament for loneliness, are prominent in his poetry. These, and personal despair, and sorrow for the sorrows of his country and her sons, are his chief themes. In "Twenty Golden Years Ago" the lament is softened to that over the passing of youth, and by contrast with the vehemence of his usual outpouring of feeling, this poem's cynicism seems almost genial.

The translations from the German in his *German Anthology* (1845) and the so-called translations from Oriental languages are most of them tainted with artificiality. Mangan wrote his best only on the sorrows of his country or his own sorrows. Perhaps had he written in Gaelic he could have found a means of expression less artificial than the English in which he usually cast his poems. There is always in his writing the suggestion of the foreigner's use of English.

What you carry away from a study of Mangan is a memory of his story and a permanent impression that there is no poet in English whose verse is so consistently downhearted. On wild days in winter when the wind is loud without and the rain and sleet drive against the panes, certain lines of his "O' Hussey's Ode to the Maguire" come to me: "Gray rain in roaring streams," "Showery, arrowy, speary sleet," "Triumphs the tyrannous anger of the wounding winds," as on winter nights when the wind moans I think of the saying of another Irish poet, "There is much evil in the crying of wind." Such is the intensity of the best poems of Mangan that you remember their gist when the lines fade from your recollection, and thinking over their subjects and his imaginative realization of them, the poems bulk larger and larger until you persuade yourself they are great poems. The materials of his poems are the materials of great poetry, the passion breaking out in them is the passion of great poetry, but he failed through lack of architectonic power and of inevitability of phrase to make his poetry great poetry.

MARTIN FARQUHAR TUPPER

It is not easy to-day to discover why Martin Farquhar Tupper (1809-1889) appealed so to his day and generation. He sold both in America and England as few poets have sold. His name was well known to Americans who could name you less than a dozen poets, a Longfellow and a Whittier, a Tennyson and a Patmore, a Byron and a Burns, a Thomson and a Pollok, a Milton and a Shakespeare. You find both an early version of the *Proverbial Philosophy* (1839-1882) and the American edition of *The Complete Poetical Works* (1851) wherever you go in the States from San

Francisco on the Pacific to Portland way down east on the Atlantic, and, for that matter, on into Nova Scotia. The first "picker" of antiques I ever met, at Smith's Cove, that looks out through Digby Gut to the Bay of Fundy, bought cups and saucers of Crown Derby from a settler who boasted kinship with Tupper.

This American edition of *The Complete Works* was one of the books in a library of less than a hundred in a remote farmhouse in the White Mountains, where there was little verse else. *The Seasons* was there, a parsing book, the old man selling out called it, and a Whittier with first and last pages worn off as well as both backs. The Whittier was there, perhaps, because the Quaker poet used to summer in the neighborhood and write of its hills and rivers and lakes. I have spent more evenings over this volume of Tupper's than it is worth, and though I have often fallen asleep over it I think I have read it through. That there is not a poem in it I am quite sure. There are obvious platitudes in plenty, unrestrained sentimentality, not a line that requires a second reading to be understood, and expressions of appreciation for America and Americans very pleasing to national pride.

Tupper was very much interested in the Channel Islands, where his people stopped over on their way from Germany to England; in Liberia; in dogs that pulled trucks; in the friendship of England and America; in the laboring millions—there is no end to the list of topics. Perhaps that is why he was so popular. No matter who you are, pauper to prince, you will find a set of verses to your condition, verses consolatory, flattering, reassuring. The wicked are excoriated, the virtuous commended. In my copy of *The Complete Poetical Works,* bought at the break-up of my neighbor's home in middle New Hampshire, I found corners of leaves turned down at "Britain to Columbia," "Never Give Up!" "Our Thanksgiving Hymn," "Cheer Up!" "Ancient" and "Modern," and "Days Gone By." These marked sets of verses are fairly evenly distributed throughout the book, showing that it had been read through. This is not always the way with old books so found. In the hundreds of volumes of poetry I have bought I have discovered in most instances the larger number of marked passages in the first quarter of the book. The reader had wearied in well-doing and made progress not half way through. Not so with Tupper. However poor his stuff, it was eagerly read, A to Z, by Mid-Victorian folks.

William Edmonstoune Aytoun (1813-1865) is remembered for his *Lays of the Scottish Cavaliers* (1849); the *Bon Gaultier Ballads* (1845-1857) that he wrote with Sir Theodore Martin (1816-1909); and for his edition of the *Ballads of Scotland* (1858). Popular as he was for his wit and for his power of telling narrative, it was as a lecturer at the University of Edinburgh that he was at his best. No song or ballad of his, or quip or anecdote, has lived, however, as has the version of "Old Long Syne" by his ancestor, Sir Robert Aytoun, the version that Burns revamped into the song that all the world still sings. A good deal of the Victorian Aytoun is the lament for yesterday:

> The olden times have passed away,
> And weary are the new.

An antiquary with a flair for verse, a rhetorician rather than a poet, Aytoun is to-day no more than a name.

THE BRONTËS

There never has been, in English literature, such good copy as the Brontës. The facts of their lonely lives, and the fiction that grew up about them, the succumbing, one after another, of the three youngest of them, with powers unproved, the quick and lasting success of the oldest, Charlotte, as a novelist, made a spectacle such as the world loves and will not willingly let lapse into obscurity.

Charlotte (1816-1855) was a considerable poet in prose, witness the moorland mood in Chapter XXX of *Jane Eyre* (1847); and Emily (1818-1848) only less a one, as all who read *Wuthering Heights* (1847) cannot fail to note. Even the gentle Anne

(1819-1849) had her lyric moments. You can find them in Chapter XLV of *The Tenant of Wildfell Hall* (1848). There have arisen champions, George Moore, for one, who have declared her the greatest of the sisters, and still others who have declared Bramwell (1817-1848) the genius of the family. It is Emily only, however, who has challenged as a poet in verse. Yet she has written no poem of sustained power. There is a stanza close to poetry in "The Prisoner"; another such stanza in "Honor's Martyr"; two such stanzas in "A Little While"; and the line that gives title to "No coward soul is mine." There is little else in her verse that is poetry. There is a great deal else there that is poetry in intention. You can feel her fiery spirit now and then, but never at the high pitch of *Wuthering Heights*. What has brought about her reputation is her story. Her loneliness, her long struggle with disease, her power to feel, her love of her moorland home, have so excited her readers to pity and wonder that they have exalted all she did into a something far finer than it was. Emily Brontë is a picturesque figure in the history of literature; a romancer of power in *Wuthering Heights;* a writer of verse visited infrequently by the spirit or technical accomplishment of poetry.

PHILIP JAMES BAILEY

If only the verse of Philip James Bailey (1816-1902) were as poetical as his appearance in old age he would have been a great poet indeed. He affected the cloak and soft hat made famous by Tennyson in England and by Hawthorne in America. He had a head of white hair that rivaled the mop of William Morris but that was well kept, and his features had about them something of that aspiration and rapt sensitiveness that made George Meredith's face so notable. The great span of years his *Festus* was before the public between its initial publication in 1839 and its fiftieth-anniversary republication, in expanded form, in 1889, and the very bulk of the epic, added to the effect made by its high intention and by the distinguished appearance of its author. Again and again it was said of him: "He looks the part of poet and prophet." Poet and prophet Bailey tried to be, but he was neither. His attempts to justify God's ways to man, to create a liberal and reconciling Christian philosophy, to give the world an optimistic creed that would content it with modernity, are to-day but Victorian twaddle, tiresome and almost unreadable. I have tried again and again to read *Festus,* but I have not read it. My copy is the anniversary edition of 1889, bought in that year by one F. R. Coulson and carefully read and annotated up to page 179. After that he marks a few passages to page 211, but he is, I am afraid, skipping, as I have been guilty of skipping in my reading forty years later. Page 276 bears his last X opposite a passage he wishes to remember. From there on the pages are cut but they bear no signs of being read or even of a rehandling. The condition of this book is, I take it, symptomatic of Bailey's position forty years ago. Then echoes of his earlier fame were still reëchoing, and people who cared for poetry made a try at reading him, few of them, I am afraid, with as much success as the purchaser of the copy now come to me. Perhaps the price, two shillings and sixpence, that I paid for this *Festus* in England is an indication of its present literary as well as market value.

Mr. Coulson liked the descriptions in these early pages of *Festus* as well as the aphorisms. He marked many of these descriptions but more of the aphorisms. It is only the latter that have even momentary value to me. Bailey's flights in blank verse seem to me cheap and weak, and his rhymed lyrics nothing at all. If he has any value to-day other than as an exhibit of Victorianism it is for his aphorisms. They are not revealing enough to be written down readings of life. Many of them are spoken by Lucifer, who conducts Bailey's particular kind of Faust through the universe. It is Lucifer who tells us that "manner's a great matter," and that:

> The sole equality now on earth is death;
> The rich have never enough of everything;
> The poor have never enough of anything.

It is Festus himself, however, who discovers that "The worst of men can give the best advice"; that "Night brings out stars as sorrow shows us truths"; and that "The worst way to improve the world is to condemn it."

There is no more poetry in Bailey than there is in these sayings. He is a poor craftsman in verse and no prophet at all. He is of his age. He loves the Macaulayan antithesis and such platitudes as delighted the author of *Proverbial Philosophy* (1839-1882). And yet Bailey was praised by Tennyson and Bulwer and Thackeray, and his *Festus* ran through edition after edition in both England and America!

SYDNEY DOBELL

If Sydney Dobell (1824-1874) is read to-day by anybody but the professional student of poetry it is for "Keith of Ravelston." That ballad has a place in several anthologies, and it is praised now and then in some book of criticism. It is not so good a ballad as such prominence as it has would indicate. In sporting parlance, it is an "in and out" ballad, fair to middling in one stanza and poor in another. Its recurrent:

> O Keith of Ravelston,
> The sorrows of thy line

burdens us with the fate that has overcome an old and distinguished house. This Scots family has a ghost very like the banshee of Irish families:

> Her misty hair is faint and fair,
> She keeps the shadowy kine.

There was perhaps a romance between the lady who became the ghost and Andrew Keith. We are not told. He is spoken of as if he were dead, but how and when and why he died, if die he did, we do not learn. There is no such uncertainty about "The Haystack in the Floods," or "Sister Helen," or "The Ballad of Judas Iscariot," or any other modern ballad of power.

De La Mare includes two other of Dobell's poems than "Keith of Ravelston" in *Come Hither*, his anthology of English poetry. One is "How's My Boy," and the other is "The Orphan's Song."

You can read the one so that it takes on drama, and you can senti-
mentalize over the other, but neither is more than second-rate.
There is not the fundamental brainwork or the architectonic power
of the master-poet in Dobell. He attempted two long dramatic
poems, *The Roman* (1850) and *Balder* (1853). *The Roman*, having to do with the liberation of Italy from the Austrians, won him
a literary success in England, and a warm welcome in Italy when
he visited there in later years.

Balder, a story whose subject, in his own words, was the "Progress of a Human Being from Doubt to Faith, from Chaos to
Order," is a fragment toward three hundred pages long. What
we have is only a third of what Dobell would have written if ill-
health had not fallen on him before he was thirty, and ended,
practically, his literary career at that early age. Its rather Byronic
hero is but a lath-and-plaster figure to-day. What you can applaud
is a certain freshness in the descriptions of nature. His highest
level in rendering human emotion is to be found in such a passage
as this that follows, in which his hero, Balder, is recalling their
trysting time to Amy, his wife:

> quick smiles that every word of mine
> Stirred up anew so often that they met
> Like sudden roses caught in a warm wind,
> And did provoke each other, ruffling sweets
> In dear confusion.

It may be, of course, that his invalidism cut him off from a
rich life, but he certainly did not utilize fully in his verse all that
his life brought him. There is nothing so interesting in all his writing as his hobby for raising "a rare and peculiarly beautiful breed
of deer-hounds."

The spectacle of Dobell may well give us pause. Here is one
who loomed large as a poet to his own day, and who, rightly, has
dwindled to almost nothingness in ours. Within a year of his death
in 1874, Dr. John Nichol put out, in two volumes, *The Poetical
Works of Sydney Dobell* (1875). In the "memoir," the professor
of English literature in the University of Glasgow could say, "His

Chamouni rivals that of Coleridge, as his Coliseum rivals that of
Byron. His descriptions of Spring have the luxuriance and truth
of Shelley's. The pastoral loveliness of the long summer's day on
the hills (Scene XXIV) recalls the idyll in the Bohemia of the
Winter's Tale."

What was there of his age, what of the qualities of the accepted "spasmodic" school of poetry, that would lead a cautious
Scot to such overenthusiasm as this? As we turn dull page after
dull page of *Balder* to-day it is difficult to answer. It seems, save
for the descriptions of nature, rhetorical, thin, cold, labored. There
are few felicities of phrase, no passages of dramatic power, no readings of life. And yet it took the years to put Dobell into his proper
place. Let critics be humble, and admit that only the years can
judge. This writer or that of to-day whom the world hails as a
poet may be no more than the hard-working and intelligent versi-
fier that Dobell was.

Alexander Smith (1830-1867) had ceased to be a verse classic
even in the decade after his death. As a boy I heard of the essays
of *Dreamthorpe* (1863), as a youth preparing for college I read
them, but only in college itself did I come to know of him as a
poet. *A Life Drama* (1853) was held up to us as a nine day's wonder that was forgotten as quickly as it came into notoriety. That
it was wholly forgotten was not true, however, for passages from
it retained then, and they still retain, a place in the anthologies.
Why I cannot understand. There is a line to remember in his
verses now and then, but there is no whole poem of sustained
power or beauty. One anthologist has cut out two-thirds of the
stanzas of "Love" before including it among his country's best,
but it remains a poor poem even after such heroic treatment. Two
lines and no more of it are worth a little something. They are:

> All things have something more than barren use;
> There is a scent upon the brier.

"Barbara," another favorite of the anthologists, is almost as
bad as a song by Weatherly. Largely because of the name fastened

upon Smith and his like by Aytoun, "The Spasmodics," scholarly interest in him and Bailey and Massey revives about once a generation, but Smith himself has hardly even a historical significance now. It was given to him, in a moment of irony, to foresee his fate. In *A Life Drama* he wrote:

> And thus they judged the dead: "This Poet was
> An April tree whose vermeil-loaded boughs
> Promised to Autumn apples juiced and red,
> But never came to fruit. . . .
> Poet he was not in the larger sense;
> He could write pearls, but he could never write
> A Poem round and perfect as a star."

There is no comment meet for that last line.

ELIZA COOK

Eliza Cook (1818-1889) made a noise in the world from 1835 to 1865. In the former year she published *Lays of a Wild Harp,* when she was seventeen. It was accepted instantaneously by the sentimentalists, and its successors, *Melaia and Other Poems* (1838) and *New Echoes and Other Poems* (1864), were just as popular. The earlier poems were reprinted in America, at Philadelphia, in 1845, and made a giftbook, in cream and gold, that the swains of the period gave to their inamoratas. With additions, the poems of this volume were again reprinted in America, again at Philadelphia, in 1856, with a frontispiece showing the authoress in curls and discreet gown of black, standing over an empty arm-chair. This volume became one of the "leading" parlor table books of its day. The old arm-chair, distressingly Mid-Victorian, was there in the frontispiece because of "The Old Arm Chair," her most popular set of verses. It is a thing of pathos, this set of verses, but not a poem.

None of her rhymes are poems. All are simple, straightforward, unaffected, and tame. They depend, for their effect, on their material, which is brought directly but artlessly into contact with the reader. There is no beauty in her verses, no discovery about life, no vision, no distinction of rhythm or of phrasing. In these verses we meet country things that win us and a soothing humanitarian spirit. "Old Dobbin" celebrates the farm horse, plodding and benign, and "Old Pincher" the faithful dog, which was given as a puppy to his mistress when she was "a youngling, wild, rosy, and fat."

Other favorites of the thousands on thousands of her readers were "God Speed the Plough" and "The Englishman." She celebrated Washington as she did John Bull, and held her American readers fast in their allegiance for a generation. My copy of *Poems of Eliza Cook* (1861), "selected and edited by the author," has eighty-two steel engravings by the brothers Dalziel, John Gilbert, Harrison Weir, John D. Watson, and their ilk. These engravings give you as many glimpses of English home life and of English countryside as do the verses of Miss Cook. This "sumptuous" volume, with its 408 pages and with its binding of blue and gold, and with an autograph letter of the "authoress" inserted, cost me only six shillings, in 1929, in the university city of Cambridge. Miss Cook is no longer the institution that she was in the mid years of last century, on both sides of the Atlantic. Her name is now less often on the lips and in the memories of men than the names of Mrs. Hemans and the Hon. Mrs. Norton, her rivals in her heyday.

CHARLES MACKAY

"Tubal Cain" of Charles Mackay (1814-1889) was the second set of verses, barring nursery rhymes and the like, that I got by heart. Even to-day, more than fifty years after I learned the stanzas, I can compass the first of them without stumbling. I had picked up "Paul Revere" by hearing my sister study it for recitation, but Mackay's chant about the smith of the Bible was taskwork set for me only. It was for dame-school I had to commit it to memory, as afterward at an academy I had to commit "Horatius at the Bridge." Longfellow, Mackay, and Macaulay! They fall together pleasantly as providers of recitation pieces. Mackay is no more than such a one, and he can be worse. He is fairly represented by "Cheer, Boys! Cheer!" "Louise on the Doorstep" is pathos at its cheapest. There is no set of his verses that does not brand itself as rhetoric on first reading. The man never had an inkling of what poetry is. *Songs and Poems* (1834) introduced him, and he had a vogue for a half-century thereafter.

CHARLES KINGSLEY

There is as little of the poet of first power in the verse of Charles Kingsley (1819-1875) as there is of the novelist of first power in his stories. He had the gift of writing songs that were quickly on all English-speaking lips, but neither "The Sands of Dee" nor "Three Fishers Went Sailing" is poetry in the sense that "Sweet and Low" or "Mandalay" is poetry. "Airly Beacon" is in many of the anthologies, but it is the surprise of its last line rather than its poetry which puts it there. There is nothing new in the old, old story, and no freshness of phrase in the quick telling of that story.

Lines of *Andromeda* (1858) and of the "Ode to the North East Wind" have been in my memory since childhood, but I cannot call either poetry of a high order, vigorous as is the tumbling measure of the one and sonorous as are the hexameters of the other. A man of towering temper and of irresistible energy who could do many things well, Kingsley made popular successes in novel and verse and nature essays, but he has proven of lasting appeal to the critics in none of the three forms.

DR. THOMAS GORDON HAKE

There is something sympathetic about Dr. Thomas Gordon Hake (1809-1895). Just as soon as you begin to read his verses you want to like them. The pity is that you cannot like them as much as you wish to. They are stories most of them, such stories as a country doctor would come upon in his rounds. They are told by a man who cares greatly what happens to the characters in the stories, the victims I had almost written. Many of the stories are sad. That, too, is what you might look for in a physician's verse. All the three professions of clergyman, lawyer, and doctor have much to do with the last days of life, but the doctor is most immediately concerned with death.

"The Cripple" is a typical poem. It recites the passing from his mother's care to the poorhouse of a cripple who had been happy in doing little chores for tips, holding a horse before the tavern or running an errand. People in and about the village where he lived were nice to him, and to his mother, who chored for the keep of the two of them. The cripple liked to play on his fife, too, for the ha'penny that helped to eke out their living. His mother falls ill, and dies, and the poor boy is on the parish. There is nothing for him now but the poorhouse. Almost all the poem save the end has to do with the life of the cripple, and with the fear of the mother that the poorhouse will get them in the end. Hake has known such a case. The country doctor, like every one else in the country, knows how many people live in fear of poorhouse, or workhouse, or county farm, or whatever else it may be called in this place or that. He knows, too, what unhappiness is ahead for the boy in that

> workhouse, bare and gaunt
> Like the drear soul of poverty,

with "mossy fen" before it "where willows crouch like aged men." All the life of the little village is presented as background to the cripple's insignificant life, made significant by the poet's concern with it. There is no sentimentality in the telling, but all the life of the community is oriented toward the least of its lives.

A year before his death Dr. Hake was complimented by having a selection made from the many volumes he had published from 1839 to 1890, with his portrait by Rossetti as frontispiece, and a preface by Alice Meynell. It did not, with its five hundred copies, do much toward spreading abroad his reputation. Only the man who gave me Mrs. Meynell's selections, and Mrs. Meynell herself, have, of all the reading people I have known, ever read a line of him. There is little injustice in that, or little loss to the public. His writing is his own, the result of a rich experience of life, but it is only a bare garnering from that rich experience.

Dr. Hake is not only a minor poet, but a minor poet of the second class. He is one of a hundred Englishmen whom love of English countryfolk and English countryside have made a writer of verses. Some quality of their time in their verse has made certain of such men well known for a time. Dr. Hake had no such adventitious aid to reputation, and his quiet and sincere writing was known only to a little group of cultivated people, most of whom were of his circle of acquaintances. Nor is it likely that Dr. Hake will have any large recognition in the years to come. It is only the lyric poet who can come into his own through the anthologies. Hake is not at his best as a lyric poet. Perhaps because of his friends his will continue to be a known name to students of the nineteenth century. One who knew Borrow and Trelawny, Gordon of Khartoum and Rossetti, Philip Bourke Marston and Theodore Watts-Dunton may be kept alive by readers of memoirs.

One wonders whether one ought to say a word about Gerald Massey (1828-1909). There was illimitable energy in the man, deep emotion, human fellowliness of a sort particularly engaging, a life interesting to follow in its many ramifications from wharf to rostrum, but almost no sheer poetry in all his lengthy verses. You will find "Not I, Sweet Soul, Not I" in certain anthologies, its three stanzas often cut to two. There is a real lilt to the lines, dewiness, freshness, the glow of spring, but there is not wholeness of good tissue to them. He never wrote a set of verses without a flaw, a flaw of poor workmanship or of rhetoric to discount the poetry. In 1889 what was thought to be the best of him was collected in *My Lyrical Life,* two volumes of the second-rate and third-rate.

It is hard reading to-day the most of it, even the verses in praise of Thackeray that Matthew Arnold remembered and those on Hood that Landor praised. It is facile stuff most of it, not too well finished, written out of no deep pondering, genuine but superficial, humanitarian, obvious, Mid-Victorian in tone and outlook.

Robert Leighton (1822-1869) is the man who wrote "The Bunch of Larks." The portly one who had the four-and-twenty dead birds for a pie cries "Give me the substance of the thing." Lark pie in London was rare, in Rome a regular Christmas dish as long as there were larks to serve. Leighton, a business man himself, found the real substance of things in beauty and celebrated what of it came his way. This once, and this once only, though, was it given him to write memorably, well as he paid his respects to Lincoln and Cromwell and other strong men of the race.

There were a mob of gentlemen who wrote with ease in Mid-Victorian times as there have been at all times since Pope created the phrase. You will find them all receiving their due in the anthologies that would be representative of their times, but you will not find them in Palgrave or Quiller-Couch or De La Mare.

One must mention William Brighty Rands (1823-1882) because of "Polly"; Mortimer Collins (1827-1876) because of "My Thrush"; Walter Thornbury (1828-1876) because of "Smith of Maudlin"; and Joseph Skipsey, the collier poet (1832-1903), for "See, Essie Goes."

WILLIAM BELL SCOTT, LINTON AND DOYLE

There are piled up before me on my desk twenty volumes of Victorian poets from indifferent to bad. I bought some of these volumes shortly after their time of publication, in the old age of their writers, who felt if they did not collect themselves they never would be collected. Such books did not sell, of course, and I bought them out of curiosity, some of them, and others of them out of some ill-defined sympathy with the unwanted volumes. They all came cheap, of course. About half of these volumes of verse, however, I bought during the ten years I have been writing this book. Had I not the book in prospect I had never bought such third- and fourth-raters. The authors of these books write on so many different matters and in so many different manners that it is not easy to tuck them away with a mere mention as Tennysonians or Pre-Raphaelites or even among that loosely connected group that Stedman called "spasmodics." They are most of them men of so little individuality, men who have made so slight discoveries of beauty of their own, men who have had so few moments of vision that they have been forced to imitate this man or that to be able to write any verse at all.

There are among them "one poem" men, like that Rev. Charles Wolfe of an earlier generation who wrote "The Burial of Sir John Moore" (1817). Such a one is William Bell Scott (1812-1890). I did not find "The Witch's Ballad" for myself, although I did mull over time and again various volumes of his verse in second-hand bookshops and libraries, and one that I bought. It registered with me first in De La Mare's anthology *Come Hither* (1923). By some miracle of atavism he recaptured a moment of old years in an untoward town of his native Scotland, and saw as in a vision as eldritch a witch's dance as there is record of in our literature.

William James Linton (1812-1898) survives, if survive he does, by reason of "Faint Heart," an attempt, after the manner of Sir John Suckling, at variations on the theme that "Faint heart never won fair lady."

There are those who hold that Sir Francis Hastings Doyle (1810-1888) wrote other ballads than "The Red Thread of Honor." Such advocates cry up "The Private of the Buffs." There is just the one ballad, though, popular as a declamation piece. Good boyish stuff and no more that "The Red Thread of Honor" is, I have heard it wildly applauded at a college alumni meeting, on its masterly presentation by a born and trained elocutionist.

The verse of the Rev. Richard Watson Dixon (1833-1900) is as slight as any that has come out of Lakeland. He is a Wordsworthian with one little lyric that survives in the anthologies, "The feathers of the willow."

WILLIAM ALLINGHAM

You find William Allingham (1824-1889) in the anthologies with "Up the Airy Mountain" and other verses about fairies. He is written down in the literary histories as the friend of Rossetti, and volumes of his verse are interesting to collectors because of illustrations by Rossetti and Millais. What is most worth while in his verse itself is the home call to his native town of Bally-shannon in the northwest of Ireland. "The Winding Banks of Erne" has its spell from the charm of this corner of Donegal caught in its long lines. The emigrant who is leaving for America now at last realized Ballyshannon as "the kindly spot, the friendly town, where everyone is known." It lies at the Erne's mouth, and near-by are the beaches along the Atlantic "Level and long, and white with waves, where gull and curlew stand." Near-by, too, but inland, is "all the brown uneven country lit with waters here and there."

Clearest of all his memories of the west country, most poignant, most fully realized is that bit of seven lines from *Day and Night Songs* (1854):

> Four ducks on a pond,
> A grass-bank beyond,
> A blue sky of Spring,
> White clouds on the wing:
> What a little thing
> To remember for years—
> To remember with tears.

Set to music, this is known the world round. Allingham felt keenly the nearness of music to poetry, and he wrote several sets of his verses to old Irish airs. He broadcasted some verses, too, in the form of ballad sheets, and these were taken to heart by many people, gentle and simple alike, in his countryside.

Allingham thought *Laurence Bloomfield in Ireland* (1864), an agrarian tale in decasyllabic rhymed couplets, his best work, but you must be interested in the land question in Ireland to follow it through to the end. It is the predecessor of many stories and plays of like concern, *Naboth's Vineyard* of Somerville and Ross and *The Founding of Fortunes* by Jane Barlow, *The Land* of Colum and *Birthright* of Murray.

Allingham is important historically, for the influence of his short lyrics on Yeats. "Twilight Voices," both in its form and in its content, has been taken to heart by the younger poet. Allingham is the best poet of the generation in Ireland immediately preceding that of Yeats, "A. E.," and Gogarty. He has not the interest in old Irish legend of Aubrey De Vere (1814-1902) and Sir Samuel Ferguson (1810-1886), but there is more of the stuff of poetry in him than in either. The succession in primacy of the Irish poets in Victorian times is Mangan, Allingham, and Yeats.

"Owen Meredith" (1831-1891) descends from Byron as well as from Bulwer-Lytton. It was on the heroes of his father's novels that he modeled his man of the world, Lord Alfred Vargrave, of *Lucile* (1860), but his ladies, even to the sainted heroine of this most famous poem of his, have about them some suggestion of the scented wickedness and dalliance of the Byronic fair. There has never been a story in verse more widely read in America than *Lucile*. Hardly a city auction where there are books put up but includes a copy, and printings of all sorts from the cheapest to one with illustrations by Du Maurier are to be found in the old bookshops. There is character-drawing of a sort in *Lucile*, but there is no sense of reality in the portraits. There is ease in the versification, and *mots* prettily turned, and a passage or two almost proverbial, but there is no poetry in it. Its cynicism is cheap, and its smartness dulled by the years. Not unworthy to stand as representative of it, and of all his verse is:

> We may live without poetry, music and art;
> We may live without conscience, and live without heart;
> We may live without friends; we may live without books;
> But civilized man cannot live without cooks.

Frederick Locker-Lampson (1821-1895), in the preface to *Lyra Elegantiarum* (1891), his anthology of *vers de société*, states that in such verse "sentiment never surges into passion," and "humor never overflows into boisterous merriment." He himself has done his hundred sets of verses of that description, from *London Lyrics* (1857) on, but he has done verses, too, that are poetry. "At Her Window" is exquisite in the manner of Herrick, and tenderer, as the nineteenth century is tenderer than the seventeenth. "To My Grandmother" is almost a fellow to "At Her Window" in tenderness, but it is arch, and, at the same time, close to tears. Locker-Lampson is more of a poet than any of the confraternity of nineteenth-century writers of "society verse," save Austin Dobson alone.

It is strange that Jean Ingelow (1830-1897) is not a better poet than she is. Her verse has freshness, command of the exact word, a sense of the picturesque, unworn figures, attack and verve. She was not, of course, a skilful craftsman, she did not labor over her lines, and she was cursed, like so many of her fellow Mid-Victorians, with extreme voluminousness. What might have been concentrated into a poem is thinned out to wordy verse in set on set of tedious stanzas, as in the thirty-one four-liners of "Divided."

Yet Jean Ingelow was cared for by her age. In the library left by Admiral White, long surgeon in the United States Navy, to his native town of Sandwich, New Hampshire, a collected edition of her works has place with collected editions of Swinburne and Browning and Byron. Dr. White was a man who knew the books he bought. They show that they were frequently turned to, handled, read. Jean Ingelow was to him a writer to be considered along with the accredited poets of her age. To most of us, perhaps, of a generation later than his, she was the poet of "High Tide on the Coast of Lincolnshire." That was a recitation piece in the seventies and eighties of last century, and its fame so wide-spread that cows in many American countrysides were called Whitefoot, Lightfoot, and Jetty after those that Elizabeth was calling when the great tide on Lindis carried her and her babes to their death.

Jean Ingelow wrote the rhymed novels of her period, and

its dramatic lyrics, and its Pre-Raphaelite ballads, and its drawing room songs. She brought heartsease to hundreds of her generation through such verses as "Comfort in the Night" and "Failure." She has left us not a single set of verses that any one would to-day put into an anthology of the best of Victorian verse.

LORD DE TABLEY

John Leicester Warren, Lord de Tabley (1835-1895), during his later years never missed a sunset. At least so says his biographer. There is nothing so notable in his verse as this habit of his life. Wisely, he never tried to "do" these sunsets in a series of poems, as nine versifiers out of ten would have done. He did try, however, nearly all the stock subjects, studies in the Greek manner, bits of rural England, the quick passing of life, the nothingness of glory. "Rural Evening," in Volume I of his *Poems: Dramatic and Lyrical* (1895) is as good a set of verses as he can do. It is a true enough picture, but it has no individuality. It might have been done by any one of a hundred fair craftsmen in verse. You make, on widely separated readings, no new discoveries of lines to remember. I find no more in him to-day than when I first read him a quarter of a century ago.

Sentimentality and poor taste and uncertain craftsmanship cheapen the verse of Sir Alfred Austin (1835-1913). From *The Human Tragedy* (1862) to *Flodden Field* (1903) there is no attempt of his at epic or dramatic or lyric poetry that has won its way into popular acceptance or the appreciation of the critics. His prose has sold, *The Garden That I Love* (1894) and *Haunts of Ancient Peace* (1902), despite faults like these in his verse, both being "successes" of their respective years. As poet laureate, to which post he was appointed by the Conservatives in 1896, he defended the Jameson raid into Boer territory in his best-known poem. This "ode" is as bad as may be, commonplace, banal, and no vindication of the foray that brought on the Boer War. In all the wide range of English literature there was never a minor poet who took himself more seriously than Sir Alfred, or who figured more prominently in his brief heyday.

WILLIAM JOHNSON CORY

There are just two poems of William Johnson Cory (1823-1892) that make for my happiness, "Mimnermus in Church" and "Heraclitus." It chances that they are printed the one after the other in the first collected edition of *Ionica* (1891). I have never seen the first edition of *Ionica* (1858), or *Ionica II* (1877), but I am told that both these poems of my choice are found in the former. There are lines in other poems that appeal to me for one reason or another, but only these two lyrics are written in the "carved perfect way" that outlasts the years.

Cory writes about the boys at Eton, where he taught from 1845 to 1872; the classics that he taught them; trips in vacation to Holland and Germany, to Switzerland, and to the Madeira Islands; and the quiet happenings of his own personal life. As a teacher for long years I am naturally interested in what Cory writes about his boys, who, by the bye, included Rosebery, Halifax, the Lytteltons, Frederick Pollock, Herbert Paul, and W. H. Gladstone. He evidently had his moments in the classroom, for he can refer to:

> The wonder flushing in the cheek,
> The questions many a score,
> When I grow eloquent, and speak
> Of England, and of war.

This is from "Academus," the close to which is his hope that those who knew him might say of him dead:

> He gave whate'er he had to give
> To freedom and to youth.

That Cory knew his boys is proven by several sayings of his, and by none more surely than his declaration of them that "They toil at games, and play with books."

Every teacher, too, will thank Cory for his claim that the teacher keeps younger-hearted than men of other professions:

> One's feelings lose poetic flow
> Soon after twenty-seven or so;
> Professionizing moral men
> Thenceforth admire what pleased them then;
> The poems bought in youth they read,
> And say them over like their creed.
> All autumn crops of rhyme seem strange;
> Their intellect resents the change.
> They cannot follow to the end
> Their more susceptive college-friend:
> He runs from field to field, and they
> Stroll in their paddocks making hay:
> He's ever young, and they get old.

"Heraclitus" is after Callimachus, but it is a something more than translation. "Two minds shall flow together, the English and the Greek," wrote Cory elsewhere, and what he prophesied came true in this poem. All men who know good companionship, social and mental, will recall times when "you and I Had tired the sun with talking and sent him down the sky," and all know how true it is that the words of the dead, were they worthy words, live after them:

> Still are thy pleasant voices, thy nightingales awake;
> For Death, he taketh all away, but them he cannot take.

There is no more human poem in English literature than "Mimnermus in Church." There is nothing of your lonely poet anywhere in Cory, your man aloof from life. He is not of that sort of modern poet to whom Dr. Johnson referred in that interview with Rossetti, brought about by Sir William Watson among the asphodels beyond Styx. Cory is not one who communes only with ravens and seamews. He must have friends with him in his pleasures. To walk and talk with friends was to him one of the great joys of his life. It is this side of the man he has been able to give most notable expression to of all the sides of himself he tried to express. It is the overflowing of the companionableness of the man in "Heraclitus" that gives its material a distinction comparable to that of its fòrm. Cory was of the Cambridge of his time, of the Eton of his time, of the landed gentry of his time. He loved England and all things English. He knew the history of his country in detail, but he lived largely in the old world of the classics for all that. The great figures of Greek and Roman legend and history were daily in his thoughts. So it was that, friendly human though he was, he wrote even of modern life in terms of the old life of Greece and Rome.

The preacher that Cory quarrels with in "Mimnermus in Church" cannot persuade him that the world to come is as good as the world of now, "This warm kind world is all I know." That last line is the final line of stanza one. The final line of stanza two is "I cling, a mere weak man, to men." Throughout, the tone of the poem is that of a most companionable and friendly man, unquestionably the gentleman, but what we call in America, "Just folks." It was given this pleasant gentleman and scholar to write two poems, not a little thing to do.

ARTHUR MUNBY

It was a good many years after Arthur Munby (1828-1910) began to publish verses before he found anything of his own to write about. *Verses New and Old* (1865) are in many manners, but no one of the many is original with Munby. There are verses after Byron, and after Wordsworth, and after Tennyson, and after Patmore, and none of them very good. He has already, however, found the material that he could handle sympathetically and freshly, the life of peasant girls on the farm and in service. Margery of "Maid Margery" is the stout and willing wench who reappears later as Dorothy, and as Ann Morgan. She has the same large hands, the same habit of falling on her knees to scrub, and she wears a like cotton print. There is already in this first volume the insistence on the virtues of homely ways, the revolt against the fine-ladyishness of Mid-Victorian ideals for women, and the worship of ruggedness in women that were to mark all his writing. There is little here, however, in any of his verses that even the most easily pleased could call poetry. When he tries to be sardonic he is cheap; when he tries to be tragic he is only melodramatic.

Dorothy (1880) marks an advance toward the kind of bare and simple narrative in which he was to do what was in him to do, and *Susan* (1893), marks an advance on *Dorothy*. He is more at ease in the rhymed couplet than he was in elegiacs. The heroine of *Dorothy* is red-armed and horny-handed and apt at ploughing, though she had, like similar heroines in a certain sort of Mid-Victorian novel, a gentleman for father. Munby did her over again as Ann Morgan, apparently because he had too narrow an experience to know other kinds of girl, or because it is the one type only he could admire.

In *Ann Morgan's Love* (1896) she is pure peasant and better drawn. Here her story is that of the servant girl who marries her master, but will not try to change her class. After a brief attempt on his part to school her into a lady, he gives it up, and goes to live with her in the little village on the Welsh Marches in which she was born. It costs him, of course, the society of most of his old set, but his close friends still come to visit him, and since he is a writing man he has plenty with which to busy himself. It was his own story Munby was telling, but that did not come to light until his death.

The telling of *Ann Morgan's Love* is all so far from the modern way that the poem seems much older than the nineties. It fails to bring you very close to either of the two, and the man is very slightly sketched indeed. Munby has tried hard to render all faithfully. He knows country ways and country things, but despite his knowledge the writing is all from the outside. You never feel you have the story from the standpoint of either of its two chief characters, but from the standpoint of some half-interested outsider, like the doctor we meet at its outset.

That is hardly the reason, however, why it did not meet with the response that greeted *Dorothy*, especially in America. *Dorothy* went through two editions in Boston in 1882, and a third cheap edition won a place in "The Seaside Library," published in New York in that same year, a rare triumph for a book of verse. In three readings of *Ann Morgan's Love* I have marked only two passages, and one of these chiefly for its philological interest. His blank verse is seldom as sententious as it is in:

> She had in her the making and the mould
> Of better things than fashion or than fame.

It is difficult to give a sense of what strength the poem has by quotation. Its strength lies in its design and proportion and material rather than in its detail. There are no purple patches of landscape description or of the heroine's beauty. It is just a plain and unvarnished tale that cites with little distinction, and from the outside, a bit of life. It stays in memory about to the extent of a fairly interesting story that you have heard of as happening in a place you do not know. It has not the instancy in memory of a story that has for background a place that you do know. Munby generally writes in the English of literature, but he likes to puzzle us with dialect now and then. In *Ann Morgan's Love* he indulges himself in the

> folkspeech of the Marches, full of words
> Vivid, expressive, picturesque; unknown
> To southern ears, but old and accurate
> As Chaucer's English; aye, and often fair.
> She was no gosterer, yet he knew full well
> How she could snape a rodney, hiking him
> Back to his work; and how with lusty arms
> She bested other women, when agate
> Keeving her barrer, thrutching at the coals;
> And how, on Easter Tuesday, she would oss
> To clip and heave her sweetheart up on high.
> Ah, and he knew that she was never fause,
> Nor fratchety, nor pizy; she was still
> Herself, as peart and jannock as the best.

Vestigia Retrorsum (1891) brought us the poet's portrait, but no verse that marked any advance in his art. It is, indeed, an undistinguished collection, such as might have been written by any cultivated man that took the trouble to master the technique of verses. *Ann Morgan's Love* was the best that Munby could do.

DAVID GRAY

They tried hard to make another Chatterton out of David Gray (1838-1861). There was really little likeness, however, between the weaver lad of Merkland and "the marvelous boy" of Bristol. Both were born in the provinces, Gray in Scotland, Chatterton in the west country; both suffered hardship in London; both had a certain genius for poetry. Chatterton was the creator of a quality that had not been in poetry before, a quality of romance, and a new movement of the line, or one that had not been in verse since the writing of the old ballads. Gray was an echo of what had gone before, a boy who fashioned himself into a compound of a thin-blooded Keats and a Wordsworth in homespun.

Proof of the first page of *The Luggie and Other Poems* (1862) was put into Gray's hands on December 2, 1861, the day before he died. Monckton Milnes had sent the poem to the *Cornhill Magazine,* but Thackeray would not accept it; Sydney Dobell encouraged him through correspondence and helped him with money; and Robert Buchanan was his friend from his Glasgow days. Milnes, afterwards Lord Houghton, wrote the "introductory notice" to his volume of verse, and Buchanan never lost an opportunity of crying him up in the many journals for which he wrote. The likeness of Gray's struggle against consumption to the struggle of Keats made him good newspaper copy, as did his many verses with full awareness of his near death. There is true pathos, too, in his story, and true pathos in his poems.

There is an innate interest and strength in his poems. They have an appeal in themselves entirely apart from the fact that they were written in the shadow of death. "The Luggie" is a pastoral in blank verse that puts much of Scotch life before you in its eleven hundred lines. The Luggie is the stream that flowed beside his father's cottage and weaving shop at Merkland, a little cluster of houses eight miles northeast of Glasgow. All his boyhood and youth had been spent on its banks and in the countryside environing it, and he knew all its moods and conditions at all hours of day and night and at all seasons of the year. Worshiping Keats and Wordsworth above the Scotch poets, it was inevitable that he should write the poem in literary English. It is a little strange, though, that there are so few native words in it, only a bird name, or a name for some country thing now and then.

There are in "The Luggie" a dozen items that have at once beauty and the smack of the soil. There is one of the best snowstorms and landscapes under snow in our literature. Put it side by side with Emerson's, or Whittier's, or Wilfred Gibson's, or whose you will, and it holds its own. There is the best description of a fieldfare's song that we have in English. Even W. H. Hudson says it "is not known to us in this country." But Gray had heard it and described it accurately and in words that are poetry. There are a ploughing contest, dances "In lone farm-houses set on whistling hills," lovers by Luggieside; autumn nights of full moon, but with "Orion like a frozen skeleton," and Cassiopeia glimmering "cold and clear Upon her throne of seven diamonds"; old Scotch songs; clacking hand looms, "whereon sit maidens homely fair, and full Of household simpleness"; a boy who was his companion in school and out; and an old couple and their lad that's dead. "The Luggie" never had, of course, Gray's final revision, but there are many finished passages in it, and bursts of poetry here and there.

There is a good sonnet to Gray's credit, too, an invitation to Robert Buchanan to come to Merkland that is full of the north-country April. There is another sonnet, not quite so good, on the evening star, and still another on "The land o' the leal" that appeals for itself, and for that phrase in the old song, "Thou art wearin' awa' " that was only too true of the poet as he wrote. It was his mother's singing of the old song to him as he lay ill that inspired its writing. But I am getting back to the pathos that his story lends his verse. It is better to remember the homely strength of that verse, the real knowledge of the countryside in it, the good workmanship. Too much stress has been laid on those boyish letters in which he boasted of the power he felt in himself. It is better just to read his verse. It has a quiet beauty that cannot be gainsayed. It has won him a modest place in English poetry.

ARTHUR O'SHAUGHNESSY

It was Louise Chandler Moulton who middlemanned Arthur O'Shaughnessy (1844-1881) for America, as she had previously middlemanned Philip Bourke Marston. O'Shaughnessy had married Marston's sister. O'Shaughnessy was a little the better writer, with an individual fall of line and a tone of his own. Generally his words either mastered him, running away with the meaning he would express when he began the poem, or they sufficed in their color and surge of sound for a burden of thought or an emotion that somehow eluded him. "We are the music makers" sums up, with some beauty, the old contention of the prophet and man of words that the world is made over in the mould of his thought. "We are the movers and shakers Of the world," he claims. He claims further:

> We build up the world's great cities,
>   And out of a fabulous story
> We fashion an empire's glory:
>
> .   .   .   .   .
>
> We, in the ages lying
>   In the buried past of the earth,
> Built Nineveh with our sighing,
>   And Babel itself with our mirth;
> And o'erthrew them with prophesying
>   To the Old of the New World's worth;
> For each age is a dream that is dying,
>   Or one that is coming to birth.

There are six stanzas more of this poem, but both thought and emotion are fully expressed by the end of this third stanza. The anthologists are right in clipping off the poem with the last line we quoted. There are sayings worth while in the remaining stanzas, but they are, at bottom, but restatement of ones in the first three stanzas. This poem is from *Music and Moonlight* (1874).

There is good work of sumptuous sort, very Swinburnian, in his *Epic of Women* (1870). One thinks, too, of Gautier as one reads of Cleopatra:

> She was reclined upon a Tyrian couch
>   Of crimson wools; out of her loosened vest
> Set on one shoulder with a serpent brooch
>   Full one white arm and half her foam-white breast.

It is ironical, in the light of such good work as these poems from which I have quoted, that O'Shaughnessy's most recognized contribution to literature should be to criticism rather than to poetry. His phrase "music and moonlight" has been taken from the title of his third volume, and used, ironically again, in a way that he would hardly like. It is a commonplace to say there is more than "music and moonlight" in poetry, or other sort of poetry than the "music and moonlight" kind. That was, however, exactly his kind, a natural development of certain Pre-Raphaelite characteristics through the medium of a temperament that seemed in many ways a composite of Rossetti's and Morris's and Swinburne's.

PHILIP BOURKE MARSTON

The pathetic story of Philip Bourke Marston (1850-1887) has done as much to keep his name alive as any of his verses. That story has been told most sympathetically by Louise Chandler Moulton, and by William Sharp. Marston was cruelly overpraised by Rossetti, who said of his "Garden Secrets," from *Song-Tide* (1871): "They are worthy of Shakespeare in his subtlest lyrical moods." They are many times less than that. There is no keen penetration of life in his verses, no deep realization of things as they are, no pushing-back of the horizon of the unknown. There are excellences of expression, but the slight experience of life, the deficiency of imagination, the absence of individuality result in an effect of feebleness. At his best Marston is a faint echo of Rossetti. His blindness did nothing for him except to bring a new sorrow into a life all too full of sorrows before. He had no Miltonic sense of black night and far stars, and no realization, such as blind men have so often had, of the rushing of the world through space and of its immensity. What verse he did is worthy of criticism is to be found in *Wind Voices* (1883), which had a vogue in America. That vogue is over now, and about all that remains of it is the reputation of good craftsmanship it made for its maker. The fragile charm of the man was not carried over into his verses. In that damning phrase of Davidson's, Marston has gone the way of all "souls called beautiful."

THEODORE WATTS-DUNTON

It is not every critic of poetry that can write poetry, either in prose or verse. Theodore Watts-Dunton (1832-1914) has proved by *Aylwin* (1898) that he can write poetry in prose and by *The Coming of Love* (1897) that he can write poetry in verse. His success in both forms, though long withheld, added a great deal of weight to his two deliverances on poetry, the article *Poetry* in the *Encyclopædia Britannica* (1885) and *The Renascence of Wonder* in *Chalmer's Encyclopædia of English Literature* (1903). Coleridge, Arnold, and Watts-Dunton have told us more about the nature of English poetry than all the other critics put together, and Watts-Dunton has not told us least of the three.

There is so much that is striking about his career that we are apt to make more of his verse than it deserves. His friendships with the poets, Tennyson, Rossetti, Morris, and Swinburne; his fellowship with George Borrow and his knowledge of gypsy ways; his courting of obscurity; the strange combination in him of lawyer and man of business and critic and poet; his hesitation and diffidence in putting out his "sonnet" sequence and his novel—the whole story of the man piqued curiosity and interest, made him, in short, a good newspaper story. The man who rescued Swinburne from himself must be a force indeed.

I have lived with his *Coming of Love* more than thirty years now, and I have read and reread it several times during that period. It has always seemed to me to fall short of its high intention, which is to show, in a gypsy setting, the triumph of love over death. He has created a character in Rhona Boswell, his heroine, as he has in Sinfi Lovell in *Aylwin,* and he has given us pictures of English countryside that are delightful in their dewiness and morning light, but there is hardly a completely accomplished poem in all the book. The material of poetry is there, the feeling of poetry is there, the elevation of poetry is there, but that final fusion which metamorphosizes what is poetic into what is poetry is in evidence in only a poem or two. I can hold no brief for *Christmas at the Mermaid,* from which certain anthologists make excerpts for their collections. The first sonnet in "The Daughter of the Sunrise" is far better poetry, about the best thing he has done. It lifts to greatness after a halting onset. There is a rapture of love here that is truly Meredithian and a warmth and color of landscape that suggest Turner. There is an ecstasy all his own in the close:

> Can this be Earth? Can these be banks of furze?
> Like burning bushes fired of God they shine!
> I seem to know them, though this body of mine
> Passed into spirit at the touch of hers!

EDWARD CARPENTER

All Edward Carpenter (1844-1929) is included in Walt Whitman. In the Englishman's verses you find the Old World countryside, sometimes in his own island, and sometimes in some traditional playground of the Englishman such as the Maritime Alps, instead of Long Island farmland or the prairies of the Middle West, or the sea beaches of New Jersey. All the musings, though,

of Carpenter, and all his preachments are Whitmanic, as are the
verse-forms in which musings and preachments are expressed. The
weaknesses and breaks that Whitman strayed into are deliberately
cultivated by Carpenter, but the vigor that underlay all the American's writing is unattainable by the Englishman. *Towards Democracy* (1882) is little more than Whitman and water, and none of
the later volumes is of a headier brew. What is perhaps pardonable in an untutored man such as Whitman is less pardonable in
the Cambridge man turned proletarian by malice aforethought.
There was a good deal of sound and fury about Old Walt but it
was all genuine, and it ended, generally, in something memorable
being said. The "strong" passages of Carpenter seem often forced,
and, as often, they fail to "come off." Most of his sets of verses
seem preludes to something that is never reached.

The nearest approaches to poetry you find in Carpenter are
certain of his descriptions of nature. He knows a willow wren
when he hears one sing, and bugloss when he sees it, but
there is no sustained writing in him about any natural thing.
He is not nearly so much of a nature poet in his loose rhythms
as are Thoreau, Jefferies, and Hudson in their several kinds of
prose.

Carpenter assumes a sympathy with all sorts and conditions
of men that Whitman really feels. He has borrowed a certain
spaciousness from his master, the trick of bridging the world in a
phrase. He has caught, too, the arrogance of Walt, his exclama-
tory manner, and his elephantine gamboling. There is no penetration to the truth of things in him, though, such as you find in
Whitman, none of the pictures of backwoods folks and things,
none of the tramp's lust of travel. Carpenter tells few stories.
Most of his attempts at them are only shells of stories. He shies
away instinctively from what is concrete. In "After Civilization"
you are led to expect some definite picture of a new world after
the wreck of cities and the old order that it foresees. No such
picture is painted for you. Such beauty as the lines have is found
in their transcripts from nature. It is difficult to understand from

any of his poems that Carpenter could be taken as a prophet, but he was so taken, it appears, and by more than a few people. By his written word, however, he can hardly long continue as other than a mild and Cantabrigian Whitman, the holder of an inconspicuous place in Victorian literature.

WILLIAM CANTON

There was a time when William Canton (1845-1926) was hailed as a poet who had bent science to the usages of poetry. That was back in the late seventies when "Through the Ages" appeared in *The New Quarterly Magazine*. A fight to the death between a primeval savage and a saber-toothed tiger, "a grey-haired pinched Professor droning to his class of girls," "a gentle shellfish" in a "cell of blue,"—these were materials rather unusual in the poetry of the last quarter of the nineteenth century. There was a time, in the nineties, when his verses about his daughter set the reviewers to saying he was a master of child verse. So liked was his "Father, whom I cannot see" that it was suggested as a substitute for the universally used child's prayer "Now I lay me down to sleep." Toward the end of his life he began a long narrative poem, "The Mask of Veronica," that seemed to promise new powers, but he never finished it.

Being an Englishman of his time Canton wrote, too, on Greek subjects and Biblical ones, on centaurs and on Solomon. All his long and busy life, a life spent largely in hackwork and journalism, he was casting about for a field of his own, but he never found such a field, and so he had slight chance of real success, of making discoveries in familiar material, in finding patterns of beauty in what daily concerned him. The best of his verses are those made out of memories of a little girl lost, or out of pictures retained of landscape seen or birds silhouetted against an arresting background. "Heart-ease" strikes home poignantly, and "The Crow" catches the nature and look of that "ungodly rogue." There are a dozen other poems, mostly nature poems, that are good to read, but they, unfortunately, do not compel you to remember them.

JAMES THOMSON THE SECOND

With all the will in the world to find it, I have never been able to find a poem of James Thomson (1834-1882) of first power. I have been reading him off and on for the forty years since I heard as a youth that he was a sort of British Poe. The story of his life; the death of Mathilda Weller, his child-love in Ireland; his struggle with drink from his early days as a schoolmaster in the army; his revolt from the faith of his fathers; his lonely years in London; and his death in hospital—all this made his so interesting a story that I wanted to like him. Particularly I wanted to like him because it seemed the world was against him, and to sympathize with the rejected of the world is a natural human impulse.

It so happened none of my friends had a Thomson I could borrow, and that I never came across one at a book-store, so I had to fall back on library copies for my first reading of him. It was, of course, *The City of Dreadful Night* (1880), that I sought out to read. It was Kipling's use of its title and his quotations from the poem, I think, that drove me to it after much talk of it had failed to send me there. I remember well how disappointed I was in it when I did get down to reading it. It seemed to me to say what it had to say of the abomination of desolation over and over again.

So it seems to me to say, as I read it now. It seems to me second-rateness long drawn out, the essence of mediocrity, reiteration after reiteration of memories from the *Inferno* and *Paradise Lost* and "Child Rolande to the Dark Tower Came." Its worst fault is its diffuseness. The verse is well enough wrought, but it is without felicities. There are no revelations of vision in it, few discoveries about life, and few pictures. His city is a kind of London in eclipse, its street-lamps lighted, but almost no windows bright from lamps within. The "vast forms" that move fantastically beyond Poe's "red-litten" windows are dwarfed or distorted here. Parts of it seem worked out almost mathematically, part XX for one. Here we see

> A couchant sphinx in shadow to the breast,
> An angel standing in the moonlight clear.

As we look again, the angel's wings have fallen, and a warrior leans on his sword where the angel stood. An unarmed man replaces the warrior, and a shattered figure the unarmed man. Thomson tells us he has written the poem:

> Because a cold rage seizes one at whiles
>   To show the bitter old and wrinkled truth
> Stripped naked of all vesture that beguiles,
>   False dreams, false hopes, false masks and modes of youth;
> Because it gives some sense of power and passion
> In helpless impotence to try to fashion
>   Our woe in living words howe'er uncouth.

My quarrel with the poem is not this half-childish reason he gives for writing it, but that, in that writing, he has not been able to reach impassioned speech.

There is almost nothing to remember from a reading of it, from many readings of it, except a general sense of a half-dead city under darkness, a few statuesque figures of perhaps allegorical significance, and a very few lines that concentrate experience of life. Only now and then does he say much in a few words. This is one instance:

> No secret can be told
> To any who divined it not before.

Thomson sums up rather well the things that count in life in part XVI, in only eighteen lines. There is, too, in the poem one night-piece that stands out a little from its monotonous gloom:

> How the moon triumphs through the endless nights!
>   How the stars throb and glitter as they wheel
> Their thick processions of supernal lights
>   Around the blue vault obdurate as steel!

Thomson, perhaps remembering the dictum of Poe that a long poem "is simply a flat contradiction in terms," has divided "The

City of Dreadful Night" into twenty-one parts; but the divisions are only an evasion. It is all one poem.

Thomson has been more successful in breaking up "Sunday up the River" and "Sunday at Hampstead." Or rather I should say that the general title in those poems covers in each case a group of lyrics, lyrics of sufficiently differing moods for each to have an entity of its own. These two poems are not just variations on a theme, as is "The City of Dreadful Night."

You find in these two series of poems the lyrics of Thomson generally included in the anthologies, "In the Tram," from "Sunday at Hampstead," and "Give a man a horse he can ride," "The wine of Love," and "My Love o'er the water bends dreaming" from "Sunday up the River." There is no one of them, however, a lyric of first power, that could stand being put side by side with Heywood's "Pack clouds, away," or Herrick's "Gather ye rosebuds," or Wordsworth's "Daffodils," or Hodgson's "Gipsy Girl."

Though "The City of Dreadful Night" was not published in book form until 1880, it had had a considerable reputation from the time of its appearance in *The National Reformer* in 1874. There was a sufficient response to the collected verse of *The City of Dreadful Night and Other Poems* (1880) for Thomson to take heart and begin to write again. He had done little verse from 1874, when he finished "The City of Dreadful Night." There was enough of old and new for another volume in 1881, *Vane's Story, Weddah and Om-El-Bonain, and Other Poems.* Though the unsold stock of Thomson's books was destroyed by fire in 1890, and though first editions of the two collections of verse, and of the collected prose *Essays and Phantasies* (1881), are scarce, I was able to buy a first of *Vane's Story* in 1928 for four shillings and sixpence. That price indicates how little demand there is for Thomson among collectors.

The two-volume edition of his poems published in 1895 with an introduction by Bertram Dobell sold slowly, too. I bought it from Dobell in 1912, and I saw it advertised long after that. Never man had a better friend than Thomson in Dobell, but, for all the latter's effort in his behalf, the place desired for Thomson among the English poets has not been won. The simple truth is that the story of the man's life is more interesting than his verse. Thomson has none of the attributes of the poet of first power. He has not a great style. He strikes no new note in poetry. He has no new magic or music of words. There is no lyric of his that makes itself a part of you from your first reading of it as does Housman's "With rue my heart is laden" or Kipling's "Lichtenburg."

I sometimes think that satire was Thomson's greatest asset, and it is axiomatic that satire cannot lift verse into poetry. His "Supplement to the Inferno" must have gotten under Bulwer's skin if he came across it. That picture of England ten thousand years ago that Thomson painted in "Sunday at Hampstead" is newer and fresher than anything else he did. I have wondered was not Shaw's Brittanus in *Cæsar and Cleopatra* a memory of that line in part V about the wild man who

> Strutted full drest in war paint. . . .
> Blue of a devilish pattern laid on thick.

These verses are the only ones of Thomson that do not suggest some other author to me. The group of young people having tea on Hampstead Heath are told by one of their number about another party in prehistoric England of four men and four women who ate a wild boar half-raw, and then built up the entrance of their cave against the wolves that howled and the wildcats that wailed without. It is only fooling, perhaps, but it is original fooling. It is these verses I should put into an anthology if I wished to reveal what was new to English poetry in the verse of James Thomson the lesser.

T. E. BROWN

Had William Morris not been written down "Our Modern Chaucer" the title must have been given T. E. Brown (1830-1897). Certainly it more truly describes the Manx poet, for Morris had only of Chaucer's qualities his easy narrative and a like acquaintance with old tales good to steal. It would seem that Brown found more of his stories in life than in books, where Chaucer found them, but his habit was apparently to show such situations as novelists had made familiar. "Peggy's Wedding" and "Bella Gorry" are the tales that make you feel they must be first hand from fact. "Bella Gorry" is told with the large ease and clarity and dignity we call classical. There is in it none of the sob that shakes most of his stories or the laughter so like it in quality, and effect. "Peggy's Wedding" is told as racily as Chaucer would have told it, but its irony is always close to a pathos that the four-teenth century had not learned to feel. "Captain Tom and Captain Hugh," in its recital of the close friends divided by the better for-tune of the more generous, takes us nearer to themes proven by use, but it is still far from threadbare, as are many of the themes of these "Fo'c's'le Yarns."

The first story of the first series, "Betsy Lee," which called attention to Brown when it appeared in *Macmillan's Magazine* in 1875, is the old, old story of lovers parted by a lie of the girl's rejected suitor, and of the girl's death because of her sorrow. "Christmas Rose" tells of the parting of two brothers through love of their foster sister that loves neither. "The Doctor" shows the results of an unfortunate marriage—the degeneration of the man through his union with a weak woman, when circumstances parted him from the girl he loved; his first love's subsequent love-less marriage; and the compensation that followed in the happy love of her son and his daughter, that compensation for which the Reverend Mr. Bell and Helen Pendennis so heartily prayed. Familiar as these stories are, they are freshened by a new back-ground, the Man of the days before it was a summer resort, and by the individual outlook on life of their author. It is usual to compare him to Hawker, but the vicar of Morwenstow, original as he was, a creator of a new way of living life, could make no new beauty in words or thought, and was only a fairly efficient rearranger of old effects. Hawker was not even a minor poet, and Brown, if you allow that narrative poetry admits to the company of the great, you must call all but major.

In essaying narrative poetry portraying stories of country life Brown was almost alone among his contemporaries. In the mid years of the nineteenth century the versified novel was not uncommon, but none of those who tried their hand at it, among whom Tennyson, Mrs. Browning, and Patmore were chief, had knowledge of the ways of peasants or such grip of the realities as Brown. Buchanan is nearer him, and Hardy, though he usually condenses his stories to shorter than ballad form, has given a kindred study in one, "The Fire at Tranter Sweatley's." Of these names those that are held great in verse are not held greatest for their story-telling, or for any qualities of this class of their writing, but for their lyrics. You must go back to Wordsworth, to "Michael" and "The Brothers" for analogues, but even here the treatment is nothing like so full as Brown's. Crabbe is nearest in material and method of treatment, but he knows none of the Manxman's cheeriness. Of younger writers Jane Barlow has told pleasantly tales in verse, but not so successfully as in prose. Masefield, of course, is a master in his kind, but his narratives are told with the swiftness of the short story, while most of Brown's move with the leisureliness of the old-fashioned novel. Brown did not get a hearing in his life from many who care for the best poetry because he was a narrative poet in a lyric age. His lyrics, which came later, were obscured by the reputation of his narratives, as Patmore's odes were obscured by the reputation of *The Angel in the House*. And then Brown was provincial, a Manx poet, writing oftenest in Manx dialect. And the provincialism of a period is seldom forgivable to that period. Only provincialism whose practiser has the personality of a Burns can overcome prejudice in his own generation.

Brown was by choice a provincial poet, the poet of the country of his birth, his youth, his vacations from Clifton College. As Oxford man he was, of course, acquainted with the old way of the poets, but he chose to write in homely fashion of home sub-

jects, to put his province, so far as he could, into poetry. In the
"Dedication" to the second series of *Fo'c's'le Yarns* he wrote:

> Dear Countrymen, whate'er is left to us
> Of ancient heritage—
> Of manners, speech, of humours, polity,
> The limited horizon of our stage—
> Old love, hope, fear,
> All this I fain would fix upon the page.

This object he could best accomplish in narrative, and it was for
narrative he had genius. Narrative brought in the habits of the
people, fishermen, miners, farmers; the customs peculiar to each
class; their ways of work and pleasure, their appearance and men-
tality; it brought in folklore, descriptions of places, the mountain
valleys, and the shores, rocky or sandy, of his mother isle, its flora
and fauna. He is in protest against the islanders' loss of their old
ways, their absorption into the empire to which he is most proudly
loyal.

Even the little of Brown's verse that is not outwardly narrative is often narrative in essence. His pictures are apt to be pictures
of incidents, but he can paint landscape without figures in it. He
wonders at the ways of God, he writes epistles to friends living
and elegies to friends dead. Some of his very best work is in his
character sketches and personal lyrics. His songs are infrequent,
for he is seldom content to confine a mood or a thought in so
brief compass. He is so curious of all which crosses his way that
he must analyze it or hunt out the story in it and carry his writing
into ramifications which a song may not contain.

Brown writes few poems about his art, except the dedications
and preludes to the *Fo'c's'le Yarns*. These reveal much of his aim
and their narrator, Tom Baynes, much of Brown's own tenderness
and downrightness. Tom is, in fact, for all Brown calls him
"old salt, old rip, old friend," very much the poet himself, in his
humor, his volcanic activity, his passion for all things Manx. Like
Sir Walter, Brown talks of old blood, but, like him, he writes

with gusto only of peasants and parsons. Though he attains as
surely in English verse as in his Manx dialect, he would rather
write his poems in the latter, and so the Manx poems have the
greater energy. It has been given to him to answer in his own
work his admonition to the future Manx poet:

> Trench deep within the soil
> That bore you fateful: toil, and toil, and toil!
> 'Tis deep as Death; dig, till the rock
> Clangs hard against the spade, and yields the central shock.

So Brown himself has dug, with the result that his poetry
clangs with "the central shock," the shock of the underlying
realities; and since the underlying realities are underlying realities
the world over, though the criers for cosmopolitanism seem always
to forget it, his poetry has universal appeal.

It is not every poet that can hope to put the whole life of his
country into his poetry, but since Man with its two hundred and
twenty-seven square miles is after all only a county, and since it
was his homeland, and since power of character portrayal and of
clear narrative was given him, with the supreme gift of lyrical cry,
Brown had done what he set his hand to. Great heart, large sympathy, ruddy humanity, racy vulgarity with nothing of common
or cheap in it, but with the tonic coarseness no age could need more
than Queen Victoria's—these are his basic qualities. From them
flower up all sorts of beauties, intellectual and spiritual. In almost
every poem there sobs the pathos of parting, and again and again
there escapes the cry of the strong man for the little son he has
lost. He never wrote more greatly than in "Roman Women,"
wonderful pictures that Browning would have loved. A few lines
flashing with insight and color, and the portrait and personality
of each woman is rendered:

> Ah! naughty little girl,
> With teeth of pearl,
> You exquisite little brute,
> So young, so dissolute—

Ripe orange brushed
From an o'erladen tree, chance-crushed
And bruised and battered on the street,
And yet so merry and so sweet!
Ah, child, don't scoff—
Yes, yes, I see—you lovely wretch, be off!

Brown's treatment of sex in this poem, as in the rest of its series, and in his Manx tales, is as frank as Meredith's and as unoffending, and always it is honest as the sun. His idylls of young love are perilously close to sentimentality, but you forgive all for the charm of his girls, Manx girls as pretty and simply natural and lovable as Hardy's Wessex girls, but most of them better fated. It is in his stories of them and their lovers, and of the older and younger members of their families, that I like him best. They seem to be a people as "kindly Irish" as their fellow-Gaels to the westward. Brown makes me feel I know his Manx folk, I who know no more of the country and its people than comes from the sight of its mountains on the horizon, the stories of a friend whose ancestry is proven Manx by the Manx family Bible, and the reading of Hall Caine's novels, which unhappily in later days had less and less to do with his homeland.

There is no barrier of dialect to cross in most of his personal lyrics, the statement of the moods that come to him, a questioning modern, though often the old ways of the warm-hearted Celtic land are the background. At other times Clifton College or Dartmoor are the places back of the poems. "Sunset at Chagford" is as analytical as the narratives are simple. The pathos of "Mater Dolorosa" and "Aber Stations" is almost intolerable. Beautiful as they are, I would reread them no more willingly than I would *Jude the Obscure*. Till his death Brown carried the heart-ache he told here, and the reader is haunted, days after he has put the poems by, with their cry of sorrow unappeasable. Yet no lover of poetry can but feel the masterfulness of their form. They are a revelation to those who hold that Browning exhausted the possibilities of the dramatic lyric.

Almost all that Brown wrote tempts you, as you read, to read aloud; you want some one to laugh with you and rejoice in the style; to rejoice with you in this new truth the poet flashes before you; to wonder with you at the imagination of the man, but most of all you read aloud because his writing is living speech, with the cry of the spoken word reverberant in it. With the strength, there is the weakness of the spoken word, and there are other weaknesses than this in Brown, but all save "the wallowing naked in the pathetic" are on the surface. The greatest strength of these poems is in their very constitution. Exteriorly, too, his lines are beautiful, the statement of striking story, or unstudied emotion, or deeply analytical thought, is in words that count. He uses old symbols and new to bring home his meaning. It is now:

> And a star come out like a swan on a lake
> White and lonely.

and now it is:

> And foxgloves, like numerous celled revolvers,
> Shoot honey-tongued quintessence of July.

This poetry is very seldom merely decorative; the words take on beauty because below them lies impassioned thought. This thought is never far from what concerns "the business and the bosoms of men," so that one can understand all his allusions readily and sympathize with his emotions from an average experience of life. Brown is companionable always, illuminating in his lyrics in English, and entertaining after the fashion of a Mid-Victorian novelist in his narratives in dialect. He is more of a poet in these lyrics than in the narratives. He could have been still more of a poet had he chosen to give his energy earlier to work in the English lyric. As it is, this work is only a by-product of a life given almost wholly to the celebration in the Manx dialect of the life of the Isle of Man. And he has paid the penalty that all but the man of first power must pay when he deliberately chooses to be provincial in manner as well as matter. The world of the center has passed him by.

WILFRID SCAWEN BLUNT

Poetry is no distinguisher of persons. It chooses a gager in Burns, a parson in Emerson, a tramp in W. H. Davies. It chose in Wilfrid Scawen Blunt (1840-1922) a man about town who was also a country gentleman and a champion of lost causes. Yet Blunt was hardly of the full stature of the poet. He was rather of the mob of gentlemen who write with ease. No one of them, however, since Byron's day is so nearly a poet. Blunt was not quite a poet because there was no ecstasy in him, no passionate love of beauty, no artistry of high order. He was impatient of hard work in writing, of rewriting on rewriting. And Blunt had not, as Scott, equally impatient of rewriting, had, a fund of romance to compensate him for the lack of the first powers of the poet.

Blunt had passion in him, the passion of love, passion for freedom, passion for the rights of man, but he could not, for all his feeling, often get feeling into his verses. That Blunt had powers of analysis of emotion *The Love Sonnets of Proteus* (1881) stands for witness. He could draw character. You see and remember the little woman in black of "Esther." He had the gift of telling a story, as "Griselda" is proof.

In none of these stories in verse, whether sonnet sequence or rhymed novel, do you see that other phase of his gentility, his country gentleman phase. This squire was just as sure of his place as the finest beau who strutted it on the mall, but he was as well versed in country things as any farm-boy turned poacher: the hunting of the hare, which he liked better than the hunting of the fox; the blackbird's shriek as it is flushed from the strawberry bed; the far-off crowing of cocks; ducks asleep by the pond; pheasants stirring in their sleep; and a hundred other country sounds and sights. He was a Catholic and a Conservative:

> The new world still is all less fair
> Than the old world it mocks.

Blunt was not always so proud of his poetry as he was of his propaganda in behalf of Arabi Pasha or of Ireland in the Land League days. He did oversee the collection of all his verse in *The Poetical Works of Wilfrid Scawen Blunt: A Complete Edition* (1914), some nine hundred pages in all. There had been a time, though, in his youth, that he had written:

> I would not, if I could, be called a poet;
> I have no natural love of the "chaste muse."
> If aught be worth the doing I would do it;
> And others, if they will, may tell the news.
> I care not for their laurel but would choose
> On the world's field to fight or fall or run.
> My soul's ambition will not take excuse
> To play the dial rather than the sun.
> The faith I held, I hold, as when a boy
> I left my books for cricket-bat and gun.
> The tales of poets are but scholars' themes.
> In my hot youth I held it that a man
> With heart to dare and stomach to enjoy
> Had better work to his hand in any plan
> Of any folly, so the thing were done,
> Than in the noblest dreaming of mere dreams.

This, of course, is only a variant of Browning's "Sing, riding's a joy! For me, I ride," but there is no doubt of it being the personal creed held strongly by Blunt. Such philosophy of life as he had was distinctly hedonist. It was all summed up in that line from "Esther": "I have tasted honey, and behold, I die!" His church was not a vital thing to him but just a tradition that he thought, as a gentleman, he should hold to. What there was of surety in life was the joy of the senses. There is happiness, and happiness defeats the years.

> He who has once been happy is for aye
> Out of destruction's reach.

Blunt had read and remembered his *Omar*, as he had his *Don Juan*. And he had won a response from his readers akin, in its lesser way, to that of the still popular Byron and Fitzgerald. Wherever you pick up a copy of *The Love Sonnets of Proteus* you find it shows signs of having been read hard, whether library copy, or that which has found its way into a second-hand book-shop. You find worn and turned-down pages, marked passages and notes scribbled on the margin. Youth has responded to youth as it always will.

Blunt had no illusions. He put all down as he had seen it and experienced it. He balked at nothing, but his breeding saved him from details that might have been offensive. In "Griselda" he justified himself for what he told, declaring: "And who would gather truth must bend him low." And yet it is not in describing the landed gentry among whom he was born, their daring and avid lives, their follies and foibles, that he was at his best. He was at his best when a vision of old times fell on him in a forest in Bosnia, out-of-the-world Bosnia. Blunt was as near to poetry here as he ever was:

> Spirit of Trajan! What a world is here,
> What remnant of old Europe in this wood,
> Of life primeval rude as in the year
> When thy first legions by the Danube stood.
> These are the very Dacians they subdued,
> Swineherds and shepherds clad in skins of deer
> And fox and marten still, a bestial brood,
> Than their own swine begotten swinelier.
> The fair oak-forest, their first heritage,
> Pastures them still, and still the hollow oak
> Receives them in its bosom. Still o'erhead
> Upon the stag-head tops, grown hoar with age,
> Calm buzzards sit and ancient ravens croak,
> And all with solemn life is tenanted.

AUSTIN DOBSON

Austin Dobson (1841-1921) is remembered to-day as a con-noisseur of eighteenth-century art and as the first of the late Victorian writers of *vers de société*. He is very like in the two fields, the field of the familiar essay and the field of familiar verse. Always there is in his writing the art that conceals art; the labor of the file so skilfully applied that we sense rather than see the evidence of it, the semblance of ease, urbanity, clarity, reasonableness, and complete self-control. There is true feeling in Dobson, but there is seldom real exaltation of spirit; there is fancy in plenty, but little imagination; there is prettiness galore but almost no beauty.

Dobson, for all these limitations, might be more than a writer of society verse. What prevents him, in all save a few poems, from being more, is a slight forcing of the note on which he writes, a play-acting at deeper feeling than he really has, an artificiality that tight-laces his muse. "A Gentleman of the Old School" has been a daily friend of mine these forty years. It professes a code with which I have the greatest sympathy. It delights me still at each rereading, but I cannot rid myself of a suspicion that it is a little affected. I like it as much as I ever did, but I cannot admire it as I did in my teens. Its sentiment has been so stressed that it has become something like sentimentality. "A Gentleman of the Old School" is full of good things, though, exhibits from the eighteenth century as worthy of a place among your collections as any Wedgewood figure or Sheraton cupboard. No man has written better of doves, whose "ruffling, puffed content" he has caught exactly. In key, too, is what Dobson tells us of his hero's liking for the chase. He

> held
> That no composer's score excelled
> The merry horn, when Sweetlip swelled
> Its jovial riot.

It was in the eighties of last century, when America was beginning to tire of Mid-Victorian things and to recapture from garret and cellar and barn eighteenth-century objects of household art, that Austin Dobson came into vogue among us. *Proverbs in*

Porcelain (1877) were popular pieces for amateur acting; *Old World Idylls* (1883) was a parlor table book; and ballads and rondeaus, triolets and villanelles of his were imitated at valentine parties, and at the "progressive" tortures that did duty for games in that period.

"A Gentlewoman of the Old School" is another pleasant poem, but it is obviously a reiteration of the effects, with but slight change of subject, of "A Gentleman of the Old School." *The Ballad of Beau Brocade* (1892), with illustrations by Hugh Thomson, was a favorite gift book of the nineties, and the ballad that gave title to it a recitation piece almost as popular as "The Highwayman" of Noyes in the nineteen-twenties. "The Sundial" is another one of his sets of verses that are close to poetry, but it is marred at the close by a sentimentality.

There is a good deal to be said for the position of those who hold that the best verse of Dobson is that directly descriptive of the eighteenth century and critical of its authors. His allegiance to Pope and to the times of Pope should be set over against the rather derogatory criticism of Sir William Watson in *Wordsworth's Grave* (1890). Says Dobson:

> Take up the *Lock*, the *Satires*, *Eloise*—
> What Art supreme, what Elegance, what Ease!
> How keen the Irony, the Wit how bright,
> The Style how rapid, and the Verse how light!
> Then read once more, and you shall wonder yet
> At Skill, at Turn, at Point, at Epithet.
> "True Wit is Nature to Advantage dress'd"—
> Was ever Thought so pithily express'd?
> "And ten low Words oft creep in one dull Line"—
> Ah, what a Homily on Yours—and Mine!
> Or take—to choose at Random—take but This—
> "Ten censure wrong for one that writes amiss."

That is keen criticism and apt quotation. This that follows is almost a credo:

> So I, that love the old *Augustan* Days
> Of formal Courtesies and formal Phrase;
> That like along the finish'd Line to feel
> The Ruffle's Flutter and the Flash of Steel;
> That like my Couplet as Compact as Clear;
> That like my Satire sparkling tho' severe,
> Unmix'd with Bathos and unmarr'd by Trope,
> I fling my Cap for Polish—and for POPE!

"The Ruffle's Flutter and the Flash of Steel" tries bravely to give the age in a line. The trouble is it is a little too general. It might serve as well as a description of Jacobean or Elizabethan times.

Dobson makes no attempt to be other than he is by nature and taste. He is content with his limitations and he is sometimes slightly contemptuous of the finest things. In "An Epistle to a Friend," the prologue in verse to *Eighteenth Century Vignettes: Third Series* (1896) he owns:

> For detail, detail, most I care
>   (Ce superflu, si nécessaire!)
>
> .   .   .   .   .
>
>   My aim
> Is modest. This is all I claim:
> To paint a part and not the whole,
> The trappings rather than the soul.

In "The Poet and the Critics" he is equally frank. In his poems is

>   the best he had:
> Much Memory,—more Imitation;—
> Some Accidents of Inspiration;—
> Some Essays in that finer Fashion
> Where Fancy takes the place of Passion;—
> And some (of course) more roughly wrought
> To catch the Advocates of Thought.

It is a "Household Art" that Dobson would celebrate, as he tells us in the verses under that caption:

O Art of the Household! Men may prate
Of their ways "intense" and Italianate,—
They may soar on their wings of sense, and float
To the *au delà* and the dim remote,—
Till the last sun sink in the last-lit West,
'Tis the Art at the Door that will please the best;
To the end of Time 'twill be still the game,
For the Earth first laughed when the children came!

This is the art that he has celebrated in both verse and prose. He himself was a very part of the "household art" of the English-speaking peoples for a quarter of a century. From *Vignettes in Rhyme* (1873) to his *Collected Poems* (1897) Austin Dobson had a prominent place among the read and quoted poets of his tongue. His books, prettily bound and prettily illustrated, were in thousands of homes. They were proper birthday presents and Christmas presents and philopena presents. They vied with bonbons as safe and noncommittal presents to girls. They entered into and became a part of the life of late Victorian times, in its phases both lively and severe. They appealed to the every-day instincts of nice people. They were decorative, well-bred, homey, domestic without namby-pambyness.

His prologues and epilogues, the verses dedicated to his friends and the gossipy letters in rhyme he sent to them, are in the very vein of the familiar essay in prose. They are very happy verses of their kinds, better on the whole than his familiar essays in prose and his criticism in prose. His son, Alban Dobson, in *Austin Dobson: An Anthology of Prose and Verse* (1922), seems to value the prose higher, for he puts two passages in prose to every set of verses. Such emphasis on the prose is hardly just. It is true that the qualities of all of the writing of Austin Dobson are the qualities of prose rather than of poetry, but if it is not a bull to say it, I will say that his best prose is in his verse. By that I mean, of course, that in workmanship, interest, and power his verse outdoes his prose. His *Henry Fielding* (1883) is a sterling book, but there is all Dobson has to say in it in the short compass of his verses "Henry Fielding," dedicated to James Russell Lowell. It is of rhymed prose that Austin Dobson is master, and not of the higher forms of either prose or verse.

ROBERT BUCHANAN

Robert Buchanan (1841-1901) is to most readers the author of *The Fleshly School of Poetry* (1871-1872) rather than the poet who wrote "The Ballad of Judas Iscariot." Such a reputation is often, and sometimes unjustly, interpreted as an illustration of the fact that a man may survive as a writer because of his attack on a greater man, when, if it were not for the attack, his name would have sunk into obscurity. It is impossible to be dogmatic about such matters, but it seems to me that, if it had not been for this attack, Buchanan would be better known than he is. He would have, I think, about such a place as has Hake or T. E. Brown or Wilfrid Gibson, instead of being dismissed as a poetaster who was a calumniator of a painter and poet only short of great.

To-day, of course, we can look on the old scandal dispassionately, no matter what our personal prejudices. I happen to be more in sympathy with the ideals of the Pre-Raphaelites—which their practice did not always advance—than with the ideals of the humanitarian group to which Buchanan belonged, but that does not prevent me from seeing that there was an insistence on physical detail in Rossetti which was worse than bad taste. Though the Buchanan charges were pushed too far, there was ground for them. What weakened the charges as valid criticism was the fact they were inspired by a desire for revenge. Buchanan was out for blood in *The Fleshly School of Poetry*. Swinburne had slighted David Gray, the poet who was Buchanan's friend in youth, and W. M. Rossetti had called Buchanan "a poor and pretentious poetaster" in the controversy that followed Buchanan's rejoinder.

If Buchanan had done poetry of the first power it would, I think, have obliterated memory of the attack on Rossetti. The pity is Buchanan did not do such work. It looked, though, in his youth, as if he might have done it. *Undertones* (1863) was only 'prentice-work, but there was sharp observation of life, creation of character, satire, and flashes of poetry in *Idyls and Legends of Inverburn* (1865), a series of narrative poems on Scotch life, most of it Lowland and low-class. *London Poems* (1866) revealed no new powers, but it widened the scope of his work, and it showed he had deep sympathy with the underdog. *The Book of Orm* (1870) was an attempt to break new ground. It contains "The Dream of the World without Death," the most quoted of his poems and the one most often found in the anthologies. Like nearly all he has written, however, this poem is not fully realized, either in feeling, or in imagination, or in form. Nor is this one poem, or the volume as a whole, a thing of wonder and verbal magic. There may have been Highland blood in Buchanan, but he never seems to me the Celt in his writing. With the exception of certain lines in *Balder the Beautiful* (1877), he was nearer the poet in his earlier work than in any verse that he wrote.

Buchanan calls his *City of Dream* (1888) an epic poem, believing that the term is "applicable to any poetical work which embodies, in a series of grandiose pictures, the intellectual spirit of the age in which it is written." It seems to me he explains a part of his failure as a poet by these words. They reveal that his purpose is topical, an exposition of ideas of his time, and that the writing is "grandiose" rather than grand in its intention. To Buchanan, evidently, "grandiose" does not carry with it its own condemnation. We all know, of course, that "grandiose" may be glossed as "grand," but it has had, from before the time of Buchanan's use of it, an association with what is pompous and pretentious.

Like so many reformers Buchanan is fighting here, as later in *The New Rome* (1900), what the development of civilization would soon do away with without his efforts. The heartburnings and doubts that are so important to him to discuss seem to-day outside of what concerns us. The world accepts, pretty generally, the Christian morality, and says frankly it does not know whether or not there is a survival of human personality after death. *The City of Dream* attempts to be, Buchanan tells us, *Pilgrim's Progress* up-to-date, "for the inquiring modern spirit, what the lovely vision of Bunyan is for those who still exist in the fairyland of dogmatic Christianity." It is hardly that, but rather a succession of bouts with men of straw.

The attempts of Buchanan with American subjects are no happier than *The City of Dream. St. Abe and his Seven Wives* (1873) takes us to Salt Lake City, and *White Rose and Red* (1874) to Maine, but Buchanan had not been in America when he wrote them, and neither is important as a record of life or as literature. His reliance in both of these poems, as almost always in his verse, is on something else than impassioned writing that breaks into music. Here he falls back upon story and a life which he thinks will have the appeal of strangeness. Elsewhere it is description of countryside or humanitarian feeling or argument over religion that he falls back upon. It is to the earlier volumes that we must turn, if we would judge Buchanan by what he could do. He is in command of his subject material in the narratives of the Lowlands and of London.

Idyls and Legends of Inverburn (1865) is at its best in "The Widow Mysie: an Idyl of Love and Whiskey." It relates how Tom Love, "whiskered, well-featured, tight from top to toe" and a well-to-do farmer's son, is jilted for his father when the tavern-keeping widow finds the son cannot get the old man's money to spend on setting up house for the widow and himself. Buchanan is happier far in the ironic and dourly realistic than when doing the pathetic, as in "Willie Baird" and "Hugh Sutherland's Pansies." Nor are his attempts at the romantic in high life, in "Lord Ronald's Wife," or in chronicles of fays and elves and the like, any more successful. "The English Huswife's Gossip" and "The Two Babes" have the weakness that comes to him with a pathetic theme, but they have moments of realism that almost redeem them from sentimentality.

London Poems (1866) presents a fresher kind of work than

Idyls and Legends of Inverburn, but no more poetry. Its excellences, such as they are, and they are not inconsiderable in "The Little Milliner," "Liz," and "Nell," are not, however, the excellences of lyric ecstasy, but the excellences of characterization and story-telling. The heroine of "The Little Milliner" is a Barrie character done before Barrie began to write. She is, like Cinderella and several of her sisters, bird-like and dainty, full of pleasant make-believe, a small girl grown up without losing her girlishness or without failing to put on womanliness.

"Liz" is the story of a girl of the slums dying in childbirth. It is hardly dramatically true that one so situated should be telling the minister so unbrokenly, and with so sure a sense of proportion, her piteous story. It is an old device, a much-sinned sin, of the sentimentalist and unrealistic writer. "Nell" is better done. It is the story of a rougher girl than Liz telling her friend Nan how her man was hanged for the murder, in drink, of a fellow of his. There is less sentimentality in "Nell" than in "Liz," and better architectonics and tighter writing.

"The Scaith o' Bartle" is another Scotch story, of the general sort met in *Idyls and Legends of Inverburn,* but of the seashore, instead of an inland place. It is a sad story, like most in both these collections of narratives. Buchanan justifies such sadness in the verses introductory to *London Poems,* saying:

> And if I list to sing of sad things oft,
> It is that sad things in this life of breath
> Are truest, sweetest, deepest. Tears bring forth
> The richness of our natures, as the rain
> Sweetens the smelling brier.

That is as close to a reading of life as Buchanan comes. He is wanting in readings of life, as in impassioned passages. He bitterly resented a criticism of Richard Le Gallienne of his *Wandering Jew* (1893). Le Gallienne said the poem lacked work upon it. He was right. Nearly all of Buchanan's writing, prose and verse alike, lacks work upon it. Buchanan was too driven, by the amount of writing he had to do, to expend on that writing the loving care nearly all the poets who count have expended upon their work.

It may be, too, that Buchanan was confirmed in his belief that narrative poetry was the most important kind of poetry by a declaration of his friend Charles Reade, which he quotes with seeming approval in an estimate of Reade published at the time of the novelist's death. In a letter to Buchanan, Reade wrote: "I look on poetry as fiction with the music of words. But divorced from fiction, I do not much value the verbal faculty, nor the verbal music. And I believe this is the popular instinct, too, and that a musical story-teller would achieve an incredible popularity."

Buchanan realized, of course, that his own gift for verse was for the narrative and not the lyric, so he naturally found comfort in such a saying as this of Reade. It is just what you would expect of Reade, for his weakness as novelist and dramatist both was that there was nothing of the poet in him. And without the poet in him, it cannot be too often emphasized, no writer can be a great writer.

What there was of poet in Buchanan came out when he was most native, most the Scot. It is as an outcast Scot, a man who has broken some clan law of the old ballad world, that Buchanan sees Judas Iscariot. Admit we must there is a touch of melodrama about this ballad, of the melodrama without which Buchanan would not be Buchanan. It was the melodrama in *The Shadow of the Sword* (1876), and in *Alone in London* (1884), which sent the thousands to the library and bookstore for the novel, and the tens of thousands to the theater for the play. The striking images of "The Ballad of Judas Iscariot" are the white dove sleeping, head under wing, on the cross of crucifixion, the white bear gliding round the "frozen Pole"; and the white Christ at the open door of the hall in which was laid the Holy Supper. All three are old symbols, but used with fresh significance. Buchanan could not preoccupy himself with his dream until it would assert itself freshly to him. What he did was to rehabilitate old dreams with a certain amount of theatrical power. So it is only by chance he is a poet at all.

ERIC MACKAY

There was a volume of the verse of Eric Mackay (1851-1898) on the parlor table of two sisters on whom I used to call in my youth. I read it as I waited for the girls to prink and descend upon me in full splendor. I came to have a fine scorn for *The Love Letters of a Violinist* (1886) from these brief readings, but I could not own my scorn in that house, the sentimentalities of Mackay being a considerable part of the life of the younger sister. She was "musical," and she thought Mackay the musician's poet. The glad confidence of youth is gone from me now these forty years, but the rereading of Mackay once a decade since those old days has not changed my opinion of his verse. He is a sentimentalist of the school of "Owen Meredith," though without what the late Victorians thought was the "delightful wickedness" of *Lucile* (1860). Mackay was of his time. He knew his audience, and it responded to him. He had his ten years of adulation, and he is now forgotten, and deservedly forgotten. There is nothing, really, for which to remember him. There is no new music in his fluent and vapid verse, no readings of life, no findings of beauty undiscovered by the poets before him.

Charles Stuart Calverley (1831-1884) is like Dr. Johnson in that he never wrote anything worthy of his reputation. There was a spirit and a glow in the man that warmed everybody with whom he came in contact, and that made his acquaintances regard what he wrote more highly than it deserved. He was apt at parody, but there have been those more apt. "J. K. S." (James Kenneth Stephen), who almost worshiped him, was a better parodist. Frederick Locker-Lampson had a lighter touch in *vers de société*. Austin Dobson held the level of his light verse far nearer poetry. Praed brought to satire of fads current more jollity and verve.

There is good fooling and sound criticism in *Fly Leaves* (1872), but it cannot be said of one of his sets of verses that it is the perfect parody of its original. *"Butter and eggs and a pound of cheese"* comes closest to the perfect parody, but it is a little

obvious, a little heavy-handed, a little cheap. There are those who
think Calverley's "The Cock and the Bull" an utter annihilation
of Browning. It is clever, it is to the point, it is amusing, but
"J. K. S." does Browning up more neatly. It is more memorable,
perhaps, that he was the first to rhyme "blossom" and "opossum."

"J. K. S."

James Kenneth Stephen (1859-1892) cared greatly for the
higher forms of poetry, but he proved himself master only of
vers de société. Even within this field the range of his successes
was narrow. He was the parodist and the turner of pleasantries
about better men. A confessed student of Calverley, he made
himself known as a rhymer while at Cambridge, where he matricu-
lated in 1878. His first collection of verse was *Lapsus Calami*
(1891) and his second *Quo Musa Tendis* (1891).

His *mot* on Kipling and Haggard is Stephen at his best:

> When the Rudyards cease from kipling
> And the Haggards ride no more.

He makes a frontal assault on Wordsworth in "A Sonnet." Here
he begins with the first line of "Two Voices," agreeing that "one
is of the mountains," but declaring that the other is "of an old
half-witted sheep." He derides Browning often, but he is juster
to him than to Wordsworth, admiring him only a little less than
Shakespeare.

Outside cf parody Stephen is only, he admits:

> a common man
> Who says what other people say.

He is sane, lucid, concise, a good craftsman, an anti-sentimen-
talist, and to the point on the main matters. No man has been
clearer on the vexed question as to the nature of love.

> I have a meaning for love, that is plain:
> Further than passion, and longing, and so on, it
> Means to me liking and liking again.

There is proverbial wisdom in him, too:

> It isn't what one *hasn't got*
> That ought to quench the light of life:
> It's what one *loses:* is it not?
> It's death, or treason in a wife.

Not a Prior, not a Praed, not a Dobson, "J. K. S." remains a minor in a minor art of verse. He holds his place, though, a reprinting of him in 1928 getting a good press more than a generation after his death.

If Mathilde Blind (1847-1896) is referred to to-day it is as the biographer of George Eliot (1819-1880). Yet after her heroine's death she had her own little hour as a writer of verse. Those who liked *The Spanish Gipsy* (1868) liked *The Prophecy of St. Oran* (1881) and *The Heather on Fire* (1886), an outlander's narratives of Highland life. Mrs. Emily Pfeiffer (1827-1890) was having recognition, too, in these late Victorian years, earlier than Miss Blind, later than Miss Evans. The verse of all three was of their time, with a minimum of intrinsic worth in it to last on to to-day. My copy of Mrs. Pfeiffer's *Rhyme of the Lady of the Rock* (1885), a second edition, is a well-thumbed book. Its addenda of press notices but serves to stress for the *n*th time how a reputation real and living in its day can die out completely in a generation.

AUGUSTA WEBSTER

It was the habit of the critics of her time to say that Augusta Webster (1837-1894) had the greatest dramatic power of any woman since Joanna Baillie. It was their habit, too, to say that she was in lyric power not far below Mrs. Browning. To-day, when she is all but unknown, hardly even a name, such ratings must seem fantastic, but they were rather generally supported in the eighties of last century. She wrote a great deal, she commanded publication by the leading publishers of her day, she sold well, and her name was one you came upon frequently in the papers and periodicals. It may be that her very versatility was her undoing. She made a good fist at lyric, introspective sonnet, problem poem, narrative, drama, but there are no lines of hers everywhere quoted, or any set of verses that cannot be denied a place in the best anthologies. You can pick up nearly any volume of hers for three-and-six in the English bookshops. That was what I paid for *A Book of Rhyme* (1881), and for *In A Day* (1882), her ambitious play. Both have been by me now several years, but neither has been read more than the once that duty demanded. I have no marked passages in either, no impressions written in the blank pages at the ends of the books, as books that have appealed to me compelled me to write. Impressive as her poems and plays look gathered together on a library shelf, there is not one of all, of them one recalls as one recalls Lady Nairne's "Land of the Leal" or Mme. Darmesteter's "Spring and Autumn."

A. MARY F. ROBINSON

Emerson tells us that no young man ever really believes he will die. A. Mary F. Robinson (b. 1857) is of a contrary opinion. She declares in "Spring and Autumn" that:

> God in His heart made Autumn for the young;
>
> .   .   .   .   .
>
> That thus the inevitable heritage
> Might come revealed in beauty, and assuage
> The dread with which the heart of youth is wrung.

That is a deep and understanding reading of the season, if one that will not be accepted without challenge in many places, for the old deplore autumn almost as often as do the young. What shall we say, then, to the even more surprising and dubiously comforting thought in:

> And for the consolation of the old
> He made the delicate, swift, tumultuous Spring;
> That every year they might again behold
> The image of their youth in everything
> And bless the fruit-trees flowering in the cold
> Whose harvest is not for their gathering.

That is the one poem of Madame Darmesteter, as she was when she published it in *Retrospect* (1893), that remains in memory. I came across it in 1899, when I picked up the book at an after-Christmas sale. It set me looking her up, in her early years, when she was Miss Robinson, in *A Handful of Honeysuckle* (1878), and in the several volumes she wrote after she married, in 1888, M. James Darmesteter, the famous French authority on Persian. I found no other poem to put beside it in the Pre-Raphaelite verse of her early years, in her later Italian studies, or in the poems that record her deeper experiences of life.

I looked forward eagerly to her *Collected Poems* (1901). She was now Mme. Duclaux, having married the director of the Pasteur Institute in Paris in 1901, and she was the presiding genius of a group of wits that made up a real salon. None of the verses included in this volume and unknown to me before I met them seemed, however, a fellow to "Spring and Autumn." She was still to me, as are a half-hundred other English poets, the poet of one poem. And no verses of hers I have come upon since then, in all her pensive and well-wrought writing, are the equal to that epigram of my first liking.

Mme. Duclaux has been translated, we are told, into French and Italian and German, and she has become as well known on the Continent as any English poet of her generation. In England only Mrs. Meynell among the women poets rivaled her in late Victorian times. Mme. Duclaux has written many kinds of verse well, from ballades to ballads, from epigrams to a translation of Euripides, but they have a way of fading out of memory, all of them save only "Spring and Autumn." You remember that poem for its poetry, however, rather than by reason of subject or by accidental coincidence of its mood with some passion of the hour, as is the way with every other single poem that has given its author a passing fame.

"MICHAEL FIELD"

Rare spirits that write good verse are not always poets. And yet if the world will not own them poets there are always stout partizans who will maintain that they are neglected geniuses and that the world is blind. Two women who have so been passed by are the aunt and niece who wrote as "Michael Field." They were Katherine Bradley (1846-1914) and Edith Cooper (1862-1913). Appreciation of a kind they met almost from *Callirrhoe* (1884), their first joint publication, but it was only a coterie appreciation. Such it has remained. They took their art very seriously, they learned to be good craftsmen, but they had nothing new to say nor a manner of their own to establish. They had several manners, after this model or that, but no manner. There is no lyric of all their careful many that shows beauty of a kind that had not been before they began to write. There is no play of theirs that has in it figures against the sky. Their posthumously published *Deirdre* (1918) is dwarfed at mere thought of the versions of Yeats or Synge.

I met their versions of Sappho in *Long Ago* (1889) in my youth, in the Mosher reprint, and I enjoyed them. They were sound work, but they are no more. *Long Ago* seems to me now after many years to contain their best writing, but there is no one of their renderings that one would choose for an anthology of the best. Miss Sturgeon writes a warmly appreciative book on them in *Michael Field* (1922). She marshals praise of them by several of those in the high places of poetry. Despite all her effort, however, her book failed to win them a wider hearing than they had had. Their verse lacks always spontaneity of feeling, freshness of expression, and those qualities that keep poetry in memory.

ALICE MEYNELL

There is an elusiveness and faint coldness about the writing of Alice Thompson Meynell (1850-1922), whether in prose or verse. There is, on your first reading of either essays or poems, a feeling that here is a studied aloofness, a determination not to be of the vulgar herd, but as you read her a second time you come to feel that her avoidance of the usual and the recognized is instinctive. Save for a moment or two of exaltation, she picks her way as daintily through life as she would through a muddy crossing.

Alice Meynell was, though, in no sense a superior person. She believed in the ways of nature and in the common lot of men. She was the mother of seven children, a good housekeeper, and the contributor of a weekly column to *The Pall Mall Gazette*. And with all her cares she found time to help her husband in the rescue of that other Thompson of genius, Francis the poet, and no relative of hers, from the streets of London, and in the fostering of him through the writing and publication of his exuberant poetry.

Alice Meynell was almost an infant prodigy. Her first volume of verse, *Preludes* (1873), won her a real but a restricted reputation at about the time that her sister, Lady Elizabeth Thompson Butler, the battle-painter, was being besieged by crowds on the street because of the fame of her *Rollcall*. After Alice Thompson married Wilfrid Meynell in 1877 she put away poetry for a long time, no volume of verse following *Preludes* for twenty years. Then she published *Poems* (1893), the earlier volume with five omissions and seven additions. After another eight years she published nineteen sets of verses as *Later Poems* (1901). Twelve year later she "collected" herself in *Poems* (1913) with a total of only seventy-six titles. The little sheaf, *Last Poems* (1923), gathered together in 1923, after her death, brings the total of all she would wish to be judged by to hardly more than a hundred poems.

Six poems stand out above the rest, "A Poet of One Mood," "The Garden," "Renouncement," "Spring on the Alban Hills," "November Blue" and "The Shepherdess," though they are very like in tone to all their fellows. Alice Meynell is, as she says in one of the six:

> A poet of one mood in all my lays,
> Ranging all life to sing one only love,
> Like a west wind across the world I move,
> Sweeping my harp of floods mine own wild ways.

That is, she is what she says she is in the first three lines, but there are no "wild ways" in these poems. It is not so much the love of the woman for the man that sounds in her poems as the love of woman for love. It is the effect of the man's love, and of her love, on herself, which she cherishes.

> And snatches of thee everywhere
> Make little heavens throughout a day.

She hugs to heart what love brings her. Comparing her love to an incoming tide she writes:

> But inland from the seaward spaces,
> None knows, not even you, the places
> Brimmed at your coming out of sight,
> —The little solitudes of delight
> This tide constrains in dim embraces.

She gives us, too, in "A Poet of One Mood," a just description of the colors of her verse, which are "the colors of a dove" and "a flash of silver greys." She works in black and white, and in combinations of these, with only a flush now and then of rose-ash or pearl.

Another love poem, and again a sonnet in form, is "The Garden"; and love-poem and sonnet, too, is "Renouncement," her most impassioned poem. I shall attempt no praise of it. It is enough that Rossetti had it by heart and that he told William Sharp that it was "one of the three finest sonnets ever written by women."

Alice Meynell spent a large part of her youth in Italy, and she has written of it in both prose and verse out of deep intimacy and keen sympathy. Read "Ceres' Runaway" in her *Essays* (1914), and "Spring on the Alban Hills" in her *Poems*, if you would know her at her best on England's most loved foreign land. You would expect both of these writings to be studies in greens, but only the essay is predominantly that. The greyness through which she sees everything dims the landscape in the sonnet. She, most curiously, sees spring "flush" hill and plain with "a dust of flowers."

"November Blue" is a lyric. It praises the color that the elec-

tric lights give to the streets of her beloved London. It shows her
of our day, inquiring, picking out adroitly the loveliest feature
that modernity has brought to the cities.

"The Shepherdess" is, like "November Blue," of her *Later
Poems* (1901). It is the most musical and the happiest of all her
lyrics. There is a precious epithet in it, to mar it for some, to give
it a pleasant suggestion of the seventeenth century for others.

Mrs. Meynell was deeply read in poetry, and she has the
courage of her likes and dislikes. She relies on authority in theory,
and scouts authority in practice when it clashes with her own standard of values. She excludes Gray's "Elegy" from *The Flower of
the Mind* (1897), her anthology of poetry from Spenser to
Wordsworth, and she gives place there to only two poems of
Burns and to one of Byron. Her introduction, brief as it is, is one
of the fundamental statements on the English lyric, and her notes
are a mine of delight.

Alice Meynell was proud of the reticences of her father, T. J.
Thompson. Her own pride led to even greater reticences, but
there were reservations from that pride that are difficult to explain.
She wrote frankly of her love for her husband, or rather of the
effect of his love upon her. She is almost silent, in her verse, on
her love for her children, she who was the devoted mother of
seven. There are two poems only, "The Modern Mother" and
"Maternity," in which she breaks her code of reticence on mother
love. She is deeply stirred in them. Perhaps she was afraid to
speak out her feelings. She is very English. Perhaps that explains
the restraint, the bleakness, the insistence on Novembry grayness
in her verse. Perhaps she is taking refuge in colorlessness, and in
the perfection of her art. That one must keep one's poise is what
speaks clearliest in Sargent's sketch of her.

That there have been omissions of writers of verse that should
have had consideration in this book, I am only too conscious now
that I have read the proof. How I came to miss Sebastian Evans
(1830-1909) I cannot account for, since I have had good talk
over his *High History of the Holy Graal* in the farmhouse of

the White Mountains next to that in which I now write. The Hon. Roden Noel (1834-1894), too, I have known for years, buying him, and kindling a little in young years over some of his verse descriptive of nature. Alfred Domett (1811-1887) we all know was Browning's Waring, and a gallant and picturesque figure who brought Maori themes into English poetry. Andrew Lang (1849-1912) has done society verse and verse descriptive of his beloved Lowlands of Scotland almost memorable. Thomas Ashe (1836-1889) has an elusive sort of charm; and Frederick Myers (1843-1901) did good verse in the manner of Wordsworth as well as the memorable prose of his *Human Personality and Its Survival of Bodily Death*. It is easier to bear having neglected Sir Lewis Morris (1833-1907), even if one's Welsh blood interests one in some of his narratives. There are others one would rather forget than say hard words about.

THE PLACE OF VICTORIAN POETRY

This Victorian era has claims to be considered as the period of third importance in English poetry. For its intrinsic lyricism and for its breadth of scope the Elizabethan Age stands unquestionably first. Spenser and Sidney, Shakespeare and Marlowe, Dekker and Campion, Ben Jonson and Donne remain incomparable despite all the attempted changes in the standards of critical judgment. True lovers of poetry read them over and over, as they read all the other masters from Chaucer to Masefield, for the sheer delight there is in their writing.

The Georgian period, with Wordsworth and Coleridge, Byron and Landor, Shelley and Keats, cannot be denied second place. The heydays of the seventeenth century and the eighteenth century have both been undervalued. The time in which wrote Milton and Herrick, Crashaw and Cotton, Marvell and Vaughan is a time of great poetry. Nor can the attitude of the dominant critical writing since Wordsworth's day toward the time of Burns and Blake, Cowper and Crabbe, continue forever to minimize its importance.

There is, however, in Tennyson and Browning, Rossetti and William Morris, Arnold and Meredith, Swinburne and Patmore, such a wealth of romance, such a freshness of rhythm, such a deep reading of life, such an impassioned lyrical feeling, such a vision, and such a lordship of language that their time must be given precedence over the time of Milton and the time of Burns.

The late nineteenth century and the early twentieth century are one time. That time is not far behind the Victorian age in its poetry of power. It is admittedly difficult for a critic contemporary to a poet to appraise that poet objectively. If, however, one's method has been to put a poet over against his predecessors of like kind, and to look for the qualities in him that they possess and that seem to have kept them alive, one is less likely to err in one's judgment. Looking so at Yeats and Hardy, Francis Thompson and Masefield, A. E. Housman and Ralph Hodgson, one cannot write down as of less than first moment the time in which they wrote.

We can, however, be surer of our Victorians. They have survived that lessening of appeal which is so sure to follow the enthusiasm over a poet that his death provokes. We see them in the perspective a generation that has passed affords. They continue to be read in a time of different critical taste and of different assumptions of critical values. The seekers after strange gods have attempted to belittle the Victorians, but they remain as sure of their place among the great in English poetry as do the Elizabethans and the Georgians.

INDEX